'Did you go to school?'

The question asked of suspected
Old Etonians by Old Etonians

CONTENTS

PROLOGUE

British playwright Alan Bennett first arrived at Cambridge University in 1951, fresh out of Leeds Grammar School. His most striking memory of his Oxbridge experience was not the colleges' historic architecture or even the warm greetings from the avuncular dons. No, Bennett's abiding memory is his first unhappy encounters with something he had never met before – a public schoolboy.

On his return to Cambridge in 2014, Bennett was still irritated and angry at what he witnessed sixty-three years earlier. Speaking to an audience tightly squeezed into King's College Chapel, he not so fondly recalled:

> If the Dons were genial, some of my fellow candidates were less so. That weekend was the first time I had come across public-schoolboys in the mass, and I was appalled. They were loud, self-confident, and all seemed to know one another, shouting down the table to prove it, while also being shockingly greedy. Public-school they might be but they were louts. Seated at long refectory tables beneath the mellow portraits of Tudor and Stuart grandees, neat, timorous and genteel we grammar-schoolboys were the interlopers; these slobs, as they seemed to me, the party in possession.

In March 2016, an unnamed undergraduate writing in Oxford University's student newspaper *Cherwell* gives an uncannily similar description of his own encounters with public school alumni. 'Going to Oxford University from an inner-city comprehensive school,' he wrote, 'is like living on another planet, one populated by strange people in bow ties with no concept of what it's like to live in the real world... People seem surprised in Freshers' week that you haven't met their mate Tarquin from St Paul's, or you didn't know about Humphrey from Eton's gap year excursions in Goa.' The student continues:

> this public school network is real, and it affects your life as a student from a state school. Oxford's famous drinking societies are where this network comes into its element. The most famous of all is the Bullingdon, but Keble College have the 'dissolved' Steamers, whose misogynistic antics arguably earned the college the chant: 'We are Keble, we hate women.' There's nothing wrong with a couple of lads going out for a meal, but when these lads all went to public schools, and meet in an all-male dining club, it projects an image of exclusivity that the university is keen to distance itself from. Yet this exclusivity is real, and is perpetuated by the students themselves, dishing out invites only to those who went to the top public schools, leaving those who were not fortunate enough to attend searching for where we fit in this posh puzzle.

Britain's public schools started life in medieval times as schools for the poor. Closely tied to the church, they found favour as institutions of social mobility which took bright and pious children from their local community to the government of England. But they soon became victims of their own success, hijacked first by the aristocracy and then the merchant middle classes, who had profited so handsomely from the country's industrial revolution. A premier league of private schools, which educated fewer than 3,000 boys, became the academy of the ruling elite which ruled an empire and waged and won two world wars.

Even as Britain faced its darkest hour, George Orwell urged action against the public schools, saying: 'It is all too obvious that our talk of "defending democracy" is nonsense while it is a mere accident of birth that decides whether a gifted child shall or shall not get the education it deserves.'[1] At the same time the Nazis, waiting patiently across the Channel for the Battle of Britain to be resolved in their favour, were speaking admiringly of the English public schools, where they fully expected to be sending their own *privilegierte Kinder*. Adolf Hitler had modelled his own elite schools for *Führerschaft* on the English public school.[2] The German invasion booklet even included useful tips on how Nazi parents could put their children's names down for Eton, although it noted disappointedly that the school was booked up until 1949. Its author was Walter Friedrich Schellenberg, a member of the Nazi high command, who advised his fellow senior officers of the SS: 'The one half of a per cent of children who attend public schools will eventually occupy about eighty per cent of all important social and political posts.'[3]

Imagine a world where all the leaders of that world are able to pass on their power directly to their children. These children are plucked from their nurseries and sent to beautiful buildings far away from all the other children. Here they are given all the codes and taught all the skills they will need to wield their parents' power and protect it for their own children. They are provided with all the teachers they need, the best buildings, the best doctors and the best food. They are introduced to the greatest thinkers and allowed to see and touch the finest art. Each day the children are told that the reason they are here is because they are the brightest and most important children in the world.

Before they are returned to society they are shown how to use secret languages and how to recognise the expressions, manners and countenances of their tribe. To make it easier they are also equipped with a uniform of brogues, blazers and badges. In the outside world they are presented with the best jobs, the grandest houses and most of the money. Through their networks of friends and family they control the government, the army, the police and the City. The leaders tell all their people that everyone is equal and that everyone has the chance of becoming a leader. But this isn't true because the leaders have made it impossible for the people's children to become leaders.

Today all the great institutions of state – government, judiciary and military – are run by an elite who have attended private schools. The bankers, hedge-fund managers and financiers who control the money markets in the City went to these schools. Our professions continue to be dominated by privately educated doctors, lawyers and accountants. And the same is true of the country's fourth great estate, the national newspapers and broadcasters which set the political weather.

The figures speak for themselves. Only 7 per cent of the population attend a private school. Yet private school pupils represent 74 per cent of senior judges, 71 per cent of senior officers in the armed forces, 67 per cent of Oscar winners, 55 per cent of permanent secretaries in Whitehall, 50 per cent of Cabinet ministers and members of the House of Lords, and a third of Russell Group university vice-chancellors.[4]

Other influential sections of society are similarly affected. Nearly half (44 per cent) of the captains of industry and businessmen and women on the *Sunday Times* Rich List attended public school. Following closely behind are 43 per cent of newspaper columnists, 36 per cent of cabinet ministers, 33 per cent of

MPs and 22 per cent of shadow cabinet ministers. Eton College educated more MPs (twenty) than any other school.[5]

Even within the rarefied world of private schools, there is another, smaller, more powerful hierarchy. The further up society's food chain the narrower and more selective the private education background becomes. This is particularly so among the judiciary, often regarded as the guardians of the state. One in seven judges attended one of just five independent schools (Eton, Westminster, Radley, Charterhouse and St Paul's).

The private school sector has long recognised that the golden ticket to success is a degree from Oxbridge. A cadre of very expensive public schools boast Oxbridge admissions rates as high as 40 per cent. Just twelve private schools in London and the home counties send 500 students to Oxford and Cambridge each year – 7 per cent of all Oxbridge places.[6] Most state schools don't send a single student to Oxbridge.

But these figures are meaningless until you see what damage this unfettered privilege is doing to our country. Our 'leaders' have used money and patronage to tightly control access to education so that we now have the biggest ever gap between the richest and the poorest in British history. Britain's billionaires have seen their net worth more than double since the recession, with the richest 1,000 families now controlling a total of £547 billion. At the same time four million UK citizens are deemed so poor that they are said to be in persistent poverty. If you are born poor in Britain, the chances are that you will die poor.[7] Millions of people will go to their graves never knowing there are charities called Eton, Harrow and Charterhouse whose sole purpose is to improve the lives of rich and privileged children.

The American philosopher John Rawls said that a just society is one you would be happy to enter without knowing your social position in advance. Against that measure, can we really claim that Britain is a just society? The widening gap between private schools and 'bog-standard' state schools means that a child today has less chance of breaking through the class and career barrier than their grandparents born in the 1950s.[8] The subtle networks of the privately schooled help to create a system of self-perpetuating advantage and social immobility.

When David Cameron announced he was resigning from parliament because he considered himself a 'distraction', the veil was lifted. The former member for Witney returned to his London club and the grouse moor. His friend and chancellor of the exchequer, George Osborne, capitalised on his position by taking six jobs, including the editorship of a national newspaper. They left Boris Johnson behind in charge of the country's foreign affairs at a critical moment in the nation's history. An Eton education teaches bombast, bluster and buffoonery. All harmless in the debating chambers of parliament and on TV game shows, but in the real world, where real lives are at stake, such playfulness can be catastrophic.

We want accountable leaders who understand the problems facing a deeply divided country, not egotists and charlatans who can't see beyond their own self-interest. Britain crashing out of Europe, the splintering of the Labour Party and an indebted and unbalanced economy are the direct consequence of public schoolboys of all parties playing politics with our lives. So the question must be asked – is the public school system, which for so long has commanded the heights of British society, fit for purpose? Is it helping to bring us closer together to build a fairer society or is it driving us apart?

If you take your children out of the community in which you live then you are no longer part of that community. Children who are educated away from the children next door can never integrate properly. In golden-gated estates, hermetically sealed from the plebeian masses, they are expressly told they are the chosen ones. So when they leave their protected 'green zones' and rejoin the world community they are bristling with unconscious prejudice. They are not part of any big society; they are the few who have been programmed to ignore the interests of the many. The time has come to end this corrupt trade in life chances. Because while Britain remains governed by the narrow interests of the public schools there cannot be a true democracy.

PART ONE

SELLING EDUCATION BY THE POUND

In 1540, the year Thomas Cromwell was executed for treason, the two men charged with the procurement of his death, Archbishop of Canterbury Thomas Cranmer and Richard Rich, chancellor of the Court of Augmentations, were deciding whether poor children had the right to be educated alongside the sons of gentlemen.

Rich argued: 'As for the other, husbandmen's children, they were more meet, they said, for the plough and to be artificers than to occupy the place of the learned sort. So that they wished none else to be put to school but only gentlemen's children.'

To this Cranmer replied: 'Poor men's children are many times endowed with more singular gifts of nature, which are also gifts of God, as with eloquence, memory, apt pronunciation, sobriety, and such like, and also commonly more apt to apply their study than is the gentleman's son delicately nurtured.'

Rich: 'It is meet for the ploughman's son to go to plough and the artificer's son to apply the trade of his parent's vocation, and the gentleman's children are meet to have the knowledge of government and rule in the commonwealth; for we have as much need of ploughmen as of any other state; all sorts of men may not go to school.'

Cranmer: 'I grant much of your meaning herein as needful in a commonwealth, but yet to utterly exclude the ploughman's son and the poor man's son from the benefit of learning, as though they were utterly unworthy of having the gifts of the Holy Ghost bestowed upon them as well as upon others is as much as to say that Almighty God should not be at liberty to bestow his great gifts of grace upon any person... Wherefore if the gentleman's son be apt to learning let him be admitted; if not apt, let the poor man's child, being apt, enter his room.'[1]

1

POOR SCHOOLS

Private education was first established in the British Isles by wealthy Roman families who came here shortly after the imperial conquest. Where Greek children primarily received their education from the community, a Roman child's first and most important educator was chosen by his or her family.[1] In Rome the first private schools were populated by paying pupils from the less well-off Roman families who pooled the fees to secure cheaper rates.[2]

The Romans even wrote into law the link between fees and private schools. Emperor Diocletian's edict on pay scales established set fees for each class of education. It meant that elementary schools could charge 10 denarii (around £50 today) per pupil per month, while schools that taught grammar and rhetoric charged up to five times more.[3] Under this system the Roman conquest of Britain brought reading and writing to the British elites on a scale never seen before. But when the Romans departed in 410CE Britain sank into its Dark Ages and education was neglected.

It wasn't until the arrival of St Augustine and Christianity in 597 that the torch of learning was reignited and an army of monks and clerics brought about a mass conversion of the heathen English.[4] This was not a piecemeal undertaking but a systematic and professional operation directed by Pope Gregory in Rome. Where Augustine and his followers established a church, they would also found a school. For the British people it meant education would be forever synonymous with the practices of Christianity. And at the heart of the new religion was a new written language. As the Victorian historian Arthur Leach said: 'To understand the rudiments of the new religion, to take part in the new religious worship, it was necessary for the English to learn Latin.'[5]

Local grammar schools were established to teach Latin to the novice priests while song schools educated children in singing the praises of God. One of the first was King's School in Canterbury, an Augustinian grammar school which became the subject of a famous debate between Thomas Cranmer and Richard Rich about who deserves education.[6] The other great Saxon churches of Rochester and York followed suit, founding their own grammar and song schools. These are England's oldest schools, still in existence today.

Alfred the Great restored the place of schools in Britain after the Viking invasions of the ninth century, which had resulted in many monasteries being razed to the ground. At the heart of Alfred's vision were strong community centres of learning organised by the local priests. And he helped make reading and writing more accessible to ordinary people by overseeing the translation of Latin texts into Anglo-Saxon. Nevertheless, by the early twelfth century, under Norman rule, these Christian schools had reverted to Latin. A Norman education remained focused on vocational training and most pupils were still aspiring monks or priests, though there are rare cases where members of the young nobility were sent to school.[7] But the more typical apprentice came from the community and from the common stock.

St Paul's Cathedral school was established in 1123, when eight needy children were given a home and education in return for singing in the cathedral. Indeed, in the twelfth century most cathedrals and collegiate churches had schools founded in the same vein. The schoolmaster was one of the country's most important officers and teaching was one of the most important functions. Some schools – like those at Bedford, Christchurch and Waltham – were removed from monastic control and handed over to secular canons. Bury St Edmunds, for example, which had probably been founded as part of a collegiate church before Canute's time, was given an endowment at the end of the twelfth century to convert it into a 'free or partially free grammar school'.[8]

More than 300 years after the Norman Conquest only 5 per cent of the population could read or write. The lords and earls still regarded education as a threat to the feudal system of serfdom upon which they relied to run their estates. Some lords of the manor even enacted laws banning local serfs from attending school. Yet by the fourteenth century the English church had established a network of schools that served its own staffing needs as well as the wealthy ruling classes, who started to use them to educate their sons. Soon the grammar schools and song schools were joined by chantry schools. Established by wealthy benefactors or guilds, 'chantries', each with their own priest, were effectively independent of monastic rule and so offered individuals access to liturgy outside the controlling influence of the clerical elites. These schools allowed Christian philanthropists to personalise their dedication to Christ and mould schools in their own image. In this way the first independent or public schools were born.

The founders and patrons of the public schools set out with the intention to provide free education for the poor, hence the apparently oxymoronic use of the word 'public' today. At the time, these schools would have been revolutionary and arriviste. The first was Winchester College, founded by William of Wykeham in 1382. Wykeham came from a family of Hampshire farmers and was educated, for a few years at least, at the local grammar school. It was here that Wykeham acquired useful contacts which helped him secure a clerical position at Winchester Castle. By the mid-fourteenth century this farmer's son had worked his way up to be King Edward III's most trusted adviser. In 1363, the King was so well disposed to William that he described him as 'his secretary, who stays by his side in constant attendance on his service and who with all his servants is under the king's special protection'.[9]

Wykeham's first foray into education reform was the establishment of New College at Oxford University in 1379 for the study of 'theology, canon, civil law and the arts'. To support his institution, he also founded a new school in Winchester that acted as a feeder to the college. But he was determined this was not to be another vehicle for the aristocracy to foist their own scions on the government of England. Wykeham envisaged a fair admissions system that catered for boys from the same humble beginnings as his own.

Winchester welcomed its first pupils in 1382, less than a year after the Peasants' Revolt, the country's first mass socialist movement. The city, and no doubt Wykeham himself, had been profoundly affected by the national protests which included calls for a return to the social equality of Alfred the Great and the 'laws of Winchester.'[10]

Under Wykeham's enlightened reforms, the first public schools came to provide an ecclesiastical education for the community's poorest and most needy children. Acutely aware of the necessity to exclude the sons of barons and aristocrats, he even capped parental income so that pupils could only take up a place at the school if their father earned less than £3,500 a year.

Wykeham's school began with just seventy free scholars – the number of disciples sent out by Jesus to spread the word of God according to the Gospel of Luke. The central tenet of Winchester's own charter proclaimed the rights of 'the many poor scholars engaged in scholastic disciplines, who suffering from deficiency, penury and indigence, lack and will lack in the future the proper means for continuing and advancing in the aforesaid art of grammar'.[11]

Winchester's system of professional schooling secured such strong ecclesiastical and academic results that many of Oxford's brightest scholars were drawn from its ranks. Today Winchester College continues in this tradition of enrolling bright and influential students. Two of Jeremy Corbyn's closest advisers, Seumas Milne and James Schneider, are Wykehamists who went on to Oxford.

The success at Winchester spurred on other medieval philanthropists. Education was suddenly the new charity of choice for independently minded movers and shakers of the medieval period. The establishment of the first public schools gathered pace with Eton (1440), St Paul's (1509) and Westminster (1560). St Paul's School was committed to providing education for 153 free scholars, this being the number of species of fish believed to exist in the world as told in St John's Gospel. Its statute also envisaged an international dimension to its charity, promising to educate 'all nations and countries indifferently'. Later, Harrow School's foundation can be traced to an endowment bequeathed by John Lyon for a free grammar school in 1572.

Among the guilds and professions, City of London School was established in 1442, upon the bequest of John Carpenter, 'for the finding and bringing up of four poor men's children with meat, drink, apparel, learning at the schools, in the universities, etc., until they be preferred, and then others in their places for ever'.[12] The charter of Merchant Taylors' School, founded in the City in 1561 by the eponymous livery company, stipulated that it should cater for 250 pupils, of whom 100 must be 'poor men's sons'. The rest of the school was expected to pay, although only small sums.[13] Meanwhile, City of London School's endowment was so fecund that the governors' time was mostly spent dreaming up ways to spend it.[14]

These were England's first public schools and their statutes expressly barred the genuinely wealthy from entry. But alas, the Wykeham model of social and religious education quickly became a victim of its own success. The social advantage secured by entrusting a young heir to an institution that guaranteed a place at Oxford, even six centuries ago, was irresistible. And Wykeham and the other early benefactors, despite some reservations, were not blind to the monetary needs of their schools.

Soon the landowning aristocracy forced amendments to the public school charters to defeat the financial caps. Winchester's revised charter now read: 'We allow, however, the sons of noble and influential persons, special friends of the said college, up to the number of ten to be instructed and informed in Grammar within the same college, without burden [i.e. free] upon the aforesaid college.'[15] It is hard to imagine a more eloquent yet shameful concession to the baronial class.

By the turn of the fifteenth century, these fee-paying scholars, confusingly called commoners, outnumbered the free scholars.[16] In this way the home-tutored sons of nobles forced their way into the successful medieval grammar schools. The other public schools quickly succumbed to the twin temptations of cash and aristo connections. St Paul's relaxed its rules on who could qualify as a scholar by stipulating that all pupils were expected to pay for their own wax candles, an essential (and expensive) part of Elizabethan liturgy. Following the dissolution of the monastery at Westminster Abbey, Henry VIII established a new foundation at Westminster School, stating that forty scholars should be taught grammar by two masters. In 1560 the school was refounded in Elizabeth I's statutes, which poetically declared: 'The scholars shall be forty in number, and we wish that in selecting them the greatest weight be given to gentleness of disposition, ability, learning, good character and poverty; and insofar as any one candidate excels in the possession of these qualities, he shall, as is proper, be preferred.'[17] The founding fathers added the stipulation that no scholar should be 'elected' to the school who could expect more than £10 in inheritance. But such high ideals were undone by a further condition of entry which imposed mandatory fees on the first year, thus defeating with a stroke of the quill the philanthropic intention behind the Queen's statute.

A Queen's Scholarship is now one of the most prestigious competitive awards in public school education but it has little consideration for the local needy. At Westminster today there are forty-eight Queen's Scholars, who pay half fees of £7,500 a year. They still enjoy great privileges, which in 2011 included an invitation to the wedding of the Duke and Duchess of Cambridge and an audience with the Dalai Lama.[18]

Eton College's royal connections (it was founded by King Henry VI in 1440 located close to his favourite castle at Windsor) immediately bestowed a cachet, drawing in the ruling classes, which in turn also corrupted its charitable mission to educate 'seventy poor and needy scholars'. The masters established houses in the town which they ran as going concerns charging commercial rates for board and lodging. Today the school has managed to advance the original foundation of seventy 'poor scholars' by just four pupils, although exactly what constitutes 'poor' is not always clearly defined, and these free pupils are heavily outnumbered by the intake of 1,230 fee-paying students.

Charterhouse School, founded in central London but relocated to Godalming, Surrey, was established in 1611 by the bequest of Thomas Sutton, a money lender who upon his death was described as the richest man in England. In an act of redemption Sutton ensured that the riches he had made out of the financial woes of others would, in part at least, go towards the education of forty 'poor' children. The school governors defined poverty as: 'no children to be placed there whose parent have any estates of lands to leave unto them, but onlie the children of poore men that want means to bringe them up'.[19]

Charterhouse today insists that these were not 'poor' boys as we would know them, but the sons of the middle classes: 'In this context the word "poor" merely meant those without the prosperity of substantial estates behind them. Thus Charterhouse was from the start the province of the professional classes – the sons of doctors, lawyers, clergy – rather than the landed gentry.'[20]

The implication is that Charterhouse was not and never has been a school for the poor. Yet the school's first intake of 'middle-class' boys, aged between ten and fifteen years old, went on to take apprenticeships rather than go up to Oxbridge. These scholars, who became known as 'gown-boys', were soon supplemented by 'town-boys' – commoners accepted from outside the terms of the charitable foundation who applied to go to Charterhouse as its reputation grew. There can be no argument these 'town-boys', whose numbers quickly overtook that of the 'gown-boys', were indeed toffs drawn from the ranks of the wealthy.

★

It was under the guiding hand of Richard Mulcaster, headmaster at Merchant Taylors' and later St Paul's in the sixteenth century, that the first traces of the modern public school began to emerge with the teaching of English and sport at its heart. Indeed, Mulcaster was the first to coin a name for football ('footeball'). Meanwhile, at Winchester, the first public school idioms or 'notions' started to take shape. Today the school still refers to sports as *ekker* and *toytime* as evening prep time. Some of the same words are used across the public school estate. For example, a *div* is a common slang for class or form and a *don* is a teacher. But there is a mutual respect for other school slang. A Wykehamist may, however, speak of 'an Eton

notion' or 'an Oxford notion' in describing the vocabulary or traditions of another institution.

This special language bestowed an instant sense of belonging
on a select community that was able to define and regulate its
own world segregated from the townspeople. Over time the argot
and ritual, played out in testosterone-charged dormitories, took
on cruel and even savage characteristics which have become associated with the initiation ceremonies of the public schools of the
Victorian period and beyond. This included beatings (*bummings*
or *tundings*) and corporal punishments meted out by the teachers
and prefects. Other customs and practices, now so familiar, can
be read in the revised statutes of the first public schools. The idea
that older pupils would have pastoral and disciplinary care of the
younger boys was established as part of the prefectorial system and
helped the teachers and governors rule over the schools.

Unsurprisingly, snobbery set in early. Just a year after Merchant
Taylors' had its first intake of boys, complaints were made to the
Bishop of London that some of the pupils were speaking with
'Cumbrian accents'.[21] The central objection appeared to be that
the masters were 'northern men' and had inadvertently passed on
their Cumbrian dialect to the boys. The clergy, who had their own
vested interest in the affairs of the school, complained: 'They did
not pronounce so well as those who be brought on the southern
parts of the realm'.[22] Later, received pronunciation, the language of
the south of England and the upper classes, became the obligatory
accent of the public school.

However, it was the town of Shrewsbury in Shropshire that
established the first old boys' network. Founded in 1552, the
school's prestige was not defined by its teaching or headmaster but
by a select set of border gentlemen who came from outside the
town. The most glamorous was Sir Philip Sidney, nephew of the
Earl of Leicester and grandson of the Duke of Northumberland,
a 'poet and Renaissance man'. Sidney formed a friendship with

another poet, the lowly Fulke Greville. Greville's continued pursuit of his poetry was wholly supported by a series of political sinecures granted to him by the wealthy Sidney family. According to the former *Financial Times* journalist and author David Turner: 'The alliance between Greville and Sidney furnishes perhaps the first clear public school example of the old boy network.'[23]

The early public schools separated the ranks of the high nobility from the arriviste scholars and sons of the moneyed burghers. Most schools, by habit and custom, ended up adhering to a rigid class structure. The poor scholars who had won places at a public school endured bullying and beatings purely because of their lowly station. They were given the worst accommodation and were always the last to eat. At Eton, dining was so strictly segregated that the poor scholars were made to sit at separate tables from the sons of the aristocracy. Dining between the senior teaching staff and the young elite became the basis of the conclaves which cruelly invented new ordeals to be visited on the scholars.

Not that many of the scholars would have complained. Seventeenth- and eighteenth-century England was a tough place to grow up and public school reflected this. A foothold on the bottom rung of society was worth almost any indignity or humiliation. For the scholars it also presented a welcome income as many were paid to act as servants. The origins of the fagging system, where senior boys used junior members as personal servants, can be found in the paid service to the newly arrived aristocracy. Even the teachers, who were poorly paid and often looking for a better position, played a subservient role to the sons of earls and dukes, whose families retained the gifts of social advancement.

The history of the English public school is littered with the names of the 'not so rich but famous' who experienced terrible cruelties at the hands of their peers and teachers. Take, for example, the school travails of Charles Merivale, the historian and founder of the Oxford and Cambridge Boat Race. A sportsman and no shrinking violet, Merivale could not claim to be descended from any notable ancestry. Throughout his time at Harrow in the early 1800s, the school impressed upon him a deep 'social inferiority' which he said scarred him for the rest of his life.[24]

Despite this iniquity the schools remained to some degree the gentle agents of social mobility that Wykeham had envisaged. Richard Neile, son of a tallow chandler, rose from his humble beginnings to become Archbishop of York in 1631 largely thanks to an education at Westminster School. Another Westminster scholar, Richard Corbet, was proclaimed Bishop of Oxford in 1628 despite his father being a lowly nurseryman. One of the most celebrated cases of public school social mobility was that of Ben Jonson who, in 1572, was born into relative poverty. His father died shortly before his birth, and his mother remarried a brick-layer. Luckily for the clever young Jonson, an unidentified friend paid for him to attend Westminster School. In 1616 Jonson was named England's first ever Poet Laureate and such was his standing that Queen Anne, wife of King James I, agreed to perform in one of his plays.

However, by the beginning of the nineteenth century the impact of the community scholar programmes had been so watered down that Wykeham's free scholars were now in a very small minority. Despite notable rags-to-respectability stories, by the close of the 1800s they were the exception rather than the rule. Those who profited from the public schools were brazen about the con-spicuous absence of any charitable purpose. When the governors of Winchester were directly challenged in 1818 about the over-whelming number of rich pupils at a school established for the benefit of the poor they claimed that all their pupils were very poor – 'it was only their parents who were rich'.[25]

Wykeham's educational ideal had been usurped by England's rich and powerful families. The word 'public' had taken on a whole new meaning so that the schools opened their doors to all the nation's wealthy families, no matter where they lived or what religion they practised.

The public schools were founded to educate the poor and ended up serving the interests of the rich. This wholesale betrayal of the founders' charitable objectives was so egregious that it reached the attention of the courts. And in 1810 a case concerning Harrow School rested on how far the school now catered for the education of the rich at the expense of the poor.[26] Seventeen years later, in a separate case, it was even argued that public schools that 'educated gentlemen's sons' should no longer be considered charities.[27]

The public schools came about because of the pre-eminence of universities which had become essential to political and social advancement in late medieval England. Had the ancient grammar schools been allowed to flourish and evolve naturally we may have had a very different system of education with stronger state schools supported by the whole community. It is true for the most part that those who were educated in the early chantries and schools attached to cathedrals and monasteries were Christian recruits preparing for a life in the church. But they were chosen from the people, and they lived among the people, keeping alive in the hearts of the community the humanising influences of letters and of religion. Few of the laity, rich or poor, could read; but the poor saw their children winning the rewards of learning without favour or affection. It is this ethos that once enriched the whole community, not just the privileged few.

2

NURSERIES OF ARISTOCRACY

The story of reform of England's public schools is largely one of vested interests battling against church, state and economic reality. But it is also one of missed opportunity and of weak-willed politicians being asked to curb the influence of their own networks. For almost half a century, abolition or even serious reform has been off the table. Yet in Georgian and Victorian Britain this was actively pursued, and later, under Harold Wilson's Labour leadership, the great public schools lived in real fear for their very existence. Eton had even devised plans for relocating to Ireland or France while also considering becoming a comprehensive.[1]

The public school movement was at its most vulnerable at its inception when it broke from the monastic rule of the church and was very nearly strangled at birth. The idea of bypassing the monastery schools and sending pupils directly to university was regarded by the senior clergy as sacrilegious. Winchester sent exclusively to its sister college in Oxford while Eton had a similar relationship with King's College, Cambridge. This amounted to a direct assault on the church's centuries-long hold on the education of the nation's upper echelons.

The first crisis point arrived in the early 1500s when the ecclesiastical courts were ready to serve excommunication notices on any new public school which failed to yield to the writ of the monasteries.[2] Yet in an increasingly secularised society there was a growing need for schools to educate the sons of the landed and city gentry in institutions independent from ecclesiastical authority. If Britain was to remain competitive, then its schools must be open to all – they could not exist solely for the education of the clergy.

Eton College came very close to abolition just twenty-one years after its foundation. It owed its existence to King Henry VI, who lavished on Eton a substantial income from land, and a huge collection of holy relics. He even persuaded the Pope to grant a privilege unequalled anywhere in England: Eton was to have the right to grant Indulgences to penitents on the Feast of the Assumption. However, when Henry was deposed by King Edward IV in 1461, the new King annulled all grants to the school and removed most of its assets and treasures to St George's Chapel, Windsor, across the Thames. A number of influential figures came to Eton's rescue and a good part of the school was saved, though the royal bequest and the number of staff were much reduced.[3]

Next came the greatest attack on education in the medieval period – the Reformation. This time it was the public schools' clerical, rather than monastic, standing within the church order, as well as their independent association with the universities, which secured their survival. Had they remained centrally and politically linked to the monasteries, there is little doubt Winchester and Eton would have suffered the same fate as the chantry schools, which were broken up under King Henry VIII's dissolution of the monasteries. The 1545 Chantries Act accused these community church schools of misapplying funds and misappropriating lands.[4] As such, all chantries and their properties were transferred to the Crown.

Now the ill wind which decimated so many monastery and abbey schools blew favourably in the direction of the public schools. Much of the dissolved wealth of the monasteries and their endowments was redistributed among the King's favoured institutions. For example, the Priory of St Andrews of the Ards, a

Benedictine abbey at Stogursey in Somerset, was handed over to Eton College. Unchecked, the public schools grew in number and influence. The monastery-run grammar schools were refounded and established with independent charters.

According to Arthur Leach, the educational historian, twenty-four newly endowed public schools were created in a single year.[5]

*

A century later it was radical Puritan ideas, stirred up by the English Civil War, that next threatened the Royalist-supporting public schools. Groups like the Levellers, who wanted to create a much fairer society, were greatly vexed by the powers wielded by the schools. Such reformist thinking attracted the Czech-born educationalist John Comenius, who came to England to champion universal education. Writing home in 1641 he said: "They are eagerly debating on the reform of schools in the whole kingdom, namely that all young people should be instructed, none neglected."[6]

Comenius left for the Continent the following year to let the English fight among themselves and with him went any chance of bringing education to the ordinary people. Instead it was the philosophy of poet pamphleteer John Milton which dominated English thinking on the subject. At its heart was a neo-Platonic academy to educate a hand-picked ruling class for the Puritan state.

It meant that the public schools under Cromwell simply turned from educating one set of aristocracy to the education of another, leaving the schools more unruly than ever. The school staff and townspeople lived in fear of the young gentlemen pupils. Many of the schools had simply become ungovernable or were ruled by tyrannical cliques of brutalised wealthy children. And tyranny quickly turned to rebellion. In 1690 the boys at Manchester Grammar protested at the length of their Christmas holidays by arming themselves with blunderbusses and barricading the school. They held out for a fortnight before surrendering to the school authorities. Twenty years later pupils at Winchester staged a mutiny over how much beer they were allowed to drink.

In the next century Eton and Winchester each suffered six full-scale revolts. But the worst case of insurrection was at Rugby where the masters were taken prisoner at swordpoint. The crisis was only brought to an end when the local garrison of soldiers, aided by constables and farmers, stormed the building and freed the masters.

In response, the masters became more brutal in their treatment of pupils. Pitt the Elder, prime minister from 1766 to 1768, was so appalled by the harsh education meted out at Eton that he determined to have his three sons home-schooled. He later claimed that 'a public school might suit a boy of turbulent disposition but would not do where there was any gentleness'.[7]

Fired up by the revolutionary fervour sweeping Europe, the school revolts took on some of the Continental republican zeal. In the 1790s, Merchant Taylors' flew the Tricolour from the Tower of London on the Queen's birthday while at Winchester the boys sent the Red Cap of Liberty up the school flagpole.[8] This was a dangerous game to play. Britain was at war with the French republic and, fearing a copycat insurrection, the government gave strict orders to crush any domestic revolt. The massacred common people of Peterloo in 1819 experienced first hand exactly what that meant, but the treachery of the public schools was overlooked.

Turmoil on the Continent gave way to the dawning of the age of meritocracy. Aristocrats were stripped of their wealth and influence in favour of advancement based on character and ability. But in mid-nineteenth-century Britain the word 'poor' had become a relative term, applying to anyone whose father did not hold a title or did not share in the new wealth created by the industrial revolution. At Eton the school was divided into two distinct groups – Oppidans, who paid full fees, and Collegers, who obtained their education through grants or scholarships. The fagging system kept the 'poor' boys in their place and legitimised a level of harsh punishment that shamed the schools and brought misery to many. Towards the turn of the eighteenth century, poaching, vandalism and violence were endemic among many public schools. 'Charity boys' at Harrow were still being victimised long after they left the school. Having endured years of abuse while a schoolboy, William Winckley, a foundation scholar from a humble background, set up business in the town only for Harrovians to attack his home and molest his wife.[9]

The misrule of public schools finally reached the ears of parliament and one parliamentarian in particular. Henry Brougham was a slave reformer, journalist and founder of the influential *Edinburgh Review* who later became lord chancellor. Brougham had been educated at the local high school in Edinburgh and now made it his personal mission to see the mismanaged public schools run by the state for the public good. He had identified numerous abuses where endowments had been taken from the free scholars and used to benefit the masters and governors. When he became lord chancellor in 1830 he told the Commons committee on education that he believed more than £500,000 of public money given to public schools (equivalent to approximately £54 million today) was being misused: 'It is difficult not to repine at the silly use which well-meaning but ill-informed persons have so often made of the funds which have been designed for charitable purposes.' He argued that a fifth of this misused money should be invested in the training of teachers 'capable of giving the people a real education'.[10]

Unsurprisingly, Brougham's ideas on state-funded education proved unpopular in parliament, and the bills that he introduced in 1820, 1835, 1837, 1838 and 1839 were all defeated. Faced with entrenched opposition, he gave up efforts to reform the public school system and instead concentrated on the education of the poor through his support for the Ragged School movement.

Although efforts at reform were consistently put off, criticism of public schools did not fall on deaf ears, and the beatings and barbarity became a popular subject in newspapers and periodicals. In 1874, when the headmaster at Shrewsbury gave a boy eighty-eight strokes of the birch for having beer in his study, there were verses in *Punch* and questions in parliament; one of the newly appointed governors resigned and, although a public inquiry cleared the headmaster of excessive severity, he was dogged by the episode for the rest of his life.[11]

At the same time the middle classes demanded a higher quality and more humane education which was beginning to be met by the new grammar schools. This combination of public scrutiny and competition forced the public schools to measure up to new standards of education. Although some of the worst kinds of torture were curtailed, efforts by the governors to halt daily cruelties were largely thwarted by senior boys and masters. The argument ran that with so few teachers per pupil a regime of strict discipline was essential to avoid the riots of the past. There was also a widely held notion that this tough upbringing was the best preparation for the tough life ahead, imposing rule over the native majorities of the British Empire.

But the greatest criticism of all was that the education they sold was out of step with Britain's dynamic and rising economy. Their reliance on Greek and Latin to the exclusion of sciences put them at odds with the grammar schools and newly established academies. Charles Darwin, perhaps the most enlightened mind of Victorian Britain, made it quite clear that his public school deserved no credit for his scientific achievements. He spent seven years at Shrewsbury but complained that when he tried to show an interest in the natural world he was 'rebuked' by his master.

'Nothing,' Darwin later wrote, 'could have been worse for the development of my mind than Dr Butler's school, as it was strictly classical, nothing else being taught except a little ancient geography and history. The school as a means of education to me was simply a blank.'[12] Thomas Arnold's reforms at Rugby School, where he was a pioneering headmaster, had tried to address this obvious shortcoming but his loyalty to the classics meant his efforts fell short of the mark. What he and other so-called progressive headmasters failed to grasp was that the public schools served a single purpose – to produce gentlemen fit for society.

'Except for a few gifted and eccentric men like Tennyson,' argues the historian Colin Shrosbree, '[public schoolboys] made little contribution to the artistic and cultural life of the country... They took little part in trade or industry, although they might invest in order to buy more land. The army, into which many of them went, was an institution on the fringes of English society and was not the nation in arms, as in France, or the embodiment of state as in Prussia.'[13]

Shrosbree argues that 'men from the public schools formed a political elite whose membership was not dependent on knowledge, or ability, or democratic approval, but was buttressed and kept in place by a restrictive educational system, in which any equality of opportunity was stifled by the classical requirements of the public school system... The classics fulfilled the same sociological function in Victorian England as calligraphy in ancient China – a device to regulate and limit entry into a governing élite.'[14]

This, of course, explains why politicians like Boris Johnson and Jacob Rees-Mogg have such a fondness for Roman and Greek historians.

Public schools had become specialists at turning out princes and prime ministers but not much else. According to David Turner, 'Repeat custom from the families of Britain's tiny political class, and those desirous of breaking into it, was not enough to prevent a marked slide in the already small number of boys entering the old public schools.'[15] Their enterprise had become so niche that some of the best-known had come close to extinction. Harrow, for example, had a total school pupil complement of 351 in 1802 but this had fallen to an almost unviable 69 by 1844. That year the governors met to consider the 'probable dissolution of the school'.[16] What saved the public schools from a deepening irrelevance was not the reluctant and half-hearted attempt at reform from within but the innovation of young men educated elsewhere.

Britain's industrial revolution transformed the world's economy, laid the foundation for the building of Empire and ensured the first steps towards globalisation. Its architects were inventors and engineers whose basic education was met by the community not the public schools. Michael Faraday, the father of electricity, was the son of a Scottish blacksmith who could not afford to send his son to a fee-paying school. George Stephenson, the great civil engineer and 'father of the railways', came from an impoverished family and was illiterate until the age of eighteen. Richard Arkwright, whose inventions and entrepreneurship shaped the industrial revolution, was taught to read and write by a cousin because his family couldn't afford to send him to a public school. Isambard Kingdom Brunel, the greatest engineer of the industrial revolution, owed his formative education to a diligent father who home-schooled him and later the French university system which he entered when he was fourteen. Indeed, almost all the notable engineers and inventors who made Britain's industrial revolution did so outside the public school system.

It is a rich irony that it was to these ordinary self-made men whom the public schools owed their survival. The enormous wealth created by the industrial revolution brought about a new class of factory owners, bankers, industrialists and entrepreneurs, all determined to use their fortunes to leave an impression on their country. To achieve this they were more than happy to ensure that their own children benefited from the privilege and advantage that came from a classic public school education. The idea of buying a position among the British aristocracy made absolute business sense.

3

EMPIRE OF THE SONS

The Golden Age of the English public school corresponded with the triumph of the British Empire. Generations of diplomats, politicians and civil servants who ruled a quarter of the known world passed through the same school gates. Prime ministers Robert Peel, Lord Palmerston and Winston Churchill attended Harrow, while George Canning, William Gladstone and Arthur Balfour received their education at Eton. For 200 years, the Empire was the playground of the public schoolboy.

Cecil Rhodes, the architect of modern imperialism, neatly summed up the British perspective by claiming in 1902: 'We are the finest race in the world and the more of the world we inhabit the better it is for the human race.' Such unshakeable confidence was expressed by public school headmasters at morning prayers and echoed across the Empire. In this way, public schools were the 'aggressive, bigoted and extreme' propagandists of British imperialism.[1]

The essential foundation of a public school education was a hierarchical system governed by house loyalty and a blind faith in Queen, country and Empire. Strict, regimental discipline was drilled into pupils from the very first day of school and gave rise to the claim, wrongly attributed to the Duke of Wellington, that the Battle of Waterloo 'was won on the playing fields of Eton'.

Public schooling was brutal and so were the means of suppression employed by the new English rulers of Asia and Africa. The massacres and capital punishments that characterised Britain's suppression of national insurrection and native mutinies were applied with a dispassionate zeal by boys who had endured canings and a multitude of tortures during their formative years.

A superiority in British weaponry meant very few died at the hands of the enemy. This is an important point because even as late as 1861 there were fewer than 3,000 boys being educated at England's leading public schools and the schools could not have survived high rates of battlefield attrition.[2] At the Battle of Omdurman (1898) in Sudan, General Kitchener's army massacred up to 12,000 Mahdists for the loss of just forty-eight men, of whom just three were British officers.[3]

Governance of the Empire was made more efficient by the fact that those in charge had gone to the same school. At Harrow, Admiral Sir Augustus Clifford, one of the longest serving Black Rods, had been a fag to Palmerston, Viscount Althorp, a former chancellor of the exchequer, and Viscount Duncannon, a lord lieutenant of Ireland.[4]

The minor public schools also trained hundreds of lesser men to become the essential bureaucratic workhorses of the Empire. Since Britain's industries and trade were wholly dependent on the subjugation of large populations spread over vast lands there was no shortage of posts to fill. In *The Invention of Tradition*, historians Eric Hobsbawm and Terence Ranger stress: 'All this produced administrators who ruled their districts like lordly prefects inventing traditions to keep the fags on their toes.' Attention to detail was essential so that, by imposing obedience on an individual, the British rulers were able to enslave villages, towns and cities. Hobsbawm and Ranger illustrate this point by telling the story of one district inspector who had the habit of taking long walks among the local community in his tall hat. Halfway out he would leave the hat on the tree and then expect the nearest villager to bring it back immediately. Anyone reported to be have ignored the inspector's hat hanging on the tree could expect a harsh punishment.[5]

The governing ethos which shaped the men who ran the Empire was 'muscular Christianity'; at its heart was the idea that participation in sport could contribute to the development of Christian morality, physical fitness and 'manly' character. This is how Thomas Hughes expressed it in *Tom Brown's School Days*, published in 1857: 'The least of the muscular Christians has hold of the old chivalrous and Christian belief, that a man's body is given him to be trained and brought into subjection, and then used for the protection of the weak, the advancement of all righteous causes, and the subduing of the earth which God has given to the children of men.'

In pursuit of this ideal many of the public schools had developed their own games. Perhaps the most famous of all is Eton's wall game, a full-contact ball game still played today, although not the brutal version of the eighteenth and nineteenth centuries in which it was not uncommon for players to be literally left for dead on the field. However, it was the game of rugby that lent true physicality to muscular Christianity at public school.

The historian Brian Dobbs summed up the appeal of the game: 'If the Muscular Christians and their disciples in the public schools, given sufficient wit, had been asked to invent a game that exhausted boys before they could fall victims to vice and idleness, which at the same time instilled the manly virtues of absorbing and inflicting pain in about equal proportions, which elevated the team above the individual, which bred courage, loyalty and discipline…it is probably something like rugby that they would have devised.'[6] One of the reasons this appealed to public school headmasters and their boards of trustees in the late-nineteenth century was because of what they saw as the problem of homosexuality. They believed that adopting the ethos of muscular Christianity would in part serve to distract boys from exploring homosexual relationships.

Academic excellence and scientific inquiry were sidelined as rugby, cricket and football were employed to define physical and psychological character.

The legacy of this ethos lives on today – in 2012 and 2016 half the British Olympic teams came from private schools. As Britain embarked on its colonial adventures, muscular Christianity was the defining virtue wholly embraced by the British Army and the legions of missionaries who sallied forth across the Empire. Winning wars, crushing cultures and converting pagans was the best way a man could flex his Christian muscles.

The Victorian figure who best represents the ideal of muscular Christianity made his name in a number of famous military campaigns in defence and expansion of the British Empire. General Charles Gordon was a courageous commander and explorer whose adventures were avidly followed by the British public as he chased and fought Britain's enemies to the very margins of the known world. Gordon did not attend one of the great English public schools but instead went to a minor private institution in Taunton, Devon, called Fullands House, before being sent on to the military academy in Woolwich, then as important as Sandhurst in training army officers. Here, religious teaching and physical instruction were as strict as at any of England's great public schools. Even by Victorian standards Gordon's religious conviction was feverishly impassioned. He was especially impressed with Philippians 1:21 where St Paul wrote: 'For to me to live is Christ, and to die is gain', a passage he underlined in his Bible and often quoted. But Gordon, who once said to a Roman Catholic priest that 'the church is like the British Army, one army but many regiments', never allied himself to any church nor became a member of one. Instead he allowed his whole life to be defined by his muscular Christianity.[7]

Following the death of his father he undertook extensive social work in Kent including teaching at the local Ragged School. Before 1870, there was no universal education system in Britain, and the Ragged Schools were a network of privately funded schools that gave a free education to children whose parents were too poor to afford fees. Gordon even took in some of the children to live with him in his own home. His religious principles made him a leading opponent of slavery and throughout his African exploits he battled the slavers, often diverting military resources to help free slaves. Yet he was also a deeply flawed character. He frequently disobeyed orders, including those that came directly from Prime Minister Gladstone.

Gordon met his grisly end after the siege of Khartoum where he had been sent to evacuate the British garrison. It was here that his refusal to obey an order cost him his life. Instead of relieving the garrison he decided to stay on to fight the Islamist army led by Muhammad Ahmad. After holding out for months in hope of a relief column sent from London, Khartoum's defences fell. Gordon was killed and his severed head paraded around the city. Ahmad proclaimed himself ruler of Sudan, and established a religious state, the Mahdiyah, which was governed by a harsh enforcement of Sharia law. Out of consideration for his Turkish, Egyptian and Sudanese troops, Gordon had refrained in public from describing his battle with the Mahdi as a religious war, but his diary showed he viewed himself as a Christian champion fighting just as much for God as for Queen and country. At the time, Gordon's military campaigns had the full blessing of the British public. In August 1864, *The Times* wrote in support of Gordon: 'The part of the soldier of fortune is in these days very difficult to play with honour... but if ever the actions of a soldier fighting in foreign service ought to be viewed with indulgence, and even with admiration, this exceptional tribute is due to Colonel Gordon.'

History has not been so kind. In *Eminent Victorians*, Lytton Strachey strongly implied that Gordon, who remained a confirmed bachelor all his life, was a paedophile who may have even preyed on the children he befriended in the Ragged Schools.

In many ways Gordon embodied the ideal of the privately educated Victorian adventurer so loved by proponents of muscular Christianity. He was a charismatic, insubordinate, repressed homosexual who was addicted to danger and, by the end of his life in 1885, had a strong death wish.

While Charles Gordon represented the overachievement of an Empire adventurer, the vast majority of England's public schoolboys played much smaller and far less glamorous roles. The Barttelot family has lived at its ancestral seat at Stopham in West Sussex since 1372 and can trace its ancestry back to William the Conqueror.[8] Since the 1820s the male Barttelots have been schooled at Rugby and Eton. Sir Brian Barttelot is the Fifth Baronet and the fourth in the line to be schooled at Eton. Sir Brian has served as military secretary to the major-general commanding London District and Household Division between 1978 and 1980 and regimental lieutenant colonel of the Coldstream Guards between 1987 and 1992. In 1989 he was appointed Officer, Order of the British Empire. Generations of Barttelots served in Britain's Empire.

But in 1885 one of Sir Brian's ancestors played such an infamous part in the Sudan campaign that his actions raised serious questions about the darker side of a muscular Christian education. In 1874 Major Edmund Musgrave Barttelot followed in his father's footsteps and entered Rugby School. He then went to Sandhurst, again behind his father, where he was enrolled as an officer in the 7th Royal Fusiliers.

After the fall of Gordon at Khartoum the emboldened armies of Muhammad Ahmad, the self-proclaimed Muslim Mahdi, cut off Equatoria and threatened Cairo, key to Britain's influence in the region. In 1885, Emin Pasha, the governor whom Gordon had personally appointed to office, withdrew further south, to Wadelai near Lake Albert, but was in imminent danger of capture by the Mahdi's superior forces. The following year, Britain assembled the Emin Pasha Relief Expedition, led by Henry Morton Stanley (of 'Dr Livingstone I presume' fame) and set about the rescue of Pasha.

Major Edmund Musgrave Barttelot was one of eight public school-educated officers and gentlemen explorers who volunteered for the mission. As Stanley's second in command, he was in charge of the rear column together with an Anglo-Irish gentleman explorer, James Sligo Jameson, an ancestor of the Jameson whiskey family. While the main column pressed on to relieve Emin Pasha, Barttelot's column was left in the jungle to wait for replacement slave porters to be brought upriver. Very quickly the stifling heat and infectious diseases took their toll on the column and the British officers struggled to keep control. Barttelot maintained discipline through floggings and executions. Officers reported that he repeatedly stabbed African workers with a steel-pointed cane and that he 'had an intense hatred of anything in the shape of a black man'.[9]

Stranded in the jungle, Jameson and Barttelot looked for ways to entertain themselves. Curious about the practice of cannibalism, they paid six silk handkerchiefs to purchase a young slave so they could witness the act first hand. The ten-year-old girl they bought was tied to a tree, stabbed twice in the abdomen and bled to death. The cannibals then sliced meat from her. Jameson captured the ordeal in watercolours which he exhibited among the column.

Neither Barttelot nor Jameson survived the expedition, the latter dying from disease and the former being shot by a man whose wife he had threatened.

The fate of the column and the actions of the British officers were thought to have inspired Joseph Conrad's novel *Heart of*

Darkness, with Barttelot the basis for Kurtz. But Victorian society and the schools which produced such men took a rather different view. Barttelot's entry in the 1901 *Dictionary of National Biography* says he 'was a severe disciplinarian, had a somewhat hasty temper, and was unversed in dealing with orientals, but his character was freed of all serious reproach'. His brother Walter, who went to Eton and Sandhurst, later wrote a book defending his younger brother's behaviour by launching a scathing attack on the self-educated Stanley.[10] In the summer of 2017 I arranged to visit Sir Brian Barttelot at the family home in Stopham to try to understand more about his ancestor. Drinking tea in the country-house drawing room, Sir Brian happily discussed Edmund's exploits: 'The general view is that it was atrocious of Stanley to leave them there, and what happened after that was inevitable – they all went mad.'

Edmund was survived by his brother, Walter George Barttelot, who died in action on 23 July 1900 (aged forty-five) at Retief's Nek, Orange Free State in South Africa, during the Second Boer War. He was shot and killed leading a charge against a Boer position. His son, Walter III, died in Iraq during the First World War. His brother, Lieutenant Commander Nigel Kenneth Walter Barttelot, was killed in the same war while commanding the destroyer HMS *Liberty* at the Battle of Heligoland Bight. Sir Brian's father, another Walter, left Eton and joined the Coldstream Guards. 'He did a short stint in China,' says Sir Brian, 'and then got married in 1937 and then World War Two broke out and he ended up in Normandy in 1944. Churchill decided that guardsmen were put into tanks, but the guardsmen are all tall men and tanks aren't suitable for tall people.' Walter died fighting in Normandy. 'He was commanding his tank battalion in 1944 and arrived shortly after the first wave of the invasion and had a big success in a battle called Caumont. And then he was promoted and took over the 6th Guards Tank Brigade – so he was acting brigadier. He was rushing about on roads that hadn't been cleared and took a wrong turning in a scout car and was blown up by a mine. So he and his driver were killed in August 1944.'

Sir Brian believes the English public schools must have had 'quite a lot of impact' on the making of the Empire. 'You find boys turning up,' he says, 'who understood through their fathers how it works – my family people went into successive regiments, so you build up a bank of how things should be done.' He says discipline was essential and laments that now it 'has almost disappeared off the map – people don't want to be shouted at, they don't think they can cope with it. We've got a lot of floppy people now. And we used to get a clip across the ear in my day and that was quite normal – and you weren't offended, you just thought I've done something wrong and I won't do it again. That doesn't happen now. People shoot their mouths off now, there's no discipline. Today's politicians have no discipline. I'm old-fashioned.'

He believes the public school system gave the Empire 'continuity and cohesion'. And he says: 'I'm sure this is true of other schools as well, but the fact is your really good friends go back to those days. You can make friends later in life but they're never the same because you haven't got the same traditions and memories.'

★

The conventional and popular wisdom of the public schools triumphantly marching hand in hand with the Empire is only part of the story. Certainly, on the field of battle the officer classes were dominated by the privately educated gentlemen of the leading public schools. But whether the spark of military genius was struck at the great public schools is very much open to question. Indeed, the greatest military leader of them all, Wellington, hated his short time at Eton between 1781 and 1784, where he felt miserably lonely and socially adrift after his father's death left the family bereft of funds. The idea that Wellington's victories were 'won on the playing fields of Eton' is fatally undermined by the fact that Eton did not own any playing fields at that time.

A more likely influence on the young Wellington was the grammar school he attended in Dublin, where he was born. The school focused on the arts, literature and music. Among its most famous alumni was the nineteenth-century songwriter Thomas Moore. This may have accounted for the sensitive disposition that Wellington occasionally showed on the battlefield – he cried when he read the list of the dead after Waterloo and often took pains to avoid needless bloodshed.

In 1785, a lack of success at Eton, combined with a shortage of family funds due to his father's death, forced the young man and his mother to move to Brussels. A year later, Arthur enrolled in the French Royal Academy of Equitation in Angers, where he blossomed as a horseman and linguist. So it is perhaps more accurate to say that Waterloo was won on the playing fields of Angers.

While Victorian prime ministers were usually products of the English public schools the same cannot be said of Benjamin Disraeli, the prime minister perhaps most associated with Empire.

Unlike his younger brothers, who were sent to Winchester College, Disraeli attended a much less prestigious school only to surpass all family expectations.[11] Many other famous names popularly associated with the building of the British Empire were either educated outside the public school system or barely educated at all. Robert Clive, the statesman and general who founded British India, was sent to an ordinary grammar school in Market Drayton, Shropshire, before a fleeting attendance at Merchant Taylors' School in London from where he was expelled after less than a year. Hardly the propitious start in life for the conqueror of India, yet there is no mention of the tenuous nature of his association on the Merchant Taylors' website, which places him on a list of the 'great men' it has schooled.[12]

A little more can be said of the schooling of another imposing figure on British rule in India. Warren Hastings, the first governor general of India, attended a grammar school and then Westminster School, where he became the first King's Scholar of his year in 1747. But two years later at the age of sixteen, the impoverished circumstances of his family forced him to leave the school to find work. His headmaster protested against the removal of so promising a scholar, but Hastings was sent to a private tutor. In October 1750 he landed at Calcutta.[13]

Cecil Rhodes, the guardian of the British Empire who extended its reach to the far corners of Africa, did not take one step inside a public school. While his older brothers went to Eton and Winchester, his family decided Cecil should attend Bishop's Stortford Grammar School. He was a shy boy but excelled in study and sport, playing for the first eleven cricket team.[14]

David Livingstone, the most famous explorer of the Empire, was born in a Scottish tenement block and spent his youth working at the local cotton mill where he was employed as a piercer. But the philanthropic mill-owner furnished the children with a school and schoolmaster so that Livingstone and his fellow piercers could study for two hours after work.

Scotland provides us with a counter-example to England – a place with few public schools and a much greater commitment to a national education system. The high level of literacy in Scotland by the end of the eighteenth century could only be matched in Switzerland and New England. It was nearly one hundred years later that England finally got to grips with a national education system that could take pupils from primary school to university. In fact, the Scottish universities committed substantial resources to bursaries and scholarships so that they could offer free places to impoverished students who showed talent or aptitude for learning.

It led higher-education historian Robert Anderson to observe that as a result they did not suffer from the social barriers imposed by Oxford and Cambridge.[15] Proof of the success of the Scottish education system can be seen in how many working-class Scots used their schooling to improve their lives. For Livingstone it meant securing a place at Charing Cross Medical School.

To some extent the received wisdom holds true that Britain's Empire was ruled and led by men educated at a small number of leading English public schools. Certainly, senior diplomatic and government posts were dominated by privately educated men. Yet the schools have also exaggerated their role and over-promoted key imperial figures who had tangential or unhappy relationships with their alma maters.

Too little attention has been paid to the vital and often overlooked contribution of the grammar schools and self-educated men. This is particularly true of the Royal Navy, which was the backbone of the Empire, securing our lifelines from the Napoleonic Wars to the Second World War. Lord Nelson began his education at a grammar school in Norfolk before transferring to a small boarding school. Officers serving in Nelson's navy mostly came from humble beginnings. Indeed, in 1939 only 5 per cent of those in the position of rear admiral and above had been to a public school.[16] The army too had far more ordinarily educated officers than the public school historians lead us to believe. A survey of 'eminent men' in Queen Victoria's reign, published in 1900, reveals that only 16 per cent of the army officer corps had attended a public school.[17]

Yet the public school system gave the Empire a set of easily communicated values and, in muscular Christianity, a conquering ethos. This ethos was extended across the Empire through a colonial network of select schools based on the public school model. In this way the schools helped prop up the Empire by educating maharajas and princes. But the shameful massacres and abuses of power raise questions about the suitability of the schools as training grounds for leadership.

Herbert Branston Gray, former headmaster of Louth Grammar School and of the boarding school Bradfield College from 1880 to 1910, was a passionate believer in the British Empire. Yet he felt compelled to write an excoriating article in which he accused the public schools of 'letting down the Empire' by mirroring society at large, which he characterised by 'lack of preparedness, insularity and complacency'. In 'The Public Schools and the Empire', published in *The Spectator*, he denounced the rigid conformism of the public schoolboy, 'his public conduct and manners' as well as the 'mind-numbing unwholesome cult of games worship'. He argued that the Empire required 'democratic and enlightened' boys for the demands of 'a new age' and if they were not up to the task then they should be replaced.[18]

Public schools have helped to write British history. They have been cheerleaders for colonialism and controlled the narrative of Empire. In so doing, the excesses and abuses associated with this period were suppressed, while the positive values of muscular Christianity were promoted. The warning was sounded by Gray in 1913.

4

A VICTORIAN RECKONING

In Victorian Britain, newspapers and periodicals were a dominant feature of political life. At their zenith in the mid-nineteenth century there were more than 150 fifty paid-for serious journals. Politicians who wanted to get their voices heard wrote articles and the government reacted to campaigns in much the same way they do when the *Daily Mail* takes up an issue today. One journalist stood above all others with a reputation for aggressive, campaigning journalism: Matthew James Higgins. And in 1860 he had the public schools in his sights.

Writing under a pseudonym in *Cornhill Magazine*, Higgins alleged that Eton masters were exploiting boys financially. They were supposed to behave like parents ('in loco parentis'), he complained, yet they ran the school as a business, working not through a sense of disinterested vocation but from vested interest. The extravagant lifestyles they supported, moreover, encouraged among boys a taste for 'expense and self-indulgence' whereas he said the ideal teacher should embrace a life of simplicity and self-denial.

He also challenged the high pupil–teacher ratio (48:1), which maximised profit but prevented personal, sympathetic relations developing between masters and boys and made the proper supervision of leisure time impossible. The underlying problems of a school were not caused by the inherent rebelliousness of boys, he implied, but by the masters' mercenary attitude to their work.[1]

Higgins's article was followed by others that went further, accusing the Eton masters of stealing funds. The *Edinburgh Review* summed up the totality of the charge: 'That the statutes of such a foundation as Eton College should be carried out to the letter in the present day is, we admit, neither possible nor desirable; but it is both possible and desirable that the enormous revenues willed by an English king for the promotion of education… should not be illegally diverted from their original destination into the pockets of a small number of individuals who are not entitled to them.'[2]

Public indignation over schools' failure to honour their charitable status was becoming impossible to ignore. The focus on Eton made uncomfortable reading for parliament, where 105 MPs were Old Etonians, including the speaker and the chancellor of the exchequer.[3] In earlier times they could have been relied upon to quash any inquiry into their alma mater, but the nature of popular politics had changed. The Reform Act of 1832 had given the middle classes the vote and not all of them were sympathetic to the notion of government by public school. Dissatisfaction turned to anger when parliament voted down a series of bills designed to provide free education for the poor.

In 1861 a Scottish politician called Grant Duff, a barrister and member of the Liberal Party, proposed the establishment of a commission to investigate the public schools and make recommendations for their reform. Duff had been educated at the Edinburgh Academy, a public school established in 1823 to offer Scottish society a classical education to compete with the very best of English public schools. Yet Duff strongly believed Germany and France had taken a lead over English schools by giving young men an education that was based on sciences, not the classics. If Britain wanted to retain its superior industrialised advantage, its schools needed urgent reform. The idea of English vulnerability was a popular topic in the media and the Eton scandal gave the reformers their chance to act.

What Duff and his supporters had in mind was a wholesale shake-up of the public schools, broadening both the syllabus and the intake – the first unsteady steps towards a national curriculum. Duff wanted an inquiry of all endowed schools, numbering some 800, which had been established or maintained for the public benefit.[4] Duff was surprised at his initial success, confiding to his Scottish constituents that he feared blocking measures led by the cry 'floreat Etona'.

The minister tasked with assembling the commission into public schools was Sir George Lewis (Eton), who was now home secretary in Lord Palmerston's government. Lewis, an editor of the Edinburgh Review, had resigned his post in 1855 to succeed William Gladstone as chancellor of the exchequer – a George Osborne in reverse. Lewis was a baronet and related by marriage to George Villiers, 4th Earl of Clarendon.[5] It was to the former foreign secretary Clarendon whom Lewis turned to chair the inquiry. A third influential member of the commission, joining Duff and Villiers, was another former foreign secretary, Granville George Leveson-Gower, 2nd Earl Granville (Eton).

Today it seems remarkable that all four men in charge of reforming public schools owed their careers to private education and that two of these reformers (Lewis and Granville) were products of Eton, the very school which had sparked the inquiry in the first place. But there were political reasons for the appointment: Palmerston viewed Clarendon as a contender for his crown and sidelining him as chair of a lengthy royal commission would keep him busy and out of domestic and foreign politics. Few disagreed that Lord Granville and Lord Clarendon were seriously interested in reform but their ambitions were modest. What Duff had wanted was a full inquiry into all 800 public schools so that, reformed, they could form the basis of a national secondary education system. To this end, he had written to all the leading schools seeking their views on a commission.

In his own correspondence with Duff, Lewis accepted that endowed schools had been brought under the jurisdiction of parliament and the charity commissioners and that they must yield to government investigation. But he distinguished what he identified as a 'principal class' of endowed school whose permission would be needed before such an inquiry could take place.[6] In so doing Lewis had found a way of protecting the elite schools from the intrusive and further-reaching conclusions of a broader inquiry which was to follow Clarendon. By 'ring-fencing' a select number of schools from this second inquiry and allowing the 'elite' to dictate the terms of reference of their own inquiry, he could offer them special protection.

When the terms of the commission inquiry were published in July 1861, it was clear that Grant Duff had been out-thought by the wily Lewis. Instead of all 800 endowed schools, only nine were to be asked to give evidence to the Clarendon Commission. They were Eton, Winchester, Westminster, Charterhouse, St Paul's, Merchant Taylors', Harrow, Rugby and Shrewsbury. They had a combined pupil population of 2,708 and each was considered the crème de la crème of aristocratic schooling, being the institutions from which the majority of parliament was drawn.

The fact there was no serious attempt by the schools to avoid the benign terms of this inquiry speaks volumes. When Clarendon finally published its conclusions they came as no surprise or concern to the public schools. There was some genuine progressive reform, which the schools themselves recognised as necessary. An improved management structure, better accommodation and the quality of the curriculum and the teaching was to be subject to oversight. It was also agreed that more must be done to embrace the teaching of science to bring the schools in line with Europe.

By accepting the modest reforms of Clarendon, these nine leading public schools had escaped the radical shake-up of 782 grammars established in the sixteenth and seventeenth centuries to help educate the community. Under the later Taunton Commission it was decided that these schools were too unevenly spread across the country, leaving neglected pockets of illiteracy and innumeracy. To remedy this, the Endowed Schools Commission was created to remodel the schools using fee-paying pupils to supplement the endowments. Overnight, Britain's grammar schools were turned into quasi-public schools open to those who could afford a fee-paying education.

Far from Duff's original intentions, the overriding effect of the Clarendon and Taunton commissions, and the acts of parliament which followed, was to preserve and strengthen the status quo of a class-based education system in England for the next 150 years. The public did not get a root-and-branch reform of public schools, nor a redistribution of their vast resources, accumulated over the centuries from state endowments and philanthropic bequests.

For the free scholars, who came from the communities the schools were supposed to serve, this was a disastrous result. By the late nineteenth century most had already been sidelined by the wealth brought in by the fee-paying pupils, but after Clarendon the very statutes upon which they could make a claim for a free education were recast to give a much gentler interpretation of what constituted charitable service.[7]

The only saving grace was that foundation boys at some schools, including Eton and Harrow, were now recognised in law: 'Speaking generally, the foundation boys are, in the eyes of the law, the school. The legal position of the Head Master of Eton is that of a teacher or "informator" of seventy poor and indigent boys, received and boarded within Eton College; the Head Master of Harrow is legally the master of a daily grammar school, established in a country village for the benefit primarily of its immediate neighbourhood.'[8] But the poor's right to a public school education was immediately undermined by Clarendon's countervailing conclusion that the free scholar owed his education to the paying pupil, the former's place in the school subsidised by the latter.

And so public school fee-paying education became a right enshrined in law.[9]

The Public Schools Act 1868 gave public schools independence from direct jurisdiction or responsibility of the Crown, the established church or the government. The following year, the headmaster of Uppingham School invited seventy of his fellow headmasters to form what became the Headmasters' Conference – later the Headmasters' and Headmistresses' Conference (HMC). The independent school movement was born.

5

ETON RIFLES

On 4 August 1914 Britain was better prepared for a world war than any other nation on earth. The British Expeditionary Force (BEF), the professional standing army, may have been small compared to French and German forces but it was capable of quick and efficient mobilisation. In its support, Britain could call upon a national network of volunteer units, at the heart of which were the public school Officer Training Corps (OTC) and combined cadet units.[1]

Since the time of the Napoleonic Wars, these schools had been on an almost permanent battle footing, turning boys into officer soldiers. The threat of a French invasion in 1804 had led to the first volunteer force at Rugby – well before Thomas Arnold had pioneered his ideas of muscular Christianity.

By the mid-nineteenth century the volunteer units were receiving substantial arms funding from the government. The most famous school corps was the 'Eton Rifles' or, to give them their real name, the 'Eton Volunteers', established in 1860. Harrow, Winchester and Marlborough founded similar cadet forces, all equipped with army-issue weapons. Although these brigades of regimented and well-trained boy soldiers were voluntary, there were plenty of senior military advisers and generals who agitated for conscription.[2]

Field Marshal Lord Roberts, the hero and saviour of the Boer War, returned from the conflict in 1902 convinced of the need for a mandatory schoolboy force of officer cadets. Edmond Warre, headmaster of Eton from 1884 to 1905, and founder of the Eton Rifles, strongly believed that public schools should do more to support the army. In a speech to the Royal United Services Institute in 1900 he called on parliament to enact legislation that made military training compulsory for boys over fifteen.[3]

Nevertheless, even ardent lobbying from such well-qualified quarters failed to move the government to action. It wasn't until the early 1900s that these school brigades became part of the Officer Training Corps movement, organised by the reforms of Richard Burdon Haldane, the Liberal imperialist secretary of state for war (1905–12). By the summer of 1910 half of Harrow School took part in the annual OTC summer camp, parading, exercising and shooting for one week. Similarly high numbers were reported at camps attended by Eton, Rugby and Winchester. Participation in these camps and OTC membership numbers were closely watched by the War Office, which regularly wrote to the schools, urging the headmasters to take the business of training cadets as seriously as possible. In turn the headmasters wrote to the parents, issuing dark warnings of Prussian war-mongering and the militarisation of the Continent.

But the War Office needn't have worried: the public school ethos was founded on an unquestioning loyalty to King and country. Most boys aspired to achieving glory on the battlefield. The schools extolled the values and objectives of the Empire by lionising Empire figureheads such as the Duke of Wellington and Gordon of Khartoum. Popular literature of the day was littered with references to battlefield valour and sacrifice in India and Africa. G.A. Henty's books, *The Dash for Khartoum*, *With Kitchener in Sudan* and *The Young Colonists*, glorified African colonial adventure, while Rudyard Kipling's *Kim* and A.E.W. Mason's *The Four Feathers* did the same for India. Out there, Britain's superior weaponry had made soldiering less risky. The last imperial war, the

Boer War, had been fought more than twelve years ago and was over in less than three years. In that time a record seventy-eight Victoria Cross war medals were awarded to British and colonial soldiers. Eton alone had sent 1,326 officers to fight in the conflict.[4]

The First World War historian Anthony Clayton says that by 1914 the cultural identity of the public schools and the army were finely matched:

> [The] preference for selection of future regimental officers [was] from the growing number of fee-paying boarding Public Schools, their discipline now restored. They were spartan, with senior boys responsible for the discipline and welfare of juniors, hierarchic and snobbish, with a curriculum classical rather than scientific, and had compulsory worship on Sundays. Sport and membership of the School's cadet corps could count more than academic achievement. Morality and self-discipline were viewed as equating with courage. The foundations for future regimental life were carefully laid and, most important of all, the attributes of an officer and a gentleman were inculcated. Family traditions of service with particular regiments were appearing. The age was one of a strong military culture with pride in Imperial expansion.[5]

By 1914 Britain had a standing army of 400,000, of whom it is estimated 10,000 (2.5 per cent) were former public schoolboys. The man in overall charge of recruitment, General Kitchener, already a hero of imperial campaigns, nervously observed the Prussian build-up of arms. His chief concern was that, while Germany could rely on conscription to bolster its ranks, Britain's leaders wanted to make their soldiers part of an army of the willing.

Kitchener set a target of one million volunteer men. Fifty-four million posters were issued, eight million personal letters were sent, 12,000 mobilisation meetings were held and 20,000 speeches were delivered by military spokesmen. That summer, when war was declared and the call went out for volunteers, the army benefited from a virulent jingoist fever sweeping the nation. The militarisation of the public schools meant there was no shortage of officer volunteers. By the spring of 1914 Marlborough College proudly proclaimed that 'almost every able-bodied boy had joined' its OTC.

At stake was a millennium of uninterrupted hegemony. Should Britain have lost the war the ruling class would have lost everything.

Alec Waugh, the elder brother of Evelyn, was typical of the younger boys at Sherborne School in Dorset who had been impatiently waiting their turn to join their heroes on the front line: 'It was impossible to feel the old excitement about the result of a house match when the morning paper had brought with it the story of Neuve Chapelle. The winning of cups and the gaining of colours ceased to be an end in themselves. For the boy who was prevented by lack of years from joining the army in 1914 school life became a period of marking time.'[6]

Waugh and thousands of his fellow pupils were cheered on from the safety of the sidelines by their headmasters exhorting them to 'play up and play the game', a popular refrain taken from the famous verse written by Sir Henry Newbolt in 1892 about a cricket match at Clifton College where he was at school. It refers to how a schoolboy, a future soldier, learns selfless commitment to duty in cricket, which he remembers in the nick of time before the regiment is overwhelmed by the mass ranks of the Mahdi in Sudan.

In the first weekend of the war in 1914, 100 men an hour (3,000 a day) signed up to fight. By the end of the year, 1,186,337 men had enlisted, hundreds of thousands from across the Empire. Among this wave of enthusiastic recruits I have estimated that 31,000 were officers, the vast majority from public and independent endowed schools.[7] As such, they would enjoy greater privileges than the average private. At that time, obtaining a commission was strictly a matter of class. Until 1870 cavalry and infantry officers secured a rank in the British Army under the purchase system, for which no formal military education was required. Every applicant's family had to demonstrate that their son had 'the education of a gentleman'. To do this they had to seek the approval of a regimental colonel and to pay a substantial fee 'which was both proof of his standing in society and a bond for good behaviour'. In this way the military became the plaything of the aristocracy. Lord Cardigan (Harrow), who led the disastrous Charge of the Light Brigade in the Crimean War, paid the equivalent of £2 million in today's money to purchase his commission. The system of promotion worked on a similar basis. When a vacancy became available the senior officer of the immediate lower rank in the same regiment had a priority claim on the position, providing he had sufficient funds to meet the sum laid down by parliament for that rank.

The route to officer class was prescribed through the military training colleges of Sandhurst and Woolwich. All officers attended as gentlemen cadets and were only granted their commission after completing the course. During their training the public school recruits held the status of 'gentlemen cadets' and were not subject to military law. Their parents continued to pay for tuition and boarding as well as additional fees for books, uniform and mathematical instruments. For the sons of serving or former officers, rates were reduced. Practical tests of aptitude for leadership did not exist and were only introduced during the Second World War. Unsurprisingly, such a system 'had the effect of confining entry to the RMA [Royal Military Academy, Woolwich] and the RMC [Royal Military College, Sandhurst] to public schoolboys, often from families with a military connection'.[8]

Robert Sherriff, better known as the writer R.C. Sherriff, attended Kingston Grammar School in Surrey, founded in the reign of Elizabeth I. After leaving school in 1914 he followed his father into the insurance business and joined Sun Assurance in London as a clerk. A week after the outbreak of war, Sherriff responded to Kitchener's call for officers: 'I was excited, enthusiastic. It would be far more interesting to be an officer than a man in the ranks. An officer, I realised, had to be a bit above the others, but I had had a sound education at the grammar school and could speak good English. I had some experience of responsibility. I had been captain of games at school. I was fit and strong. I was surely one of the "suitable young men" they were calling for.'

However, the army was unable to recognise the achievements he attained at his grammar school and his application was rejected. The recruiting officers were issued with a list of acceptable schools and Kingston Grammar was not on it. There was no intended personal slight; it was simply that grammar school men were excluded as part of the army's administrative process.

Sherriff meekly returned to his job with Sun Assurance. The following year, the British Army suffered such appalling casualties that it had to lower the officer barrier and accept those it had once deemed unsuitable. Sherriff wrote to his managers again asking for them to keep his position open as he intended to reapply for a commission. But the company refused, informing him: 'The Directors do not feel in a position to pay your salary while away from the office. You will have been regarded as having resigned your position'.[9]

Official military discrimination against the recruitment of non-public schoolboys meant that in the first year of the war the British Army was without the services of thousands of soldiers who later proved themselves to be excellent officers. While the public school officers were cloistered away, the grammar school soldiers had a much better understanding of the men they led into battle. This class barrier was not only wasteful to the war effort but was plainly irrational. Kitchener himself would have found it hard to pass muster.

In November 1915 Sherriff volunteered again and this time successfully won a commission into the East Surrey Regiment. He served at Vimy Ridge, Messines Ridge and Passchendaele where he was wounded during an artillery barrage.[10] In his famous play, *Journey's End*, Sherriff depicts the privately educated schoolboys of Britain's *haut monde* playing at being leaders of men. Stanhope, the central character, is a high-flying public schoolboy whose kind, generous nature is twisted by the horrors of the trenches. He becomes embittered and turns to drink. Stanhope is based on Sherriff's own commander, Captain Godfrey Warre-Dymond (Marlborough), whom the playwright grew very close to during their war service in France. At the close of hostilities in 1919, Warre-Dymond left the army and fell on hard times. He was divorced by two wives and became indebted to loan sharks, forcing him to set out as a travelling salesman. He later asked Sherriff for money and a reference.

Despite mounting casualties, the jingoism of the first year of the war was enthusiastically carried forward by the public schools. In fact, public schools remained stoically uncritical of the war. In October 1914 a motion proposed at a Shrewsbury School debate that 'modern weapons have destroyed the romance of war' was defeated by five votes.[11] Those who died were heroes; those who questioned the motives or the tactics were branded cowards. The pressure felt by young men like Sherriff and Waugh to join up was partly driven by the public opprobrium directed against anyone conspicuously left behind on civvy street.

To help boost morale and instil courage among the officer class the military's top brass showered them with medals. The highest award for gallantry was the Victoria Cross, which was awarded sparingly. Throughout the conflict, 627 servicemen were honoured, a quarter posthumously and significantly only 163 officers who had attended public school. Because the VC recognised acts of gallantry by all ranks, it was decided that more public recognition was needed to honour the bravery of junior officers. In October 1914 the army instituted a new medal, the Military Cross, which was only to be awarded to officers of the rank of captain or below who were judged to have exhibited acts of gallantry during active operations in the presence of the enemy. From June 1917 officers of the rank of captain but who had a temporary rank of major were also allowed to receive this new medal. This was the medal that serving officers and aspiring officers like Alec Waugh and his school friends at Sherborne hoped to win. By 1918 the rigid medal system was failing to keep up with acts of valour in the air battle and so the military struck two new medals – the Air Force Medal and Distinguished Flying Medal. Eton won the lion's share of public school medals: 13 won the Victoria Cross, 548 won the Distinguished Service Order and 744 won the Military Cross.[12]

But if the medals were carrots to sustain acts of heroism and leadership among the public school recruits, the stick was the court martial. A total of 5,952 officers and 298,310 other ranks were court-martialled. Death sentences were passed on 3,080 men (1.1 per cent of those convicted). Of these, 89 per cent were reprieved and the sentence commuted to a more lenient punishment. Of the 346 men put before a firing squad only three were officers.[13, 14] On the face of it, the death sentence had become a matter of class so that gentlemen officers were spared execution. This was partly because it was the officers who had the power to recommend court martial. In practice, officers accused of serious offences by fellow officers were simply whisked out of the front line to avoid damaging public morale.

For many young men an allegation of cowardice was much more serious a wounding than any physical injury they suffered on the battlefield. Yet the notion of the gallant, public school-educated gentleman, chivalrously leading his men into battle, is sharply undermined by the diaries of the 27th Earl of Crawford and 10th Earl of Balcarres. In March 1915, with an already distinguished political career behind him, he enlisted at the age of forty-three as a private in the Royal Army Medical Corps. For fourteen months he was a medical orderly on the Western Front, the only cabinet minister to serve in the ranks during the First World War. He wrote in his diaries:

> How disagreeable some officers are. They talk chiefly about their billets and personal grievances. One never hears a word about the men of the army [officers slept in beds, the men on the ground]... The officer of old standing is much more modest in his manner... This war is going to be won by the NCOs and men, not by the commissioned ranks. Eighteen months will develop a good soldier, a very passable NCO. But the period is too short to instil even the elements of leadership and control into the ordinary middle-class fellows who hold the commissions. And moreover I come across hundreds who have neither the character nor the decision to be competent officers even if they had twenty years training – the flabby, easy-going temperament of young men brought up in affluence, with never a struggle or effort to their credit – men for whom everything has been done in the past, and consequently find themselves helpless to act in the modern con-ditions of war. It is all too pitiful, too tragic... The average soldier comes from a different stock and even if his experience of strife has hitherto been limited to industrial troubles, he knows from the struggle for his livelihood what sustained and self-devoting effort really is.[15]

Crawford's diaries are not the only evidence that some officers behaved scandalously during the war. Sir Walter Barttelot, nephew of Edmund whom we met briefly in the previous chapter, kept up the family tradition of Eton followed by the Coldstream Guards. Badly wounded during the Battle of the Aisne, he was awarded a Distinguished Service Order and sent back to England.

Pronounced unfit for trench warfare, he spent the rest of the war as a staff officer and in 1918 was despatched to Tehran as Britain's military attaché, where he reportedly seduced a number of women and ended up being murdered in his bed by a cuckolded husband.

★

The greatest charge against the public school ethos is not that it encouraged some officers to behave badly during the war; far more serious is the argument that the militarisation of the public school system played a vital role in the belligerence that led to the outbreak of war. This point is best made by Tim Card, who was a master at Eton for thirty-three years before becoming vice-provost in 1988. In his book *Eton Renewed*, he says that the First World War could be seen as a public schoolboys' war, fought to preserve an imperial system which had been good for public schools but not the working classes.[16]

The public schools also have a case to answer over the misman-agement of the bloody conflict. The man many historians blame for Britain's misguided military strategy is John French (Harrow). French first distinguished himself leading a section of the expedi-tion to relieve General Gordon at Khartoum. While the column was doomed to fail, French showed brave leadership in the forlorn race across Africa. He also had a considerable reputation as a wom-aniser and his career was almost ended when he was cited in the divorce of a fellow officer while in India in the early 1890s. Yet he survived a succession of scandals and went on to head the British imperial army at the start of the war. Together with General Haig, the leader of the BEF from 1915 who became known as the Butcher of the Somme, he sent many men to slaughter. French's obsession with cavalry charges against guns and Haig's inability to understand the importance of the machine gun cost many lives while also lengthening the war.

Still, it was the old boys who wrote the first draft of history in their poems and polemical prose. Their privileged positions in society allowed them to control the narrative, whether it was shaped by critics like Siegfried Sassoon (Marlborough) and artist Paul Nash (St Paul's) or more idealistic voices such as Rupert Brooke (Rugby). Even the leading voices among the ranks of the conscientious objectors were privately educated. The trend continued over the next century. Basil Liddell Hart (St Paul's) and Alan Clark (Eton) promoted the attack on British leadership by characterising it as 'lions led by donkeys'. Later the TV series *Blackadder Goes Forth* – the ultimate parody of First World War public school attitudes – was created by Richard Curtis (Harrow), produced by John Lloyd (King's Canterbury), and starred Rowan Atkinson (St Bees), Stephen Fry (Uppingham) and Hugh Laurie (Eton).

Britain's military future, as well as its history, is still being shaped by the First World War. The OTC model for the military training of schoolboys was invoked by the former defence secretary Michael Fallon (a former pupil of Epsom College, site of one of the finest rifle shooting clubs in the country) in 2016 in his plan to extend the public school–dominated cadet corps to more state schools. By the end of 2017, very few state schools had joined the scheme – of the 260 cadet forces across the country 210 are from independent schools.[17]

★

The role of public schools in creating the conditions for a conflict which ended in mass slaughter on the Western Front was given a powerful endorsement in Peter Parker's book *The Old Lie: The Great War and the Public School Ethos*, first published in 1987: 'It is no disrespect to the dead to regret that many of them fought and died for all the wrong reasons… That men dribbled footballs towards the enemy trenches does not mean that the war was a game. That men died for an ethos does not mean that the ethos was worth dying for.'

Alec Waugh, like many of his generation, wrote about the war in damning terms in *The Loom of Youth*, published before the conflict had ended: 'All our generation has been sacrificed; of course it is inevitable. But it is rather hard. The older men have seen some of their hopes realised; we shall see none. At the beginning we were deceived by the tinsel of war; Romance dies hard. But we know now. We've done with fairy tales. There is nothing glorious in war, no good can come of it. It's bloody, utterly bloody. I know it's inevitable, but that's no excuse. So are rape, theft, murder. It's a bloody business.' Ironically, it was his unvarnished account of life inside a public school, rather than his verdict on the war, that caused a public outcry. For this Waugh was dismissed from the Old Shirburnian Society. He remains the only former student ever to have his membership revoked.

Following the armistice, the number of demobbed officers who suffered terribly in civilian life stood as testimony to the misery of post-war trauma.[18] But they were the lucky ones. The ultimate sacrifice made by a generation of young men between 1914 and 1919 is written on the memorials and cenotaphs proudly erected in their honour in quadrants and chapels across the country. It is estimated that 35,000 public school-educated soldiers died in the war out of a toll of 900,000. They constituted just over 3 per cent of the total fatalities.[19] Although the great majority of casualties in the First World War were from the working class, the social and political elite were hit disproportionately hard; their sons were the junior officers whose job it was to lead the men over the top and expose themselves to the greatest danger. Some 12 per cent of the British Army's ordinary soldiers were killed during the war, compared with 17 per cent of its officers. Eton alone lost 1,157 former pupils – 20 per cent of those who served.

The aristocracy and many leading public figures had been personally touched by the war with the sacrifice of their own sons. Wartime Prime Minister Herbert Asquith lost a son, while the future prime minister Andrew Bonar Law lost two. Anthony Eden had two brothers killed and a third terribly wounded.[20] Rudyard Kipling (United Services College), who so faithfully beat the Empire drum, glorified his son's death in his mournful poem 'My Boy Jack'. Kipling had intervened to persuade the military to take 'Jack' just weeks after leaving Wellington College when he was still sixteen years old and after he had failed his initial assessments because of his severe short-sightedness.

Analysis of the rolls of honour of twenty-six public schools by Anthony Seldon and David Walsh shows that just over a quarter of all deaths came during 1918 (heavily weighted to the six and a half months following 21 March).[21] (No one knows what the grammar school death rates were because no one has bothered to count them.) Nevertheless, in *Public Schools and the Great War*, Seldon writes that, 'exhausted and traumatised by over four years of war, the schools returned to a curriculum and way of life that was reassuringly familiar. The schools thus had a far greater impact on the war than the war had on them.'[22]

6

SURVIVAL OF THE FITTEST

The national sorrow that turned to bitter recrimination at the end of the First World War defined the perspective for social change in Britain. Politicians recognised that what their war-weary citizens desired most was a kinder, fairer country where the prospects of all were improved. So the government, led by Liberal leader David Lloyd George, a son of a teacher who promised a country fit for heroes, turned its attention to housing, living standards, electoral franchise reform and, of course, education.

Britain had been recognised as a divided society before the start of hostilities, but the war had highlighted the acute disparities in education.[1] Poor literacy levels were exposed during the processing and administration of a mass army. Health problems also became evident as large numbers of boys of military age were deemed unfit for service. The government responded with the 1918 Education Act, which raised the school leaving age to fourteen and linked the schools to medical inspections and further state support. It also abolished fees at all state-run elementary schools.[2]

At this time, any radical dismantling of or even tampering with the foundations of the English class system would have looked like some sort of defeat. Nevertheless, there remained a stubborn and persistent minority of dissident voices, mostly pacifists and socialists, who urged action against the system that had the power to take a whole nation to war. There was the Rugby-educated socialist reformer R.H. Tawney, who had refused a commission in the Manchester Regiment, choosing to join as a private soldier. Tawney fought in the Battle of the Somme, and was shot through the chest. For many years after the war he would wear his sergeant's jacket around his Bloomsbury flat. In his seminal work *Secondary Education for All* he called for an end to the 'vulgar inequalities' of the class system by the establishment of a national system of education.

Then there was George Bernard Shaw, who was at the height of his fame when war was declared in 1914. His subsequent diagnosis of the conflict as a capitalist folly driven by economic greed found favour across the classes, not just among working families. Part of his proposed cure was a radical shake-up of the education system: 'Schools and schoolmasters, as we have them today, are not popular as places of education and teachers, but rather prisons and turnkeys in which children are kept to prevent them disturbing and chaperoning their parents.'[3]

In calling for expanded educational opportunities, Tawney and Shaw joined such notable reformers as Sidney Webb, Matthew Arnold, Herbert Spencer, Thomas Huxley, Jeremy Bentham and John Ruskin. Remembering his misery at the Central Dublin Model School, Shaw was wary of proposals to employ mass education to break down class distinctions, and he disapproved of plans to allow promising students from the lower classes to attend expensive private schools, fearing they would feel hopelessly out of place in an institution full of 'toffs'. By 1923 he was convinced that the only way to end the 'Diabolonian' iniquities of government by a privileged class was to 'raze' the public schools and 'sow their foundations with salt'.[4]

His contemporary, John Galsworthy (Harrow), determined that British society was based on a strict caste system supported by the public schools. He described the schools as 'great caste factories' where the sense of superiority was 'set and hard as iron'.[5] At the same time Alec Waugh published his non-fiction account of private education *Public School Life: Boys, Parents, Masters*, arguing that there was a 'conspiracy of silence' and a 'policy of evasion' between headmasters and parents when confronting the failings of public schools, which he deemed in 'drastic need of repair'.[6] In another, perhaps even more radical move, Cyril Norwood, head-master at Harrow until 1929, called for state control of all public schools in order to bridge the 'deepening fissure' between the private and state education systems, which left pupils like 'strange dogs' when they met at university.[7]

Despite such vigorous public debate, parliament remained focused only on state education. Grammar schools, which formed the bedrock of the non-public school system, received a huge state cash injection while still being allowed to continue to charge fees to the wealthier parents.[8] By the middle of the twentieth century the state-aided grammar schools had become the natural preserve of the middle classes who had settled on a schooling that was not only affordable but more in tune with the educa-tion of children in mainland Europe. Many of these schools even provided facilities, such as science laboratories and art studios, which bettered or matched public schools – and all located in the local community.

One such school was Ripon Grammar School, refounded in 1555 with all the characteristics of a public school. Most of its pupils paid for their education and it followed the muscular Christian ethos developed by Thomas Arnold. There were fee-paying boarders; there was fagging; senior boys administered punishments; and the school structure was based on a house system with a great emphasis on sport. But in one vital respect it was different: all its pupils were taken from the community it served. In more recent times, reconstituted as a state grammar boarding school, its pupils have included Katharine Viner, editor of *The Guardian*, Richard Hammond of *Top Gear* fame, and the fashion designer Bruce Oldfield. Other notable resurgent grammar schools of the interwar period were King Edward's School in Birmingham (where Theresa May's former adviser, Nick Timothy, was educated) and Manchester Grammar School.

The success of these hybrid grammars in attracting wealthy middle-class families hit the public schools hard, leaving a number struggling to compete. There is no doubt that the scandals and horror stories that had beset the great English public schools had left them with a serious public relations problem, forcing relatively well-off families to think twice about sending their offspring to what had been derided as an alien and brutal institution. Demand for places at top public schools started to plummet. Harrow had to close one of its boarding houses, leaving masters to ponder its future existence.[9]

When new state secondaries opened up in competition to public schools in Dulwich, Streatham and Shrewsbury, the governing council of the Girls' Public Day School Trust, which ran a chain of private schools, protested to the Board of Education. The Trust had every reason to fear the competition as its accounts revealed it was £106,000 in the red (equivalent to £10 million today.)[10] The financial stability of these schools became even more precarious with the passing of the School Teachers Superannuation Act 1918, which gave state school teachers pensions, and followed measures to impose minimum salaries.

In May 1919 the public schools met with the government to thrash out a deal that they hoped would ensure their survival. Frank Fletcher, headmaster of Charterhouse and chair of the Headmasters' Conference, along with the heads of Eton and Marlborough, told the president of the Board of Education, Herbert Fisher (Winchester), they would accept free pupils from state elementary schools in return for government funding. Fisher politely but firmly rejected their overtures on the grounds that it appeared that the public schools wanted to be paid for skimming the cream of the state elementary school pupils. Fletcher recalled in his memoirs: 'We were told at the time there was no demand for places in our schools for ex-elementary schoolboys.'[11]

A century later history repeated itself when in 2016 public schools were threatened by Theresa May with the removal of their charitable status. It would have led to the schools being treated as income-generating businesses, making them liable for millions of pounds in corporation tax. At the same time Labour said it was planning to make parents pay VAT on their school fees.

Facing this two-fronted attack, the schools tried to placate the politicians by making exactly the same offer as Frank Fletcher had made to the Board of Education. And just like the Lloyd George coalition government of 1919 the Conservatives under Theresa May refused to entertain the idea.

★

The schools and the state were badly hit by the Great Depression. Many private schools were brought back from the brink by taking advantage of more restrictive state grants provided for in the 1902 Education Act. But these were only made available[12] on the strict terms dictated by the government, not by the schools. In return for taking in poor students from the community on a fee-free basis, the state pledged to pay the schools a grant. In 1926 secondary schools controlled by voluntary bodies could receive a grant from either the Board of Education or their local authority, or both. But they were required to meet the Board's regulations, and were subject to the same system of inspections as state-funded schools. The Board drove a fair bargain, expecting these 'grant maintained' schools to take no more than 25 per cent of their pupils free of charge from state elementary schools. Suitable pupils were selected using a scholarship examination.[13]

The social impact on the schools was immediate. 'I am grateful to University College School for teaching me to understand the lives of those who were poorer than myself,' wrote the poet Stephen Spender, who attended the school in the 1920s. 'When I was a child I was never allowed to play with poor children because my mother regarded them as not only rough, but also as perpetual carriers of infectious diseases… However, some of the boys I most liked were of working-class parents and lived in very poor districts.'[14]

Those public schools that remained untouched by the state system were able to continue educating the nation's elite. Britain's aristocracy and upper classes had developed a dependency on schools that valued eccentricity and promoted amateurism over professionalism. Amateurism meant the pursuit of noble causes in themselves, whereas professionalism tainted life because it encouraged greed.[15] For Cyril Norwood, however, what parents were actually paying for was 'a social badge, and… rights of entry to circles which people do very much desire to enter'.[16]

In the time before the Second World War, governments remained resolutely concerned with providing schools for those who were excluded from the education system rather than curbing the education of the upper classes. Critical voices of the post-war era also softened their tone. Among those who'd become reconciled to wealth-based education for the privileged was Alec Waugh. Sherborne forgave him his 'libellous' attack on the school in *The Loom of Youth* and the Old Shirburnian Society reversed its decision to expel him from its ranks. Most tellingly of all, Waugh ended up sending his two sons to Sherborne as boarders.[17] Perhaps his brother Evelyn was right after all when he wrote: 'One goes through four or five years of perfect hell at an age when life is bound to be hell anyway, and after that the social system never lets one down.'[18]

The public schools took full advantage of this more benign political climate, and pupil rolls rose to record numbers.[19] Greater demand for places even triggered a building programme, ushering in a new breed of public school which included Stowe, Canford and Bryanston, founded on very different charitable statutes. Gone was the promise so fundamental to the ancient statutes of Winchester and Eton which had pledged to serve the community by providing education for the poor. In their stead was a much more businesslike assessment of what a public school endowment should be: a modern schooling for those who could afford it. The fagging and blooding of the Victorian period were cast aside in favour of a humane religious education for the professional classes. Sadly, many of these pupils would not join the professions immediately, as another war was looming.

7

CHURCHILL, THE PUBLIC SCHOOL REFORMER

It is testimony to the resilience of the public schools that a select group of men from a handful of schools were able to dictate the terms of Britain's involvement in the Second World War. The appeasement policy of one public schoolboy, Neville Chamberlain (Rugby), helped create the conditions for conflict with Germany, and set the scene for another, Winston Churchill (Harrow), to come to the nation's rescue in its hour of peril.

The type of privately educated senior officer who had led the BEF to a bloody stalemate in France in 1914 was easily recognisable among the next generation of commanders who were once again drawing up plans to defeat the Germans across the Channel. So we should not be surprised that the war got off to exactly the same disastrous start as the previous one, with a series of morale-sapping defeats.

The first of these calamitous setbacks was orchestrated by John Vereker, an aristocrat career officer who also took the title 6th Viscount Gort. Like Churchill, he had been educated at Harrow from where he was expected to take a commission in the army. His reputation had suffered a severe blow in 1908 when, on a moose hunt in Canada, he accidentally shot and killed his guide. Nevertheless, Vereker went on to distinguish himself in the First World War and was awarded the Victoria Cross.

His experience of bogged-down trench warfare poorly served him in the next conflict. Surprised by the Germans' Blitzkrieg tactics, Vereker very nearly lost Britain its entire army. As it was, he was forced to leave behind 68,000 soldiers and abandon all the BEF's heavy equipment in northern France. Hitler's failure to give the order to chase the British into the sea gifted the Royal Navy precious time to perform a small miracle and rescue 224,000 soldiers off the beaches of Dunkirk, with the help of the flotilla of 'little ships' from the south coast of England.

While Vereker could claim some kind of victory (he had at least brought home most of the army) the same could not be said of another British general who also attended 'a very famous' English public school and was also decorated for bravery in the First World War. Arthur Ernest Percival did not come from the same aristocratic stock as Gort, but his father was a sufficiently successful land agent to send Arthur and his brother to Rugby. There, Percival excelled in the school's Volunteer Rifle Corps but left in 1906 with a single higher school certificate. In 1914 he enlisted as a private in the Officer Training Corps of the Inns of Court but, like so many public school soldiers, was rapidly promoted through the ranks. He was awarded the Military Cross following the Somme offensive when he was badly wounded by shrapnel. After the war he was sent to Ireland where he was accused by the Irish Republican Army of being responsible for brutally torturing detainees, including pulling out fingernails with pliers. He later survived an attempt on his life at Liverpool Street Station in 1921.

Following the outbreak of the Second World War, Percival was sent to the Far East to command British Empire forces against the Japanese. Like Vereker, he too was surprised by the speed and strength of the enemy. In the face of a series of bold Japanese offensives he beat a hasty retreat to the naval base of Singapore,

Britain's crucial military foothold in the region. As the Japanese began their assault on the city, Churchill sent orders to Percival to hold at all costs. But in February 1942, with his supplies and ammunition running low, the British general agreed to an unconditional surrender.

It was the biggest capitulation in British military history, involving the surrender of 140,000 Allied personnel to fewer than 30,000 Japanese soldiers. The defeat looked even worse when it emerged that the Japanese were also running low on ammunition and may not have been able to carry out a decisive assault against the British-led forces.

Such failures of command and leadership were symptomatic of a much deeper malaise facing the British Empire. Its rulers were schooled and fought in a bygone age characterised by a *noblesse oblige*, which in the interwar years had engendered a blind complacency. George Orwell said: 'The higher commanders, drawn from the aristocracy, could never prepare for modern war, because in order to do so they would have had to admit to themselves that the world was changing.' The senior officers in the British Army spent as much time engaged in a narrow class war with one another as they did fighting the real enemy. In Singapore, for instance, Percival was undermined by his second in command Lieutenant General Sir Lewis 'Piggy' Macclesfield Heath (Wellington), who believed he had the better credentials for Percival's job. He came from a military family that had served the Empire in Africa and Asia for many years. Before Percival was promoted to general officer commanding (Malaya), Heath had been his senior officer.

The local populations, governed for so many years by the British, had mixed feelings about the defeat of their masters. They may have feared the Japanese but under British rule they had experienced racism and cruelty and so 'could not suppress a spurt of glee at the humbling of the sahibs'.[1] The rubber and oil barons, public school expats of J.G. Farrell's *The Singapore Grip*, had enjoyed decadent lives on the backs of the local people and had never given a thought to it coming to an end. My grandfather, who went to Sedbergh School in Cumbria, was one of them and he never got over the shock of the loss of Burma, which ultimately sent him to the bottle and an early grave.

These defeats, and others in Crete and North Africa under the Wykehamist General Wavell, exposed the Empire's soft under-belly and also fuelled a public debate about the inadequacies of the men in command. At the outbreak of war, 54 per cent of major generals and above had attended one of twenty-six leading public schools, while most of the rest were privately educated with very few coming through the ranks.[2] Yet the government's reaction to a seemingly endless stream of defeats merely resulted in a gentle reshuffling of the pack so that by the end of the war the schooling of Britain's war leaders remained exactly the same.[3] Few historians believe that the Nazis or Japanese would have been defeated if the Americans had left Britain to fight on alone with its depleted resources marshalled by an out-of-touch officer class.

As the country faced its darkest hour, British society underwent something of a collective mental breakdown. The shortcom-ings of the education system were blamed for what looked like imminent defeat. Terence Cuthbert Worsley (Marlborough), a former Wellington master, laid the blame firmly at the door of the public schools: 'If public schools are national assets because of their leadership and training qualities, what are we to think of those qualities when we survey the mess into which their leadership has brought us?' It seemed a fair question and an echo of George Orwell's famous observation: 'Probably the battle of Waterloo was won on the playing-fields of Eton, but the opening battles of all subsequent wars have been lost there.'[4]

In 1941, Worsley, who saw action with Stephen Spender in the Spanish Civil War, made his case for urgent reform of public schools in a book called *The End of the 'Old School Tie'*. Worsley expressed a widely felt pessimism about the country's predicament. Remarkably, such criticism was considered neither unpatriotic nor defeatist, mainly because so many were angry at Britain's leaders for allowing a second war to take place so soon after 'the war to end all wars'.

Orwell wrote a foreword for Worsley's book, saying that the question of education must be dealt with 'as soon as the war is over'. He said Worsley's book 'will not please the defenders of the existing system', but neither will it please the 'more "advanced" experimentalists or the people who imagine that nothing can be achieved in England unless we rip down the whole social structure and build again from the bottom'.

Setting out the purpose behind Worsley's ideas, Orwell explained: 'The subjects he deals with in most detail are the need for some kind of uniform education system for all children up to the age of eleven, as a basis for a genuine democracy, and the special position of Public Schools... Part of his theme is the importance of not simply attacking the Public Schools, but of trying to incorporate what is good in them in a new system set free from class privilege.' But he warned: 'The one thing certain about the British education system is that if we do not ourselves change it after the war, it will be because Hitler is changing it for us.' And he cautioned against resistance from vested interests: 'It is in our power to decide whether the change shall be made consciously, as part of a movement towards full democracy, or haphazardly, with vested interests of all kinds fighting rearguard actions and holding up the course of history. This is, therefore, a book for those who want to see the notorious "two nations" of England made into one, and with as short a transition stage as possible.'

Orwell and Worsley were by no means lone voices calling for radical reform during the war. The BBC gave J.B. Priestley a prime slot on the radio which he used to proclaim the urgent need for a more equal society. Summing up the collective mood David Turner says: 'The barbs of Worsley, Orwell and others constituted a serious, potentially fatal charge against the boys' public schools: the role of the schools in creating leaders capable of defending and governing empires had, in the speeches of hundreds of headmasters up and down the land, been one of the chief justifications for their existence.'[5]

Even Winston Churchill had something to say on the subject when he addressed pupils and staff on a return visit to Harrow in December 1940: 'When this war is won, as it surely will be, it must be one of our aims to work to establish a state of society where the advantages and privileges which hitherto have been enjoyed by only the few shall be far more widely shared by the many, and by the youth of the nation as a whole.'[6] A year later Churchill told Rab Butler, president of the Board of Education, that he wanted 60–70 per cent of places at public schools to be filled by bursary boys on the recommendation of the 'counties and the great cities'. Butler, in public at least, conceded that 'some of the public schools would go.'[7]

What is sometimes framed today as a Trotskyite plot by a lunatic fringe of the Labour Party was once considered plain, old-fashioned Conservative common sense. By not tackling the malignant complacency which had allowed the promotion and advancement of a narrow class of leaders, politicians were now reaping the whirlwinds that threatened to blow down the Empire and enslave its peoples to fascism.

*

There was more bad news for public schools on the home front. While army leaders were being pummelled in Europe, Africa and Asia, their alma maters were taking an economic beating. Even before Hitler had ordered the Luftwaffe to direct its efforts against London, public schools had begun a mass evacuation from the cities.

The future of some of the most famous English public schools looked bleak. Having abandoned their school buildings for country residences, they took on additional costs while the makeshift nature of their new facilities forced them to offer reduced fees. By the end of the Battle of Britain a chain of south London girls' schools had reached the end of the financial road and handed staff their notices of termination.[8]

Even schools already safely ensconced in the countryside faced serious financial disruption during the early years of the war. Their buildings offered vital accommodation for British forces or could be affordably turned into research and development sites for the war effort. Most, however, were spared the intrusion of the war because they could still call upon support from government.

Given the existential threat facing the British people it seems extraordinary that Churchill's Conservative-led coalition government should find time and resources to tackle such a trifling problem as public schools. Yet in 1943, Labour's National Executive demanded 'acceptance of the broad democratic principle that all children of school age shall be required to attend schools provided by the State'.[9]

Few would have argued that public schools were not ripe for reform. Masters and pupils alike appear to have accepted the inevitability of change. Nevertheless, public feeling must have been extraordinarily hostile for Britain's wartime leader to do what he did next. Churchill, aware of how distracting the education reform question had become, frustratingly declared he didn't want to spend the war 'wiping children's noses and smacking their behinds'.[10] So the prime minister entrusted the task of settling the public school question to the Tory heavyweight, education minister Rab Butler.

Butler, a relative by marriage of the Archbishop of Canterbury Justin Welby, was by 1941 a wealthy aristocrat – the subsequent owner of his Gatcombe Park residence would be the Queen – who had ambitions of one day leading the Conservative Party. But his reputation had been badly damaged by his association with the policy of appeasement to Hitler.

The idea that Butler would oversee the abolition of, or even seriously reform, the public schools was risible. He had attended several preparatory schools before failing to win a scholarship to Eton and ended up plumping for Marlborough. If ever his allegiance to his old public school had been in doubt, it was firmly reasserted when he intervened to stop the Air Ministry from using Marlborough to house scientists working on the development of radar at the Telecommunications Research Establishment on the Dorset coast. They ended up finding accommodation at Malvern College.[11]

Yet despite all his public school baggage, it was Butler who set up the committee to report on how public schools could be brought to the aid of the national system of education. To ensure that nothing was done that would frighten the horses, Butler gave the job of chairing the committee to Lord David Pinkerton Fleming, an alumnus of the Glasgow High School, which through its links to the Choir School of Glasgow Cathedral, established in 1124, could claim to be the oldest public school in Scotland. Fleming ensured that his twenty-strong committee was overloaded with representatives of the public schools including the headmaster of Charterhouse and the headmistress of Roedean School.

Just like Clarendon in the previous century, Fleming sent representatives to the oldest and most prestigious schools in the country, and evidence was taken in the belief that everything was up for grabs. At its most radical, Fleming considered a proposal for public school 'endowments and premises to be appropriated by public authorities and put to a number of uses quite different from those they now serve, e.g. short-term boarding establishments; schools for advanced studies for Secondary School pupils; Youth Centres; Junior Universities; schools of instruction in special subjects like music, art and handicraft; Adult Education Colleges; Training Colleges for Teachers and Youth Leaders; Summer Schools; holiday centres; or Day Schools for their local areas'.[12] Although the thinking which underpinned abolition may seem radical today, in the war years it was part of a greater drive towards the creation of a welfare state. This was how the vast majority of Britons envisaged life in a post-war society.

And in its final report the committee conceded these were 'admirable objects and accommodation for carrying them out may well have to be provided in the future'. But in the end the committee caved in to the powerful public school lobby, concluding it did not feel these goals could or should be achieved by 'destroying schools that are doing good work'.

The report warned:

> If the Public Schools were abolished, it would be necessary also to eliminate all Independent Schools and, even if this far reaching step were taken, it would be impossible, without dictatorial interference with personal freedom, to debar parents from sending their children out of the country... to be educated, possibly in schools newly established for the purpose. There would be a great demand for private tutors, and the resulting inequalities and abuses would almost certainly compel the extension of the ban on Independent Schools to cover private teaching generally.

It also raised practical problems to abolition, saying that if a 'ban on Independent Schools were not made absolute' there was nothing to stop new public schools being founded to replace the old ones. The committee also rejected the idea of bringing the public schools wholly under the control of local education authorities (LEAs), arguing that they must be allowed to continue to draw pupils from all over the country and abroad.[13]

Instead, Lord Fleming, a senior Scottish judge, recommended that the top boarding schools should devote one-quarter of their places to state-funded bursaries. This was a serious blow to those who thought real change was in the air. The report even rejected the abolition of fees at grant-maintained state schools, an idea which had enjoyed majority support from the committee. Instead, the force of Fleming's recommendations addressed a national building programme for a raft of *new* boarding schools so that more children could benefit from a public school education.

When the Trades Union Congress, which had pushed hard for a radical solution, tried to meet with Butler to address the shortcomings of the report, the wily politician wrote: 'They are of course too late. The Public Schools are saved and must now be made to do their bit. All this is whining.'[14]

At Winchester College, where they feared the worst after a visit by a delegation of Labour MPs, one former pupil wrote: 'The Fleming report had little impact on us or the school – it wasn't radical enough to survive or make a difference.' Another said: 'The school is so well established that I don't foresee many changes. Schools like Winchester College will continue for many generations to come.' This prediction was strongly borne out by a former pupil who had attended the school in the war years. After visiting Winchester thirty years later he remarked: 'The school seemed to be a very similar place when my son went there in the 1970s.'[15]

Once again the public schools had used their influence and patronage to turn what appeared to be an attack on their independence into an opportunity to secure their financial future. What had started out as a bid to overcome the social divisions public schools were perceived to reinforce, had been turned into something very different.

Churchill and Butler had also calculated that the furore over education reform would wane as the fortunes of war turned in Britain's favour. They were wrong. The public mood was crying out for fundamental social reform. Butler was quick to recognise this and skilfully opened up the debate, drawing the focus away from public schools, by promising free education for all and thus deflecting attention from the privileged, whose wealth and influence seemed undiminished by the war. His 1944 Act was a classic piece of 'One Nation Conservatism' in the finest tradition of Disraeli, which embodied the ideal of upper-class paternalism towards the working class. In one of the most radical education acts of parliament, Butler enshrined the right to a free state education for everyone from five to fifteen.

Building on the 1918 Education Act, the new legislation established a tripartite system of secondary schooling: grammar schools, secondary technical schools and secondary modern schools. Admission was controlled by a new selection criteria based on an exam called the 11-plus. But the small number of grammar schools meant most pupils went to secondary modern schools, whether they were suitable or not.[16]

★

If the Second World War was a time when the school system was subject to reform, albeit slight, it did nothing to temper the old boys themselves; indeed, the official account seems to suggest that it was public school bluster that pulled us through. In 1940, with Hitler's invading armies camped on the other side of the English Channel, Britain's prospects had looked bleak. Few had the self-belief to think only they possessed the personal qualities needed to overcome what to everyone else appeared insurmountable odds. But throughout his childhood, Winston Churchill had never doubted his abilities or his calling. The prep school thrashings had toughened him while Harrow had inculcated a sense of confidence and destiny that bordered on the reckless. As a young fag Churchill once told a senior boy who had severely beaten him for breaking house rules: 'I will rise above you later on.' The boy responded by handing him two more thrashings. Uncowed, Churchill said: 'I am leaving now, but what I said stands.' He returned to Harrow many times during the war and the friends he had made there remained life-long (he gave many of them prized jobs).

Churchill's early career had been marked by risk-taking misadventure and military catastrophe. The 1915 offensive in the Dardanelles was typical of a Churchill military operation where the prospect of political glory blinded him to the military dangers. Indeed, his reckless decision-making during the early years of the Second World War very nearly cost Britain dearly. His campaign in Norway was an unmitigated disaster. Yet surely only a man of Churchill's unquestioning entitlement to national and personal victory could have steered Britain through its greatest ever gamble.

Such an argument gives Churchill far too much credit. His leadership and morale-boosting oratory helped inject a steely purpose to Britain's war effort but the outcome of the war was not decided by one man. Air Marshal Dowding (Winchester) proved to be a masterful tactician of the skies as he commanded Fighter Command against the Luftwaffe. And Field Marshal Bernard Montgomery (King's Canterbury and St Paul's) led Britain's Eighth Army to its first decisive victory in the war. Neither was Britain's survival secured by a narrow class of leader educated at public school. In the end salvation was delivered by the blood, sweat and ingenuity of millions of ordinary Britons who refused to surrender. While Dowding took all the plaudits, few heard of the work of state-educated Robert Watson-Watt, Edward George Bowen, John Randall and Bernard Lovell who helped to develop radar. Nor was proper recognition given to the Royal and Merchant navies, whose ships were captained by state-educated sailors. 'The men who kept the convoys free in the Atlantic during the Second World War, starved Germany in the First, and kept the Empire's maritime trading routes open for more than two centuries,' says David Turner, 'were rarely public schoolboys.'[17]

Even more decisive than the navy and radar in winning the war was the intervention of the Americans. The industrial weight of the United States of America kept Britain supplied with food and vital military equipment, including the Sherman tanks that were sent to help Montgomery chase Rommel out of the North African desert. Churchill and his generals made many tactical errors and only started winning after the Americans joined the war.

The reality is that public schools gave boys like Churchill an innate sense of entitlement and in some cases an almost patholog-ical willingness to risk everything. In summer of 1940 his gamble paid off, but in the era of nuclear weapons, how should we feel about leaders with such traits?

8

POST-WAR PRIVILEGE

Anyone who questions how much of a leg-up a public school education can give a young man should pay special heed to the remarkable tale of Brendan Bracken, an Irishman born in 1901 to a builder who strongly supported the Republican cause. His father died when he was three, and the young Bracken proved ungovernable, getting into fights and eventually running away from school. After a sketchy education, his mother sent him to Australia for work. But three years later Bracken returned to Britain determined to make something of himself.

At the age of nineteen he turned up at Sedbergh, a public school in Cumbria, at the same time as my grandfather, where he convinced the headmaster that he was fifteen years old and that his family had sent him to England to enrol. The school asked few questions, especially after he handed over the full fees, money he had earned from manual work in Australia but which he claimed had been left to him by his parents who had died in a bushfire. He further boosted his society credentials by falsely claiming to be a close relation of Montagu Rendell, the then Winchester College headmaster.

A year later, in 1921, he left Sedbergh with a History prize and a genuine foothold on Britain's rigid class ladder. On the basis of his Sedbergh connections he was offered teaching posts at other public schools, including the highly respected Bishop's Stortford

College in Hertfordshire. The contacts he made at school and the gentleman's education he received opened the doors to English society. In fact, he was so convincing as a public school gentleman that he inveigled his way into the inner sanctum of the Conservative Party, which selected him as candidate for North Paddington in the 1929 general election.

But his greatest feat of social climbing was to befriend Winston Churchill, later proving himself so invaluable to the prime minister that he was appointed minister of information during the Second World War and then first lord of the Admiralty. The two men became so close that their relationship gave rise to rumours that Bracken was Churchill's secret son. Bracken's mysterious arrival at the heart of the British establishment aroused a great deal of suspicion but each time he was challenged he was able to suppress questions by citing people he had actually met at Sedbergh. His secret life and the fraud he perpetrated on English society only emerged after his death in 1957.[1]

*

On 5 July 1945 the same public sentiment which had forced Churchill to find valuable government time to address the public school problem voted the victorious war leader and his loyal servant Bracken out of office. In a whopping defeat for the Conservatives, given the recent victory in Europe, Labour won a 146-seat majority. Churchill, who could be forgiven for succumbing to a bout of post-victory complacency, gravely misjudged the national mood by suggesting that for a socialist government to succeed in its ambitious reform programme it would need the help of the Gestapo.

The militarisation of British society had forced privately educated soldiers, sailors and airmen to rub shoulders with the lower classes. Britain's time-honoured but arbitrary social divisions were sharply exposed and, after five years of universal suffering, much harder to justify. Prime Minister Clement Attlee wasted no time in founding a new socialist nation fit for returning heroes of all classes. His government delivered to the letter on its welfare state manifesto, creating the National Health Service and nationalising a fifth of the economy including the coal and steel industries, the railways and the Bank of England.

Attlee's cabinet achieved all this with the fewest number of privately educated cabinet ministers (one in four) in British history and many who came from genuinely poor backgrounds. Surely now under a Labour-led administration the days of the public schools were numbered.

The minister with the most authentic working-class credentials was Ellen Wilkinson, born into a family of Manchester cotton workers. After persevering with her education (at home and at state school) she went to university before securing a job as an officer with the National Union of Women's Suffrage Societies. Wilkinson's socialist standing was further strengthened by her high-profile participation in the Jarrow March and several visits to the Spanish Civil War. She made no secret of her communist affiliations, stating that 'we shall have only one class in this country, the working class'. After pledging her allegiance to the Labour Party she was elected as MP for Middlesbrough East, the only woman Labour member at the 1924 general election.

When Attlee came to choose his 1945 cabinet Wilkinson was a shoo-in in for minister of education. Wilkinson, the only woman in the cabinet, made a radical education reform programme her priority. Her first task was to implement the 1944 Education Act, which would bring free education to all and the abolition of school fees at state-run schools. It wasn't enough that socially disadvantaged children should be educated for free – she also wanted to open up the public schools to working-class children. A key proposal to come out of the Fleming Report, which had been excluded from the Education Act, was for public schools to provide government-funded boarding for a quarter of their pupils. Wilkinson was determined to make sure the public schools, which had done so much to water down the final report, would at least honour this commitment.

However, it was not to be. Wilkinson became embroiled in the doomed plot of Herbert Morrison, with whom she had begun an affair, to overthrow Attlee and replace him as Labour leader.[2] She worked tirelessly to achieve her lover's dream while Morrison, grandfather of New Labour politician Peter Mandelson, refused to publicly acknowledge their relationship. Two years later in 1947, convinced she and Morrison had no future, she took her own life with an overdose of barbiturates. Morrison didn't even attend her funeral.[3]

With Wilkinson dead there was no one left to champion the public school free places measure. Certainly, Attlee himself had no appetite for a fight with the public schools. Indeed, despite the low number of privately educated ministers in the 1945 cabinet, Attlee's government soon returned to the Old School Tie order.

Attlee had been educated at Northaw School, a boys' preparatory school near Pluckley in Kent, and then Haileybury College, a public school in Hertfordshire (and alma mater of Rudyard Kipling, Group Captain Peter Townsend, Quentin Letts, Stephen Mangan, Dom Joly and key aide to Jeremy Corbyn, Barry Gardiner MP. It was while working at Haileybury House, a charity run by his old school to help East End children, that he underwent his conversion to socialism. The shock of how desperate and pathetic life was for so many ordinary people living in London convinced him that the state must be used to help redistribute the nation's wealth. Today few public schools are involved in this kind of coalface charity work, preferring to make their limited social welfare contribution at arm's length.

The architect of the welfare state, William Beveridge (Charterhouse), also carried out charitable works in the East End where he attended to the needs of the working classes. After university, Beveridge moved to Toynbee Hall, just down the road from Haileybury House, where he worked with R.H. Tawney to help establish communities that enabled the rich and poor to live more closely together. These so-called settlement houses were located in poor urban areas, in which volunteer middle-class 'settlement workers' lived, helping to alleviate the poverty of their low-income neighbours. The houses provided services such as daycare, education and healthcare to improve the lives of the poor in these areas.

However, despite Attlee's commitment to an egalitarian society, neither he nor Beveridge ever saw the need to challenge the public school order. Many Haileyburians, some of whom Attlee knew from his time there, were given ministerial jobs in his first government, while one, Geoffrey de Freitas, became his new parliamentary private secretary. According to David Turner: 'When Hugh Dalton, one of Attlee's cabinet colleagues, asked one of them about the general opinion on Attlee's 1947 ministerial reshuffle, he was told "that it seemed that, to get on in this government, you must have been at Eton, or Haileybury".'[4]

In a speech at Haileybury on 28 June 1946, Attlee stated: 'This country changes, but it is our way to change things gradually, and I see no reason for thinking that the public schools will disappear. I think the great tradition of public schools will be extended.'[5] When the Queen made Attlee a Knight of the Garter he chose Haileybury's winged hearts for his coat of arms.[6]

★

In the immediate post-war years Britain came close to bankruptcy as the economy faced the twin pressures of war debts and the maintenance of a flagging and expensive empire. LEAs had promised to

pick up the bill for public school bursary schemes but in such financially stricken times there was little cash or political will to carry
it through. There was also a serious flaw in the Fleming scheme
– admission criteria for the publicly funded places were not set
centrally, but by the schools themselves. As a proposal it could have
never achieved what Wilkinson and others wanted – state control
of the public schools. Billy Hughes, Wilkinson's former parliamentary private secretary, expressed what many feared: that places in
public schools under the LEA Fleming scheme would not go to
working-class pupils but to middle-class boys and girls who were
'looking for cheap ways to satisfy their snobbish ambitions'.[7]

But for a number of public schools these LEA grants represented a valuable lifeline. The best example is Dulwich College,
which had been badly bomb-damaged during the war. Faced
with financial ruin, the school took full advantage of the free
places scheme for 11-plus boys. By the end of the 1940s,[8] 90 per
cent of all Dulwich pupils were in receipt of a local government
grant, prompting its headmaster to comment: 'It is now possible
to choose as our entrants the best boys, quite regardless of their
father's income.' The school had almost brought about a needs-
blind admissions policy – something no public school has achieved
in the modern era.

In 1950 the Labour Party published a pamphlet which called for
universal secondary schools for all children. The way to proceed,
argued the pamphlet, was to raise the standard and status of the
ordinary schools so that all parents will send their children to them
as a matter of course, instead of sending them to private schools.[9]
But before any progress could be made, Labour was out of office,
replaced by Winston Churchill's Conservative government of 1951.

The public schools had once again escaped state intervention.
Yet only a few years later the politicians educated at these elite
schools found themselves badly out of step with the national
and international mood. When it came to Anthony Eden, the

effortlessly suave aristocratic son of a baronet, Britain had a prime minister more reminiscent of Georgian times than the nuclear age.

Eden's great-grandfather was William Iremonger, commander of the 2nd Regiment of Foot during the Peninsular War, fighting under Wellington at the Battle of Vimeiro. His illustrious ancestry included Barbara Villiers, a mistress of Charles II, whose famous descendants include Princess Diana, the Mitford sisters, former Northern Ireland secretary Theresa Villiers, and even Churchill. Eden was educated at two public schools: Sandroyd School in Cobham and Eton, where he won a Divinity prize, excelled at cricket, rugby and rowing, and gained membership to the highly coveted Eton 'Pop' society whose membership is chosen by the senior pupils. In the First World War he was awarded a Military Cross for bravery after helping to rescue a sergeant from no-man's land. In the next war he was Foreign Secretary under Churchill and emerged at the end of the conflict with his own sense of self-belief intact and a contender for the leadership of the Tory Party.

As prime minister, Eden had the distinction of overseeing the lowest unemployment figures of the post-Second World War era – just over 215,000, barely 1 per cent of the workforce, in July 1955. But Eden had little interest in domestic affairs and instead focused on the world stage where he believed posterity would judge him. And his own inflated sense of importance in the world matched that of his country. In 1956 Suez was the diplomatic calamity that exposed the myth of British foreign power and the ruling class that believed in it. Without consulting the Americans, Britain and France invaded Egypt to protect their trade lines. When America objected, Eden realised he had critically misunderstood the new world order, leaving him no choice but to carry out a humiliating volte-face. It was not just an embarrassment for Eden, who had to resign for lying to parliament about what he had known of the military operation, but raised questions about the accountability of public school government (Eden's entire cabinet was privately educated and of private means). However, for those in charge of England's public schools, the Suez crisis was merely evidence of how well 'Eton government' was working. After addressing a working-men's club in the East End of London, Eton headmaster Robert Birley said: 'I pointed out to them that while people thought of the Suez policy of the Government as an "Eton" policy, because of the number of Etonians in the Cabinet, they had not recognised that both the junior members of the Government who resigned and the majority of the "dissident" Conservatives were Old Etonians. I said that what we wanted to do at Eton was to produce men who would hold independent views and be prepared to stick up for them, not men who would take an "Etonian" line.'[10]

Seven years later, another Conservative administration suffered a similar fate in 1963 when a privately educated politician lied to parliament about his personal life. John Profumo (Harrow), a leading member of Oxford University's exclusive Bullingdon Club, enjoyed an active sex life outside his marriage. One of his lovers was the model Christine Keeler, who had also begun an affair with a Russian naval attaché. At the time, Profumo was secretary of state for war and the potential threat to national security was obvious. When Profumo was confronted about the allegations in parliament he denied the story. But he was later forced to admit the truth and, more significantly, that he had lied to the House of Commons, an unforgiveable breach of trust. The resulting scandal is credited with the early resignation of Prime Minister Harold Macmillan. But Profumo's dishonourable behaviour and the ensuing cover-up dealt a terminal blow to the country's trust in the establishment. It also marked the end of deference to the public school politician.

Yet none of this translated into any real change in the status quo. Despite all the post-war progress in welfare reform and advancement in technology, Britain's class system remained as rigid as it was before the start of the war. The higher echelons of government and the country's great estates remained controlled by a narrow class whose entry was still determined by the public school system. The post-war baby boom also meant there were more children to educate from all classes.

In the next decade public schools enjoyed something of a revival, mostly minor public schools reinventing themselves to attract more fee-paying pupils. Heads were reporting waiting lists for places at the top schools stretching to the end of the 1970s.[11] Snob value was back in business.

It was also the Golden Age of the grammar school, with children from poorer backgrounds being funded by government grants to attend otherwise fee-paying schools. The modern grammar school had been established by the 1944 Education Act to educate 25 per cent of the state school population, with admissions strictly determined by the 11–plus exam. Throughout the 1960s and '70s there were around 170 direct-grant grammar schools, aligned with the Headmasters' Conference, alongside over 1,200 state-maintained grammar schools.[12]

Among those to benefit from a grammar school scholarship was Margaret Thatcher. The future Tory prime minister attended the then very modern Kesteven & Grantham Girls' School between 1936 and 1943, which also educated a number of fee-paying pupils.

David Willetts, who was minister for universities and science in David Cameron's coalition government in 2010, was another benefit from the grammar school movement, attending King Edward's School, Birmingham, under a direct grant. He followed in the footsteps of Enoch Powell whose family paid school fees. 'My parents wouldn't have been able to pay for private education. And almost everyone at KE was there under the grant system. It was an independent foundation and, when Labour tried to abolish grammar schools, it went back to being a fully independent grammar school [a private school without government funding]. The outgoing headmaster John Claughtoun would argue that we ended up with a greater social and ethnic mix than some of the independent schools.'[13]

Willetts, chair of the Resolution Foundation, also believes that the direct-grant system helped to boost social mobility at the time: 'In the nineteenth century, Birmingham grew as this huge industrial town and King Edward's could have just become more and more socially selective. But the city fathers, who were very closely connected to their school, rightly [deciding against social exclusion] said "well, we need more schools". So they created this King Edward foundation, which by the twentieth century had seven schools within it: the original school, plus a girls' school, plus five grammar schools.' Willetts argues that 'a lot of the original charitable foundations that have become private schools could have taken a different route, they could have become grammar schools. But King Edward's took the route of expanding as the demand for British education expanded. And good on them for doing so. The others became a lot more socially selective.'

The grammar school experiment had a profound impact on social mobility, lifting some children from ordinary backgrounds to influential positions in society and challenging the public school hegemony. But while the grammar school and direct-grant system greatly benefited less well-off families, like the Willetts, who had well-supported and motivated children, the vast majority had to make do with a bog-standard secondary modern. Instead of bridging the divide between good and bad education in England and Wales, grammar schools were exacerbating it. While a few clever working-class kids escaped their poor career prospects, the life chances of 11-plus failures were more dismal than ever.

The journalist Cassandra Jardine (Godolphin & Latymer) describes in vivid detail the plight of the two-thirds of the population who were sent to the local secondary modern school: 'They were housed in decaying buildings, taught by often unqualified

teachers, given only a third of the funding per head of their contemporaries at grammar schools and barred from public exams.
The middle classes feared the system, lest their children should fail
the 11-plus; the working classes saw it as a way to keep them in
their place. Many emerged with no qualifications – only the top
stream took CSEs – to become factory fodder.'

In 1964 Harold Wilson came to power promising to end the education apartheid and finally deal with the public school problem.
Labour was committed to a comprehensive education system
that would also do away with selective grammar schools which
gave preferential treatment to a self-selecting stratum of society.
The creation of a national network of comprehensive schools was
given priority. But members of the hard-left also saw abolition of
public schools as a prerequisite for community education.

It fell to Anthony Crosland, the new education minister, to
honour the manifesto pledge to set up a commission 'to advise
on the best way of integrating the public schools into the
state system'.

Crosland very well understood the English public school system.
He was educated at Highgate public school in north London and
on his second marriage to the American writer Susan Catling he
became stepfather to her two daughters who were both being
privately educated, the eldest at St Paul's in London, with fees paid
by Catling's father. Catling later wrote: 'Nature ensures that an
elite is always asserting itself in a democracy, but the state should
do its utmost, Tony said, to make it possible for those without
money or position or a literate family background to have equal
access to the opportunity that a decent education bestows.'[14]

In his hugely influential book *The Future of Socialism*, Crosland
argued that: 'This [system of superior private schools] is much the
most flagrant inequality of opportunity, as it is cause of class inequality generally, in our educational system; and I have never been
able to understand why socialists have been so obsessed with the

question of the grammar schools, and so indifferent to the much more glaring injustice of the independent schools.'

Catling recalled how her husband frequently debated with his eldest stepdaughter, Sheila, his ideas about democratic socialism:

> At first she was taken aback by the moral concept that children should not inherit large sums of money earned by others. She thought of her piggy bank, how nice it would be if someone filled it nightly. But Tony was a good teacher. He explained the reasons for urging privileged children to attend comprehensive schools: 'Of course St Paul's gives you a better academic education, but my own view is that if a girl brought up in a home with books has academic potential, she'll develop it whether or not she goes to an intensely academic school. I daresay the headmistress of St Paul's holds a different view. Much of the argument hangs on how you define education. Some would argue that a comprehensive school offers the privileged girl better preparation for the real world, though admittedly that's not the purpose of comprehensives.'

His argument made a profound impression, as Sheila later asked if she could go to Holland Park Comprehensive.

> I called on the headmistress of St Paul's, who told me we were using Sheila as a political pawn, but that it probably didn't matter too much as she was 'rather wet'.
>
> 'In what sense?' I inquired.
>
> 'She never wants to play sports.'

Later Sheila's younger daughter followed her sister to Holland Park. Around the same time, the left-wing Labour MP Tony Benn (Westminster) and his American wife were having similar misgivings about the private education of their four children. They too were removed from private schools and educated at Holland Park.[15]

In 1965 Crosland announced to the House of Commons that the government was determined public schools 'should, like other parts of the education system, become progressively open to boys and girls irrespective of the income of their parents; that the schools should move towards a wider range of academic attainment, so that the public school sector may increasingly play its own part in the national movement towards comprehensive education; and, in particular, that the schools should seek to meet any unsatisfied need for boarding education amongst wider sections of the population.' Unsurprisingly, it met stiff resistance from the obvious quarters. The shadow Tory home secretary Quintin Hogg (Eton) reminded Crosland that there was 'unsatisfied demand for boarding education' and that the public schools had 'distinguished academic records'.[16]

Establishment of the Public Schools Commission was delayed until 1965, partly because of cabinet agenda prioritisation but also because of the controversial nature of the topic. In fact, the chairmanship came to be seen as 'education's most unwanted post of 1965'.[17] The first five people to be offered the job turned it down, before Sir John Newsom, a former chief education officer in Hertfordshire, accepted the position.

Newsom was a pillar of the public school community. He had gone to Imperial Service College, was a lifelong governor of Haileybury and Imperial Service College (the two schools merged) and sat on the Independent Schools Tribunal. But the commission was regarded as being 'carefully but firmly weighted in favour of change' and faced considerable distrust from the outset.[18] For the education reformers, there was renewed cause for optimism which appeared to be well founded.

The commission proposed for a cadre of 'suitable' integrated independent boarding schools which, within seven years, would assign at least half of their places to pupils from maintained schools. And crucially, this new influx of state pupils should not be excluded from the schools on 'grounds of low academic ability'. The scheme was to be run by a new Boarding Schools Corporation, and the costs of tuition were to be covered by LEAs on a pooled basis, partially reimbursed by the exchequer. The remaining costs would be dealt with on a means-tested basis, with parents contributing where they were deemed able to afford it.[19] Additionally, public schools would be expected to become more co-educational with 'extended opportunities of boarding education for girls'. The commissioners also called for an end to 'fagging' (though many public schools had by now abolished personal fagging), 'eccentric or archaic dress that flaunts class difference' and compulsory participation in the Combined Cadet Force.[20]

Under this programme there would be 47,000 boarding places (38,000 at secondary level and 9,000 at primary level) at around 350 secondary schools and an unspecified number of schools catering for children of primary or preparatory age by 1980. The estimated cost to the taxpayer would be no more than £12 million a year and this could be reduced further if the government chose to abolish the charitable status of independent schools. If the wealthiest parents were also made to pay fees, the cost would be negligible. This was not, however, a majority conclusion as four members of the commission gave dissenting opinions and four more formally expressed discontent with the main recommendations.

The public schools complained of the report's 'doctrinaire rigidity, its woolliness of thought, and its avoidance of some main problems'.[21] Nevertheless, their greatest fear was abolition and so, publicly at least, they supported some kind of reform. In private they may have cynically noted that the downturn in the late 1960s economy made state funding an attractive financial solution to their short-term problems.

Labour having dug its heels in on the issue, many MPs expected radical action to follow. It did not. The truth was that Labour was divided over how to implement the commission's recommendations and lacked the political will to grasp the bull by the horns.[22] Even the majority recommendation to remove tax advantages from independent schools registered as charities found little favour in Westminster and Whitehall. Some ministers had misgivings about the final cost; others believed a massive overhaul of the education system was bound to count against them at the polls. Many of Labour's privately educated ministers were also far from committed to the comprehensive cause.

While Crosland's stepchildren were educated in line with his political beliefs, Attlee, Wilson and Jim Callaghan all sent their children to public schools without causing any controversy in the party.[23] Indeed, the Labour MP Hartley Shawcross (Dulwich) had claimed in 1956 that he did not know 'a single member of the Labour Party, who can afford to do so, who does not send his children to a public school, often at great sacrifice'.[24] Shawcross sent his own son, William, to Eton – he went on to head the Charity Commission, which regulates Eton and all the other public schools which claim charitable status. The father of Tory minister Ed Vaizey[25] had served on the same commission with the headmaster of St Paul's while he was looking for a suitable school to educate his son. John Vaizey had been vociferous in his opposition to the public schools while he served on the commission. But it later emerged that he was so impressed by the headmaster of St Paul's and his school that he decided to send Vaizey junior there.[26]

Any prospect of reform ended with the election of Ted Heath's Conservative government in June 1970. Nick Hillman, director of the Higher Education Policy Institute, says that the Tory manifesto comprehensively buried the prospect of change by including a single sentence supporting the right of parents to choose independent education.[27] Later the same year, the secretary of state for education and science, Margaret Thatcher, was asked in the House of Commons 'what action she now proposes to take on the reports of the Public Schools Commission'. Her reply was succinct and unequivocal: 'None, sir.' Hillman recalls the following year she told pupils at Bloxham School in Oxfordshire: 'Please never apologise for independence. It is worth stimulating and nurturing for its own sake. You do not have to justify it. It is those who wish to finish it who have to justify their case.'[28]

Even the removal of the public school charitable tax exemption, the one Newsom recommendation which had enjoyed a consensus among commission members, was consigned to the 'too difficult' basket. Ministers had taken legal advice and wrongly concluded that such a move might be used to deprive genuine charities such as Oxfam of their own charitable tax advantage. And so yet again public opinion had cried out for change, the government had produced a report, its conclusions watered down by vested interests, and the feeblest of reforms was ignored.

Labour's turmoil over public schools continued throughout the 1970s. When the party returned to government in 1974 it was principally occupied with putting out the fires of economic downturn and industrial unrest. However, the reformers had one final hand to play.

In 1975 they forced direct-grant schools, which were funded by the state and fee-paying pupils, to choose between becoming LEA-maintained comprehensives or independents without a grant. Labour ministers calculated that few of these schools would risk giving up such a valuable source of state income. But it was a gamble that badly backfired: by picking off the low-hanging fruit for short-term political gains, Labour had cut the grammar school sector adrift. Less than 30 per cent of the remaining direct-grant grammar schools became comprehensives, while over one hundred, generally large, academically selective and high-performing schools joined the public school sector. Instead of widening access, these schools returned to serving wealthy elites.[29]

★

Direct-grant places had been popular with Tory MPs who recognised that grammar schools were the one system that had given poor, hard-working families a chance to get to the top. Others, like Margaret Thatcher herself, resented the public schoolboys who took their birthrights and privileges for granted. So in 1980 the Conservative Party set about bringing back a form of direct grant under an initiative which would provide funding for the education of a few poor, bright students at the top public schools.

Between 1980 and 1997, more than 75,000 children from state schools benefited from the assisted-places scheme (though some of the parents managed to overcome the means-testing barrier by creative accounting). Eighty per cent of these students went on to attend university, with 15.6 per cent ending up at an elite institution like Oxford or Cambridge. By 2012, four out of ten assisted-place pupils were earning £90,000 a year or more and even those who didn't go to university were in solidly middle-class occupations with a good income. Tellingly, more than half went on to send their own children to public schools.[30]

But even in the supposedly classless 'loadsamoney' 1980s the scheme had its critics. John Rae, the Westminster headmaster and leading light of the public school movement, spoke out against it: 'You do not deal with a famine by sending a few lucky children to lunch at the Ritz.'

Yet into the 1980s the pendulum had swung so far away from reform of public schools that Margaret Thatcher even countenanced outright privatisation of the state education system. In 1982 the prime minister and her chancellor Geoffrey Howe were behind a politically toxic move to dismantle the welfare state. The proposals considered by her cabinet included compulsory charges for schooling and introducing full-cost university tuition fees. One of those who worked on the Central Policy Review Staff paper was Lord Wasserman, who would later become David Cameron's adviser on crime and policing. In the paper, Wasserman, who was educated in Canada, suggested cutting 25 per cent of state school teachers. Thankfully, the proposals, including the privatisation of the NHS, were leaked to the media and the backlash was so damaging that Thatcher was forced to abandon the whole scheme.[31]

9

EDUCATION EDUCATION EDUCATION

Tony Blair's benign attitude towards private education was shaped by family tragedy. When he was just a ten-year-old prep school chorister his father, Leo, suffered a massive stroke. It would be three more years before Leo, a successful barrister and lecturer, would be able to start earning again and in the meantime the family faced real money troubles, forcing them to downsize to a four-bed 'executive home' on the outskirts of Durham. School uniforms were hand-me-downs and all foreign holidays were cancelled.

Blair later said:

> We were never poor, but it was a big change from what had gone before. And I suppose it made me aware that there were a lot more people who, for whatever hardships we might have been suffering, were a lot worse off than us... People read that I went through the private system, finishing at Oxford, and think that it must have been a bed of roses. Don't get me wrong, it was a happy childhood, but it also seemed as though I was spending every spare minute in Durham hospital, visiting either my father or my sister [his younger sister Sarah was diagnosed as having a form of infantile rheumatoid arthritis, called Still's disease].[1]

In his autobiography he recollected how he leaped around the garden when he found out that he had won an exhibition to the

Scottish public school Fettes, leaving the reader with the impression that the Blairs were still struggling and the financial burden of his fees was to be met by the school.[2] In fact, his scholarship (like most scholarships to private schools) provided only a modest contribution to his fees, the bulk of which were paid by his uncle.

But Fettes, also known as 'Eton with a kilt', was not at first to Blair's taste. In the mid-1960s it still resembled a Victorian public school with strict discipline and harsh punishments. Blair was made to fag for a senior boy, Michael Gascoigne, who recalls: 'Blair would clean my shoes, blanco my army belt and polish the brass on it. If I couldn't see my face in it, he would have it thrown back at him. He would also, if it was a games afternoon, lay out my rugger kit on the bed for me, or my whites if it was cricket. We would also summon fags like Blair to the prefects' room. There was always a requirement for toast, but we insisted it had to be one-inch thick, no thinner, no thicker, with lashings of butter and marmalade.'[3]

Blair says he was beaten on a number of occasions by prefects, including Gascoigne, although Gascoigne says he can't remember laying a hand on Blair. The former prime minister also hated the compulsory Combined Cadet Force and did all he could to dodge the mindless drills and square bashing. His antipathy to the school regime was reinforced after he watched the X-rated 1968 film *If*, a vicious satire of English public school life, famous for its depiction of a savage insurrection at a fictitious boys' boarding school. In fact, Blair was so unhappy at the school that he ran away back to his home, only agreeing to return after a meeting between the headmaster and his father.

But as he came through the school, like millions of other schoolboys before him, he forgot about the hardships and began to embrace the culture of Fettes. He played cricket and rugby for the school teams and as a budding thespian took on the part of Stanhope in a production of *Journey's End*.[4]

Blair mostly attributes his happier time at Fettes to an inspirational teacher called Dr Eric Anderson who had also taught Prince Charles at Gordonstoun. Anderson, who didn't permit beatings or fagging in his house, became headmaster and later provost of Eton where he also taught 'Blair's heir' David Cameron.[5] But Anderson left Fettes in Blair's penultimate year and the teenager's outspoken disrespect for the school rules resulted in canings and eventually a threat of expulsion. Luckily, Blair had fallen in love with the school's first female boarder, Amanda Mackenzie-Stuart. Conveniently for him, her father was a judge, who saved Blair from being expelled by arranging for him to live in the Mackenzie-Stuart house while he sat his A-levels.[6]

Before taking up his place at Oxford, Blair spent a gap year in London when he founded a rock band with former pupils of St Paul's and Westminster. Later, at Oxford, he was lead singer for another group which included two Old Wykehamists. But all the time he had his eye on the main chance and hedged his bets with a conventional career in law. He eventually charmed his way into the Chambers of Derry Irvine, another Scot educated at one of the country's ancient public schools, Hutchesons' Grammar School, founded in 1641 to educate 'twelve male children, indigent orphans'.

By the time Blair was firmly ensconced as Labour leader he had nothing but gratitude for the education system that had looked after him when many might have considered him down and out. In Blair's mind the public school had helped his 'working-class' father secure a better life for his children. It was an experience upon which Blair founded his New Labour project and his support for the aspirational classes whom he believed 'intellectual' and 'wealthy' Labour grandees, like George Orwell, Anthony Crosland and Tony Benn, had forsaken in their quest for a socialist idealism.

'My dad's greatest wish,' proclaimed Blair in his autobiography, 'was I be educated privately, and not just at any old private school;

he chose Fettes because he thought and had been told that it was the best in Scotland. The problem with the intellectual types was that they didn't quite understand this process; or if they did, rather resented it. In a sense they wanted to celebrate the working class, not make them middle class.'[7]

Fettes marked the occasion of New Labour's landslide victory by giving staff and pupils a half-day holiday in honour of the school's first (and only) prime minister.[8]

Blair later said that he didn't consider himself 'particularly naturally clever' but greatly benefited from his private education which 'opened up horizons for me'. Specifically it landed him selection for his safe seat at Sedgefield after hitting it off with Labour leader Michael Foot, who had also been privately educated, over their shared love of P.G. Wodehouse.

It is impossible to underestimate the debt Blair felt he owed to Fettes and one teacher in particular. When he was prime minister he asked to take part in a national teacher recruitment campaign, 'everyone remembers their teacher'. Blair used the opportunity to sing the praises of Eric Anderson. Much later in 2017 Blair said: 'Even today [there are] millions of young children who never really get the chance to think about what they could do because they never have these horizons put before them. The great thing about education… is you realise what you can do and many people go through their lives never realising what they can do.'[9] In this context it is perhaps easy to understand how, in the year after he won the leadership, Blair 'knocked back' a proposal from the party to remove tax advantages for private schools. Or as Blair put it: 'I tried to wean the party off its old prejudices.'[10]

This new relaxed attitude to such a historic bastion of class and privilege did not sit so comfortably with the majority of the party who had been used to talking tough on public schools. For one, David Blunkett, the shadow education secretary, found it hard to accept that parents who sent their children to public schools should be exempt from VAT on fees.[11] After making contradictory comments to the *Sunday Times*, he was called to heel by Gordon Brown on the grounds that he was trespassing on Treasury business.[12]

Blair favoured a different approach. He held several meetings with senior members of the public schools' leadership to set out a gentle programme of minimal cooperation, which Blair used to show reformists in the party that change was at hand. In reality, Blair had reversed Labour's unwritten policy of integrating public schools into the state system – this at a time when the gap between state and private schools was growing. Public schools had capitalised on the banning of grammars, which provided an alternative route to top universities for state school pupils, by increasing their share of places. In 1999, private schools sent up over half of all students to Oxford, a greater number than ten years earlier when state school pupils had achieved parity.[13]

But Blair could do little to silence calls for the reform of Thatcher's assisted-places scheme, which gave a financial boost to the private schools as well as tacit approval. Having reluctantly included its abolition in the 1997 manifesto, once elected Blair agreed to phasing out the scheme over the next five years.

★

In 1997 public schools were still being treated as charities, avoiding corporation tax, VAT on school fees and council taxes on their properties. Although financially benefiting from these huge tax concessions they were making little or no contribution to the community: only one in ten were involved in any kind of working cooperation with a local comprehensive school.

Any comfort the public schools had derived from Tony Blair's promise to protect their cherished tax status was to be shortlived. Blunkett and education minister Stephen Byers, egged on by education reformists in the party, wanted concrete action, not empty gestures. Just months after the election the schools were warned that they'd be stripped of their charitable status unless they entered into meaningful partnerships with comprehensive schools. It was estimated that their charitable status saved the schools £63 million a year, worth 6 per cent of fees.[14]

Dick Davison of the Independent Schools Information Service, representing 80 per cent of Britain's private schools at the time, vowed that they would fight such a move 'all the way'. He said: 'The money the Treasury would save is a piffling amount. Private schools give away £126 million a year in bursaries and scholarships. To remove charitable status would be very mean-spirited.'[15]

The following week Stephen Byers set out the government's plan in detail when he became the first Labour minister to address a conference of independent schools, the Girls' Schools Association. He promised the government would bury Labour's old antagonism towards public schools in return for a meaningful partnership with their state school neighbours: 'We are putting aside the old dogmas and recognising there are things to learn from the independent sector. We want the independent sector to play a full part in our crusade to raise standards for all pupils in every school.'

The public schools' official position, vigorously advanced whenever challenged, was that their charity schools were saving government tens of millions of pounds on the education of half a million British pupils. But by the same token, the assisted-places scheme had also been helping to fund some of the smaller independent schools. Vivian Anthony, general secretary of the Headmasters' and Headmistresses' Conference, representing the country's top public schools, warned that some rural schools were 'struggling hard to fill places'. He told the *Independent* in October 1997: 'We recognise that we are part of a national education system, but the government has to bear in mind that we are financed by the fees of parents who expect the fees to be used for the benefit of their children.'[16] Opponents of private schools dismissed Anthony's comments as crocodile tears.

Speaking in 2017 Fiona Millar, a special adviser to Cherie Blair in the early years of the New Labour government, says: 'Tackling private schools at that time was not a great priority. In the Blair years it was about choice and diversity, and the private sector was considered a valid part of the schools market. So I don't think there was anything hypocritical about the Blair government's education policies. When it came to private schools I don't think the priority was a radical shake-up of the class system and Labour didn't want to get in a fight with the private schools.'[17]

★

In June 2001 Blunkett was promoted to secretary of state for the Home Office, where one of his new responsibilities was the reform of charity law, affording him the opportunity of attacking the public school problem on a different front. There was no general statutory definition of a charity, as the legal concept had been developed by the courts over several centuries. The law at that time was still founded on the preamble to the Charitable Uses Act 1601, which listed purposes considered to be of a charitable nature.

Labour had been toying with a shake-up of the 400-year-old law ever since the 1997 election. Under the guise of tidying up an ancient legal doctrine they could impose a modern definition of public benefit from which it was claimed the leading public schools had become so detached. Back in the nineteenth century, the courts considered arguments that Harrow only educated gentlemen and therefore could not be called a charity. Sir John Leach, vice-chancellor, in Attorney-General v. Earl of Lonsdale (1827) 1 Sim. 105, where property had been donated to found a school

of learning for the education of gentlemen's sons, said: 'The institution of a school for the sons of gentlemen is not, in popular
language, a charity; but in the view of the statute of Elizabeth, all
schools of learning are so to be considered.'[18]

A 2003 survey by the Independent Schools Council (ISC), the
umbrella group which represented 60 per cent of private schools,
showed that two-thirds of private schools had never made their
resources such as classrooms available to state schools. One school
which had drawn unwanted attention to its anachronistic status
was Gordonstoun, the alma mater of Prince Philip and Prince
Charles, and so-called Eton of the North. In April 2004 Princess
Anne, whose children Peter and Zara Phillips attended the school,
resigned from the board of governors, citing a demanding royal
workload. But other parents were left wondering whether there
were other reasons for the Princess's departure. Despite being a
multi-million-pound enterprise, Gordonstoun was £1.7 million in
debt. In order to solve its financial problems, the governors decided
to sell North Foreland Lodge, a Hampshire girls' school it had only
acquired the year before, to GEMS Education, an international
company which runs schools in the Middle East. North Foreland
Lodge was then forced to close, causing uproar among its parents.

It was difficult to understand how such a ruthless fire sale could
possibly benefit the community. The chairman of the Hampshire
school parents' association alleged that 'there was a great body of
parents who viewed this as a big scam, a put-up job to get the
land and run the school down'. As the escalating bad publicity
threatened to damage the school's reputation, Mark Pyper, principal of the Gordonstoun Schools, who had already vehemently
denied accusations of asset stripping, claimed they had intervened
to keep the girls' school open for an extra year.[19] Such an unsavoury episode showed just how far Britain's public schools had
commercially travelled since their emergence in the fourteenth
century.

In July 2003 David Blunkett published a Charities Bill which redefined public benefit so that charities were not receiving tax breaks from the state without putting something back. No longer would it be sufficient for public schools to say they provided education. Now they would have to comply with a 'public character' check designed to 'rule out organisations which, although they had purposes falling within one or more of the list, were not demonstrably for the public benefit'.

There would also be regular reviews to ensure charities did not fall into 'disrepute'.[20] In response, the public schools warned that many small charity schools could go out of business and fee rises would end the dreams of middle-class parents who wished to have their children privately educated.

This was not what New Labour was all about. Aspiration was a key part of what Tony Blair was selling to the electorate. There was a vociferous chorus of disapproval of what was now being characterised as a petty class vendetta against public schools. Some Labour MPs wanted to stop reform in its tracks. But a far more serious scandal with far-reaching implications for the regulation of public schools was about to hit the headlines and it would implicate all the leading fee-paying schools in the land.

★

Curious about what they might find on their school's private email system, two fifteen-year-old computer whizzes at Winchester College hacked in and began exploring a trove of emails marked 'confidential'. In doing so, they stumbled upon a conspiracy. Correspondence dated November 2001 revealed that Sevenoaks School, Kent, was regularly sending emails to bursars around the country providing information on intended fee hikes in an exercise known as the 'Sevenoaks Survey'. One email from Bill Organ, Winchester's then bursar, actually began: 'Confidential, please, so we aren't accused of being a cartel.' Another suggested fee increases of between 6 and 8 per cent – well above inflation. It was followed by a more comprehensive survey by Julian Patrick, the Sevenoaks bursar, covering fee expectations from fifty-one schools including Ampleforth, Charterhouse, Cheltenham Ladies' College, Eton College, Gordonstoun, Marlborough College, Millfield and Wycombe Abbey. In one message Patrick wrote: 'I believe some bursars may have revised their estimates or have fixed their fees for 2003/04. In my own case I have revised the estimate of day fee increases from nine per cent to eleven per cent.' Oliver Delany, of Clifton College in Bristol, said in another email: 'As always, if we find the others raise the "bar" then so will we.'

The two young hackers were eventually caught in the act. To avoid bad PR, Winchester separated the boys, moving one to Westminster and the other to City of London. But it was too late. They had taken a short holiday in South America where they had disguised email accounts to contact the authorities and the media.

Their disclosures made front-page headlines and triggered a high-profile investigation by the Office of Fair Trading (OFT) into the cream of English and Scottish public schools, including Eton, Harrow, Winchester and Westminster, which later found them guilty of running a price-fixing 'cartel'. The victims in all of this were of course the parents who had scrimped and saved to give their kids what they believed was the best education money could buy but were being ripped off by the schools. Speaking to the *Sunday Telegraph* four years later, the two whistleblowers summed up this sense of betrayal: 'What they were doing was illegal – it's as simple as that… These schools are meant to be charities but we showed that they were solely interested in making money from hard-pressed parents.'

The charge that these families had been shafted by their own schools was borne out by the rocketing costs of boarding fees, which had gone from £6,800 in 1990 to £20,000 in 2002.[21]

In the end, fifty schools had to pay fines totalling £3.5 million. Under the terms of the settlement, however, each school actually paid just £10,000 and an ex gratia payment of £60,000 into a new education charity to compensate 40,000 pupils who'd attended the schools during the period of the fee-fixing. This deal was greeted with huge relief by the schools as they'd managed to avoid hefty fines that would have cost institutions like Eton, Harrow and Winchester £3 million each.

The Independent Schools Council tried to trash the OFT's investigation by calling it a 'scandalous waste of money'. Nevertheless, the whole murky episode left the schools acrimoniously divided and particularly hostile to the country's two oldest public schools, Eton and Winchester, which had both aided the investigation in return for a 50 per cent reduction in their fines.

Back at Winchester the school governors quietly took their revenge on the two teenage whistleblowers by calling in the police. In a further bizarre and particularly cruel twist, they also forced two chaplains to resign for failing to report the boys' confessions. The expelled boys faced criminal prosecution for hacking but accepted a police caution after the affair had died down.[22]

Beyond the public school community, the OFT's findings had far-reaching political ramifications. The idea that fifty charities had worked together to bump up fees only strengthened the argument that the public school was really a money-grabbing big business masquerading as a public-spirited concern. This was reinforced later in the year when GEMS Education, the company that purchased North Foreland Lodge from Gordonstoun, announced plans for a network of cheaper independent schools in Britain. Its prospective fees were to be £5,000 to £6,000 a year for co-educational day schools, undercutting the competition by up to 40 per cent.

GEMS was not a charity and its entrance to the private schools market appeared to confirm the suspicion that someone was making big profits out of the private school sector. According to the company's schools' director, however, independent schools were not profiteering. GEMS would be able to offer lower fees by centralising their finance and recruitment departments, providing more children with quality education as demand for independent schools grew.[23] In 2017 GEMS, which has just three schools in the UK, reported record profits.[24]

★

When the Charities Act became law in 2006, Suzi Leather, head of the commission that was created to ensure charities met their legal obligations, seized on the public school issue. She declared education in itself was not a charitable cause and that schools had to do more to demonstrate their public benefit to the community, particularly through the provision of bursaries to poorer pupils. There was also a new set of guidelines the schools would be expected to follow.

In an investigation of a test group of public schools, two prep schools in Derbyshire and Lancashire, each with around 235 pupils and charging £5,750 a term for boarders, were the first to fail the 'public-benefit' test. Commissioners told them to increase the amount of money they spent on free places and facilities offered to the wider community, or be taxed as businesses. The decision caused an outcry among public school heads and their influential supporters, who accused Leather, a Labour Party member, of engaging in class warfare.

When she appeared on BBC Radio 4's *Today* programme, Leather made no apology for the approach the commission had adopted. Asked by presenter Evan Davis why she was attacking families who were saving the nation money by not using the state system, she replied it was 'like saying if you drive a car you should get a tax break because you're not taking public transport… Same as every other charity in the land, they [independent schools) will have to show that they bring public benefit, including to people on low incomes. There's a level playing field for everyone now.'[25]

This was all too much for the *Daily Mail*, which went to great trouble to point out to its readers that Leather herself had benefited from a private education at St Mary's Calne, in Wiltshire. Worse still, she had sent her own children to public schools and one of them was still there while the commission was investigating other schools.[26] This apparent conflict of interest meant she took no part in the commission's initial and crucial deliberations on the public benefit of independent education.[27]

Behind their cloisters, the top public schools were rattled. An Eton College in-house magazine editorial warned that a charity like Eton could take nothing for granted and would surely have to be more 'accountable to the taxpayer'. It prompted the school's former provost, Eric Anderson, to commit the school to the impossible dream of creating a needs-blind admissions system. The school magazine wrote: 'The campaign for the new foundation is fully underway, and the project started by Sir Eric Anderson, to make Eton's fees entirely means tested, will transform the school for good.'[28]

Other leading public schools were far less conciliatory. The independent schools sector went into attack mode. Christopher Ray, the high master of Manchester Grammar School, said. 'The judgements of the Charity Commission are politically motivated. It has adopted a blinkered approach, focusing upon means-tested bursaries and seeing little else. The subtext is worrying for many parents: not only are they confronted by taxes for the state system as well as by school fees, they are now likely to face some form of surcharge as schools with limited bursary funds try to cover their backs.'[29]

More concerning for the commission was the opinion of two prominent QCs who spoke out in support of independent schools. Leolin Price QC said that its approach was 'unlawful' and that the schools were already providing public benefit. Stanley Brodie QC declared the Charities Act neither created a new public-benefit test nor authorised the commission to create one.

The case eventually came before the High Court, whose membership is dominated by judges educated at top public schools. Mr Justice Warren, the senior judge hearing the ISC case, had attended Bryanston, one of the schools found guilty of price fixing by the OFT. A second judge, Alison McKenna, worked for a firm of solicitors that had more than twenty public school clients. She had also been educated privately. The third judge was educated by the state (at a selective grammar).

The judges ruled in favour of the ISC. They said it was for the schools themselves, not the Charity Commission, to decide how they complied with the new public-benefit test. More significantly, the judges saw no reason why smaller bursaries paid to middle-class families should not be used as evidence that the school was benefiting the wider community.[30] What the judges had failed to grasp was that these middle-class bursaries were going to families who were in receipt of income up to £100,000. By working around the admissions system it was possible to qualify for financial support while enjoying a lot of wealth.

The schools were delighted with the ruling while critics said the schools had won the right to 'mark their own homework'.[31] Sir Peter Lampl, founder and chair of the Sutton Trust, which has spent millions of pounds researching the impact of private education on society, called it a 'stitch-up'. Nevertheless, the ruling did contain one small crumb of comfort for the opponents of privileged education. The judges made clear that it was no longer good enough for a public school to make a token effort towards educating the poor. Under the judicial spotlight the schools also found themselves scrutinised to an embarrassing degree. During the course of the hearings evidence emerged of the lavish resources available at modern public schools.

The Education Review Group, an unincorporated association of individuals involved in the field of education, questioned how an independent school could be said to be acting for the public benefit when it uses its money to purchase resources that go well beyond what is necessary for the purposes of providing pupils with a decent education, such as building an Olympic-sized swimming pool rather than a smaller one. The judges answered that 'any school will need to consider whether the provision of some of its facilities can really be justified as either part of or properly ancillary to the advancement of education… where facilities at what we might call the luxury end of education are in fact provided, it will be even more incumbent on the school to demonstrate a real level of public benefit.' The Charity Commission called the verdict a score draw. By the time the three-year litigation had concluded, Suzi Leather had stepped down.

Her successor was the Old Etonian William Shawcross, who demonstrated absolutely no interest in going back to court for a more favourable judgment. Shawcross said that it was up to the public schools to decide for themselves if they were meeting requirements under charity law. When Shawcross appeared before MPs he rejected pressure to follow up Leather's lead by aggressively forcing public schools to justify their charitable status.

The negative publicity surrounding the charity case and the continuing criticism of public schools led to a number of heads leaving Britain to teach abroad. One of them was Helen Wright, headmistress of Suzi Leather's old school. She told the *Sunday Telegraph*:

What is very tiresome is the persistent failure of our leaders to recognise and acknowledge and praise the excellence of independent schools. It really is persistent – almost as if there is a determination to undermine the excellence, or certainly not accept it. The vaguely threatening rhetoric from politicians has become bound up with the general public's failure to understand what independent schools are today, an idea that is stuck in the past… By being funded by hardworking parents, independent schools save the taxpayer money. Those who attack independent schools perpetuate a class divide that is old fashioned and inaccurate. You just need to go to a school to see that people from every aspect of society are there. [32]

The old argument that parents of public school pupils save taxpayers' money had been shot down in 1967 by the Newsom Commission, which made the analogy of a childless couple asking for a tax refund from the state. Accusing public school critics of perpetuating a class divide is a bizarre inversion, but Blair had redrawn the political lines: a policy once deemed Conservative might now be considered perfectly acceptable by New Labour, and vice versa.

★

In September 2016 the schools once again found their charitable status under attack, this time from a new Tory prime minister.

Theresa May, who was educated at an independent school and then a grammar school which became a comprehensive, decided to tackle the public school problem head on. Much has been made of May's state education at Wheatley Park Comprehensive, Oxfordshire, but when she started there it was Holton Park Girls' Grammar School and she remained in a grammar set throughout her time there, witnessing the change without becoming an active participant. Her private primary education at St Juliana's Convent School for Girls had helped to secure her spot at Holton Park in the first place.

In a surprising attack on a system that has served the Conservative Party well, May threatened to strip the schools of their charitable status if they didn't do more to justify their public benefit. Cameron's time in office had been dogged by claims that he was running an Eton old boys' club as so many of his aides and ministers had been educated at his former school. May was determined to distance herself. Her first cabinet had the smallest percentage (30 per cent) of privately educated cabinet ministers since Clement Attlee (25 per cent) in 1945. (Margaret Thatcher's 1979 cabinet had the most, with 92 per cent.)[33]

Setting out what the schools could lose, the government explained: 'Our proposals will ensure that independent schools are doing more to benefit ordinary families, particularly those who are just about managing. These families cannot afford independent school fees but are also often earning enough not to be eligible for direct state support. The quality of their local school is important to them. We are asking independent schools to spread their expertise through the state system to benefit families like these, by setting an expectation that the best independent schools sponsor state schools and offer funded places.'

At the Headmasters' and Headmistresses' Conference that followed, Mike Buchanan, chair of the HMC, said:

Independent and state schools cannot make our relationships work with a gun pointing at our heads. We hope the prime minister understands that – after all she had the good sense to outlaw forced marriages as home secretary. She must know then that all good partnerships are based on mutual desire, understanding, respect and cooperation… While our schools are happy to punch above our weight, independent education is a tiny sector, educating around 7 per cent of British schoolchildren up to sixteen and containing many very small and specialist schools. Quite frankly, we cannot solve the structural problems in education that taxpayers entrust to the government – to the tune of £86 billion each year – nor should we be expected to.[34]

The Independent Schools Council, representing 1,330 private schools, tried to skew the debate and even steal the government's thunder by proposing the resurrection of Thatcher's assisted-places scheme. The ISC offered 10,000 places a year to children who would otherwise attend state schools – if the government agreed to pay for them. An annual subsidy of £5,500 for each pupil was suggested – a figure similar to the funding per pupil state schools received at the time. All in all, the proposed scheme would cost £50 million a year in taxpayers' subsidies, rising to £250 million a year after five years. Patrick Derham, the headmaster of Westminster School, said the scheme offered 'real social mobility': 'This scheme… is not about choosing the brightest pupils but about providing genuine transformational opportunities for those who need them most. We all want all young people to flourish and to be authors of their own life stories.' Under the proposals, independent schools would also group together to co-sponsor new state-funded schools in one or more of the six educational 'cold spots' in England identified by the Department for Education.

The plans were immediately condemned by the unions. Rosamund McNeil, the National Union of Teachers' head of education, said: 'A system in which public funds are used to support the admittance of a small proportion of pupils from low income backgrounds into private schools is a dangerous step towards a voucher system for education.' Labour politicians derided the move as resuscitating a failed policy, with the assisted-places scheme largely dominated by middle-class children, and costing an estimated £800 million while it was running. Sir Michael Wilshaw, Ofsted's former chief inspector, told BBC Radio 4: 'I think they can do better than that and if I was in government I would be asking them to do more as a quid pro quo for their tax privileges.'

After literally hundreds of years of dithering over reform, real change finally looked like it was going to happen. Then, on 18

April 2017, Theresa May called a snap election for 8 June. While private education remained high on the Tory agenda the great surprise was that Labour, offering up its most radical left-wing manifesto in decades, devoted just half a sentence to it – Jeremy Corbyn would charge VAT on private school fees.[35]

The Tory manifesto, meanwhile, read like something penned by Michael Foot. It began: 'The greatest injustice in Britain today is that your life is still largely determined not by your efforts and talents but by where you come from, who your parents are and what schools you attend. This is wrong. We want to make Britain the world's great meritocracy: a country where everyone has a fair chance to go as far as their talent and their hard work will allow.' For the public schools it prescribed that at least one hundred of the country's leading independent schools must sponsor a state school (an academy or set up a free school) or risk losing their charitable status. The Tories warned that they would keep 'open the option of changing the tax status of independent schools if progress is not made'.[36]

For May, the election was an unmitigated disaster. The Tories saw their lead reduced to a wafer-thin majority and they were forced into a deal with the Northern Irish Democratic Unionist Party, warping their political priorities. May's chief adviser, Nick Timothy, responsible for putting the flesh on so much post-Cameron policy, stepped down from his post and any plans for a radical overhaul of the public schools disappeared with him.

For the public schools, the rich irony was that they had been effectively saved from a radical education reform programme by their old enemy.

PART TWO
BAD EDUCATION

Predicting his own (and David Cameron's) future political success in 1988, Boris Johnson candidly described the realpolitik of winning votes to become president of the Oxford Union, long seen as a birthing pool for the nation's politicians. In *The Oxford Myth*, a collection of essays edited by his sister Rachel, Johnson says the 'most natural' politicians come from 'the Establishment'. This he describes as a 'loosely knit confederation of middle-class undergraduates, invariably public school, who share the same accents and snobberies, and who meet each other at the same parties. If you are a member of the Establishment, you will know it. You cannot be recruited.'

He goes on:

As an ambitious candidate in the Establishment you will do well not to appear too party political. Working this particular machine in your favour is an exercise in social politics. To all your chinless friends in the Establishment you simply look as though you lead a dynamic social life. Indeed it is essential for success as an Establishment candidate that you do not appear too gritty or thrusting. Only you know that the nectar of goodwill that you collect as you flit from party to party will eventually be translated into votes. Until that time comes you deliberately dampen down discussion of the Union and Oxford politics. Establishment folk have an English middle-class distaste for political conversation and the stooge candidate must do a great deal of subtle playing along before he can cash his chips and ask them to vote. But when that time comes the Establishment votes with a surprising and unthinking loyalty.[1]

10

DID YOU GO TO SCHOOL?

It was one of the most tumultuous summers in world politics since the end of the Second World War. David Cameron's promise to give the public a vote on Europe triggered a bitterly fought referendum which ended on 23 June 2016 with Britain voting to leave the European Union. A few days later Cameron was gone and Theresa May was suddenly the new prime minister. In America, Donald Trump accepted the Republican Party's nomination on the final day of the party's convention in Cleveland. By mid–August the crisis in Ukraine had reached a pivotal point with Russian-backed forces preparing to cross the border to launch further military incursions. On 20 September, Russian warplanes bombed a UN convoy in Syria. A few days later the Islamic State sent bombers to Turkey to blow up the airport in Istanbul. But amid all the world chaos, pupils from a school in the south of England were quietly preparing for an educational trip of a lifetime.

In many ways it was no different to any school visit. The boys were told to wear smart dress and school ties. They would need plenty of spending money and were warned to be on their best behaviour as they would be ambassadors for the whole school. But in two vital respects this school excursion was very different indeed. The pupils in question were from Eton, invited to Moscow for a very private audience with the Russian leader, Vladimir Putin.

A secret meeting between pupils from the most elite school in the world and a former Russian spy chief was highly sensitive. The eleven sixth-formers sat around a marble table in a state room in the Kremlin and, with the help of translators, were invited to ask the Russian leader any questions they liked. In spite of the best efforts of the school and the Kremlin, news of the visit leaked, propelling the boys onto the front pages of the British and world media. Putin's propaganda machine was quick to make political capital out of the world's most famous school. Some boys were interviewed by RT, the English-language television station widely seen as the Kremlin's propaganda channel, as well as the pro-government newspaper, *Komsomolskaya Pravda*. One boy was quoted as saying: 'Our media present facts in Ukraine as being entirely Russia's fault. They say that Ukrainians don't want to have anything to do with Russians. So it's interesting to talk to Ukrainian students here who have a different opinion and consider themselves Russians.' On the subject of Syria, another boy reportedly told the paper: 'Personally, I think that Putin is right to continue defending Assad in his role as president.'

Back home the boys' visit attracted condemnation and admiration in equal measure. Chris Bryant, the Labour MP and former government minister, said: 'There's a dangerous myth abroad in some right-wing circles that Putin has been a bit hard done by. That other Etonian Boris Johnson seems to think we should press the reset button with Russia. But let's not forget the Russian state had one man killed on British soil, Alexander Litvinenko, and another who worked for a UK firm, Sergei Magnitsky… We should work with Europe to strengthen our common position over Russia, not undermine it.'[1] (Events in Salisbury 18 months later when a Russian spy and his daughter were victims of a chemical weapons attack have proved Bryant right.)

Others had to acknowledge that the boys had pulled off something of a coup, securing a one-to-one, two-hour meeting with

Putin, and scooping their own newly elected prime minister, Theresa May, who had yet to arrange her own visit to the Kremlin. Chief executives of some of the world's biggest companies can spend months, perhaps years, waiting for a call from the Kremlin.

Back in Berkshire, the Eton College authorities were seriously concerned about the visit. The Kremlin-orchestrated media appearances had made the boys look naive and foolish. More concerning was the impression that Eton was somehow abusing its privilege by using soft power to trespass on the diplomatic stage. Putin's claim that he agreed to the audience because the school had educated nineteen British prime ministers only heightened the embarrassment. The boys had broken the school's unwritten rule that the only time an Etonian should have his name appear in the paper was at his birth, marriage or death – unless of course the coverage enhanced the standing of the school.

In a desperate attempt to distance Eton from the Kremlin the school issued a terse statement: 'This was a private visit by a small group of boys organised entirely at their own initiative and independently of the college.'

Eton's circumspect approach to the visit was telling. It exposed the sensitive path that Britain's most famous and exclusive private school has to tread in the twenty-first century. Any impression that the visit had nothing to do with the school, or indeed that any other school could have pulled off such a feat, is risible. So while it may have been true that the boys' trip was not officially sanctioned, the school was being disingenuous in playing down the Eton name which had made it possible.

And the connection between Moscow and Eton is much closer than many people realise. The school proudly exhibits in its ancient Cannon Square a sixty-four-pounder Russian gun captured by British soldiers at the Battle of Sevastopol during the Crimean War in 1854. Eton is the teacher of choice for the children of Russian oligarchs, who must implicitly support Putin or face ruin. One in ten boys at the school learns Russian and a disproportionate number of British ambassadors to Moscow are Old Etonians. More significantly, a few months before the Putin meeting, a charismatic Russian monk had been invited to Eton to talk to the boys.

Father Tikhon Shevkunov presides over a Russian Christian Orthodox monastery located close to the headquarters of the FSB, successor to the feared KGB. As Putin's personal spiritual adviser, he accompanies the Russian leader on diplomatic missions. His beard and long hair lend a passing resemblance to the American actor Russell Crowe, although there have been the inevitable comparisons with Rasputin, the mad monk who held sway in the court of the Tsars. It is not clear who invited the cleric to Eton but Father Tikhon says his visit was approved by the provost after some of the boys had read his book, *Everyday Saints and Other Stories*, a surprising bestseller.

Recalling his time at Eton, Father Tikhon says:

I was given a very warm reception; after the lecture I was asked many questions about the history of Russia, about its present, about Russian and English literature and culture, and of course, about the faith, about Orthodoxy. At the end of the meeting the lads asked me whether I could help them make a visit to Russia. I answered that of course I would gladly give them hospitality in Moscow and in Sretensky Monastery. Then they asked if they could meet with President Putin. The question was unexpected, to say the least. I answered that fulfilling their request would not be a simple matter. The boys asked me, 'What do we need to do for this?' I replied, 'You need to do what anyone does when they want to meet with someone they don't know: write him a letter and ask for a meeting.' The lads wrote a very polite and sincere letter, and I gave it to the International department of the President's Administration.[2]

He says that at all times Eton College was kept informed of the progress of the boys' request:

Immediately after I learned of the young men's desire to visit Russia and meet with our president, I informed the Eton College administration of it. I asked permission of the college provost to give the students' letter to the President's Administration, and permission was granted. After some time had passed, when a preliminary positive reply concerning the meeting had come from the Russian side, the ambassador of the Russian Federation in Great Britain A.V. Yakovenko informed the provost of Eton on its progress. The Eton administration reviewed two possible variations of the students' visit − either as personal, or as an official delegation. The final verdict was that they would not be sending an official delegation. When the students heard about this they said, 'Then we'll go on our own.' That is how they came to Russia.[3]

It was a version of events confirmed by the Kremlin in an official statement.

Before the boys set out, they were advised by a former Etonian master on how to negotiate the politics of the meeting. Peter Reznikov had been a Russian government interpreter before taking up a teaching post at Eton, which he held for seventeen years. This was a man who once claimed young Etonians believed he was a trained-to-kill colonel in the FSB under Putin's command. He suggested the boys ask questions 'in the friendliest manner possible − and not to annoy the president... I suggested they ask Putin about when Russian–British relations would start warming up, and what needs to be done for it to happen.'

There is a long tradition at Eton of pupil-led societies. Boys learn to arrange events, write letters of invitation to potential guests and, more importantly, use family or other contacts to bring in prominent speakers. The footballer Gianfranco Zola and the novelist Jeffrey Archer were among the boys' guests in the weeks before the Moscow visit. There is an understanding, however, that society events happen at the school and in term time. *The Times* described the boys' 'chutzpah' as 'very Etonian'.[4] Afterwards, several of the boys uploaded to social media images of them talking to Mr Putin. David Wei, from Shanghai, wrote that it took 'ten months, 1,040 emails, 1,000 text messages, countless sleepless nights' to organise the trip while studying for A-levels. After 'checking in' to the Kremlin's Facebook app, he posted: 'Guys, we truly gave Putin a deep impression of us and he responded by showing us his human face.'

★

Thirty-one years earlier, in 1985, another Eton schoolboy had visited Russia before going to Oxford to study Philosophy, Politics and Economics. His name was David Cameron and he was travelling around the Crimea with a school friend. The arrival of two schoolboys in Russia on a gap-year break wouldn't have normally interested the Soviet authorities, but the fact that Cameron and his friend were Etonians gave the visit special significance and two KGB spies were despatched to the region's capital to make contact with the boys. The naive Cameron and his chum were happy to make friends with the spies and willingly accepted the KGB's hospitality. They were treated to lunch and dinner and asked about life in England and what they thought about the government. It was only when Cameron discussed the strange encounter with a tutor at Oxford that he realised that he had probably been targeted by the KGB.[5] It makes sense. After all, the KGB had enjoyed much success recruiting spies and double agents who had recently left English public schools and were on their way to Oxbridge.

The most famous of such operations was the Cambridge Spy Ring. Anthony Blunt (Marlborough), Guy Burgess (Eton), Donald Maclean (Gresham's) and Kim Philby (Westminster) may have gone to different public schools but they moved in the same social and business circles and shared the same communist sympathies. Using their public school and university connections, the Cambridge spies effortlessly secured jobs at the BBC, MI5, MI6, and, in Anthony Blunt's case, even a posting at the heart of the royal family itself.

Loyalty to Britain is perhaps the most hallowed tenet of the public school ethos. The Queen is regarded with a special reverence by those who have been educated privately, partly because the royal family all went to public schools where they continue to serve as official patrons. Betrayal of Queen and country is regarded as the greatest toff crime of them all. Blunt, Burgess, Maclean and Philby knew this, and although each of them had their own reasons for betraying their country, they also knew their crimes would mean their names would live on in posterity.

The ongoing quest for an everlasting place in history is beaten into the hearts of all public school pupils and this egocentrism played straight into the hands of the Soviets. It allowed the Kremlin to ruthlessly exploit a system that educated almost the entire British establishment. Why waste time and valuable resources recruiting further down Britain's rigid class ladder when the public schools delivered access to the top on a plate?

The KGB's pragmatic obsession with Old Etonians during the Cold War was no different to Putin's fascination with the eleven schoolboys he had agreed to meet in August 2016. And when David Cameron and his fellow Etonian friend arrived in the Crimea in 1985, looking distinctly out of place on a gap-year break, it is hardly surprising that the KGB tried to recruit them.

As it turned out they were really on to something. David Cameron's effortless rise from home counties prep school to become the nineteenth Etonian prime minister was proof that the Kremlin's foreign-agent recruitment policy was sound. The Soviets might have also noted that between 1900 and 1979 almost a quarter (333) of government ministers (1,489) were educated at Eton.[6]

Cameron's rise from riches to power is a parable of our times. It lays bare a system in which, for the right price and a little insider dealing, a 'good' school can propel a schoolboy or a schoolgirl to the highest echelons of society in a very short time. Born the third of four children on 9 October 1966, Cameron spent the first three years of his life in Kensington and Chelsea before the family moved to an old rectory near Newbury in Berkshire. His mother, Mary, served as a Justice of the Peace for thirty years and his father, Ian, was a City stockbroker who in April 2016 was found to have run an offshore fund called Blairmore Holdings that avoided having to pay tax in Britain.[7] The Cameron family wealth had been established by David Cameron's great-great-grandfather, Alexander Geddes, who had made a fortune in Chicago trading in grain before returning to Scotland in the 1880s where he built the ancestral home, Blairmore House. Another great-great-grandfather was Sir Ewen Cameron, London manager of the Hong Kong and Shanghai Banking Corporation, who helped the Rothschild banking dynasty sell war bonds during the Russo-Japanese conflict of 1904–5. But the Cameron family's business dealings belie the family's aristocratic connections.

His maternal great-grandfather was Sir William Mount, 1st Baronet, who died 'while crossing a meadow at Aldermaston riding with the South Berks hounds from his residence at Wasing Place', a Grade II-listed mansion in Berkshire.[8] There are even direct royal claims that show he is the great-great-great-great-great-grandson of King William IV, albeit via a royal mistress, which supposedly makes him a fifth cousin, twice removed, of the Queen. Not only this, but his father-in-law's family once owned Buckingham House before selling it to George III for £21,000.

Cameron's education followed the same pattern as that of other children of the English upper-middle classes. The question of schooling was settled long before he was born based on an unshakeable trust in the most famous public schools in England. In accordance with family tradition, Cameron was sent to a country pre-prep school as the first step in the procession to Eton. He lived at home and was ferried to school in a lift-share arrangement with the select group of other mums whose children attended the same school.[9] According to Michael Ashcroft and Isobel Oakeshott's biography of Cameron, 'He had total stability and appeared to want for nothing, either emotionally or materially.'[10] It was a world to which only a tiny proportion of the population can relate: 'He is a real, proper Englishman, who would love to defend what he sees as the real England, but his real England is different to almost everyone else's,' said a childhood friend.[11]

At the age of seven, Cameron was packed off to Heatherdown, an exclusive preparatory school. It was a small school of just eighty pupils with an unusually short history – established in 1902 and forced to close in 1982. But in the sixty odd years before David Cameron attended, it had proved itself a reliable feeder for Eton.

Cameron's classmates included the grandson of the oil billionaire John Paul Getty and Prince Edward. By rubbing shoulders with the really rich and genuinely regal, a place at Heatherdown guaranteed success in life. How many other parent–teacher associations can call on the monarch to help out with the school fete?

Most of Cameron's class of 1978 went on to enjoy brilliant and rewarding careers in the City. Peter Romilly made his fortune specialising in the futures and derivatives markets.[12] Edward Mallinckrodt, who came top of the form and went on to study at Eton with Cameron, was named a Global Leader of Tomorrow by the World Economic Forum in 2001.[13] Others followed Cameron's path. Viscount Giles Goschen was briefly a transport minister in John Major's government at the age of twenty-nine and the youngest hereditary peer elected to the House of Lords by any party at just thirty-four in 1999. Others were straightforward aristocrats who left school to return to the stewardship of their titles and estates. They included the Honourable Charles Bruce, a descendant of Robert the Bruce and heir to the 11th Earl of Elgin. It was the 7th Earl of Elgin who had seized the marbles from the Parthenon in Greece and brought them to Britain.

The Camerons had registered David and his brother Alex (now a successful QC) on the so-called Eton List which effectively allowed an Old Etonian (OE) to sew up a place for his son while the boy was in nappies.[14] By the time Cameron took his place at the school in 1979 more than half of the pupils had fathers who were OEs. There was still the small matter of the Eton entrance exam, a far less challenging examination than it is now. Cameron passed, though he was not bright enough to secure a King's Scholarship, nor did he qualify for inclusion on the second tier of gifted scholars.[15]

Cameron followed his brother to Eton in 1979, the year Margaret Thatcher stormed to power and the year the Jam's hit single 'Eton Rifles' dominated the charts. Cameron later said he loved the song, much to the consternation of the band's songwriter Paul Weller, who had used Eton as a metaphor for class war.

The financial cost of all the Cameron children's education was a mere afterthought, although it would have set the family back £5,000 a year (now more than £40,000) for each boy, minus a sibling reduction. Cameron's two sisters Clare and Tania boarded at St Mary's Calne, where fees are now among the most expensive in the country at £37,500 a year.

Academically, Cameron was a slow developer, passing a clutch of unspectacular O-levels before achieving three As at A-level, in History, History of Art and Economics with Politics. Unlike his brother Alex and older pupil Boris Johnson, he was not invited into the Pop society, who were worshipped by the junior boys and wore a very distinctive uniform of black tailcoat with braid piping, spongebag trousers in a houndstooth check, and a starched wing collar with a white bow tie – hand-tied of course.[16] It has been said that Cameron felt his failure to win a place in Pop spurred him on in later life and made membership of the notorious Bullingdon and Piers Gaveston societies at Oxford so appealing. But an Eton education amounts to so much more than academic qualifications or esoteric societies. It provides a very exclusive social market-place for the rich and famous. The price of entrance is reassuringly expensive because it continues to dominate a premier league of English public schools which guarantee success. The only reason Eton does not expressly indemnify against failure is because the school's non-academic results emphatically speak for themselves – nineteen prime ministers is only a headline figure.

Cameron's headmaster at Eton was Eric Anderson, the teacher who had mentored Tony Blair at Fettes and taught Prince Charles at Gordonstoun. Like Blair, Cameron is effusive in his praise for the role Anderson played in shaping his ambitions and saving his school career. He had almost been expelled in 1984 after being caught taking cannabis: seven boys were removed in a scandal that exposed a wider drug culture at the school than anyone had realised. It was Anderson who brought Cameron back from the abyss and saved his education.[17]

After Cameron became prime minister a photograph emerged of his Eton peer group. His forty-five housemates and housemaster are pictured in 1984 in white bow-tie uniform arranged in four tiers and squinting into the sun. It could have been taken at any time in the previous 200 years. Notably there is not a single black or brown face among them. The vast majority of the boys who gathered on that warm June afternoon to pose for their picture followed in the fine traditions of Eton and became leaders of men or high achievers in their chosen field – bankers, journalists, entrepreneurs. But there are certain well-regarded professions that are, shall we say, very conspicuous by their absence. There are no scientists, inventors, doctors, probation officers, police officers or social workers. Only one of the forty-six found a job serving the local community: Benjamin Bellak trained to be a teacher and took a job at his local comprehensive school in south London. But even he eventually returned to the private fold. He now teaches at Cranleigh School in Surrey where boarding fees are over £36,600 a year.

Missing from the picture was Hugh Powell, whose father was Margaret Thatcher's foreign-policy adviser at the time. An aspiring journalist on the *Eton College Chronicle*, Powell was looking for a story that would get him noticed. His father suggested he write to the prime minister. Interestingly, the resulting interview focused not on Thatcherism but private education:

> Powell: You sent your own son to a public school, which suggests that you believe in the public school system. Do you think it will continue to have a role in the Britain of the future?
> Thatcher: Yes, people have the right to choose private education and if the public schools offer what parents want for their children then they will continue to flourish. But as someone who believes in competition I look forward to seeing the state schools increasing the pressure of excellence. My hope is that people will become less concerned with status and more concerned with performance.

Powell's follow-up question implied he was critical of the system that had served his family so well, when he asked whether public schools needed major changes to prepare their pupils for public service. Thatcher appeared to agree, saying that 'we need changes in the qualifications of those who enter the public service, with many more technically qualified people. I hope that the public schools will contribute to producing more such people rather than generalists.'[18]

Powell also asked the prime minister's advice on becoming a career politician but Thatcher told him she distrusted 'the professional politician who has never done anything else', adding that 'too often they are preoccupied with theories of politics and with manipulating people rather than bringing practical experience to bear on everyday problems.'

The tabloids had a field day and the article was carried by a number of national newspapers, although the world was blissfully unaware of how an Eton schoolboy had secured an exclusive interview with the prime minister. To Powell's mind he had achieved everything he had set out to and was able to use the interview to burnish his CV. This is confirmed by the thank-you letter he wrote to Thatcher, gleefully telling her that the interview had 'generated more interest and controversy than any *Chronicle* in the last one hundred years'. He had also gone one better than Cameron who, the previous year, had approached his cousin Ferdinand Mount, then head of Thatcher's Policy Unit, to try to bag an interview for himself. But he was rebuffed on the grounds that his cousin was too busy writing Thatcher's Conservative Party Conference speech.[19]

Cameron and Powell were destined to meet again when, unsurprisingly, they both found themselves in top government jobs. While Cameron was working his way to Downing Street, Powell was forging a career in the top ranks of the Civil Service. By 2014 he was Cameron's deputy national security adviser. Their longstanding friendship only became public when in March of that year Powell was put under the spotlight, photographed outside Downing Street with an official briefing note sticking out of his bundle of papers. It was at the height of the Ukraine crisis and the British government was carefully and secretly weighing up its options. Caught by a long-lens camera, Powell's briefing note declared that 'Britain should not, for now... close London's financial centre to Russians.'

The diplomatic blunder made front-page news, which many interpreted as proof that the billionaire oligarchs were getting exactly what they wanted for their generous donations to the Conservative Party. It was doubly embarrassing for Cameron, who now faced calls from politicians to sack the old school chum he had appointed to a top job a few weeks earlier.[20]

The Eton College house photograph only gives a narrow snapshot of the many OEs who would have cause to know David Cameron. Such is the intense camaraderie between boys who share the Eton experience that the bonds between them are unbreakable. They have spent five long years living together, growing up together, sharing intimate personal details and personal tragedy. They regard the school as their family. And after school they go to the same universities and later secure elevated and influential positions. It means OEs tend to bump into each other much more than most schoolboys do in their professional lives. Moreover, they are encouraged to seek each other out in society. One of the world's most precious networking tools is the Eton database held by the school and available to every former pupil – for a membership fee.[21]

Similar membership lists are carefully collated and mined by other public schools. Merchant Taylors' School sets out how its 'careers directory' operates with this explanation: 'This tool enables OMTs to contact fellow alumni who work in a particular field or industry for careers advice and information. The service has proven to be extremely successful and a real benefit to our more recent leavers who can easily access the knowledge and experience of their predecessors as they make decisions about their own careers. We're delighted that so many guests who attended the City Network have volunteered to be added to the directory, and also to return to school to give careers advice to the current boys.'[22]

Over the years OEs have found subtle ways of identifying each other beyond the accent and the tie. An Etonian greeting between two men who suspect they were educated at the same place is: 'Did you go to school?' The implication being there is only one school worth going to. How irresistibly tempting and convenient it must be for all these captains of industry, deal makers, lobbyists, PR men and movers and shakers across the establishment to help each other up the greasy pole. Yet it is impossible to say exactly how much influence a school like Eton can bring to bear. Impossible to count how many occasions it has literally been a case of jobs for the boys. Well, almost impossible. In the schooling and political career of David Cameron many of these associations are exposed.

After school, Cameron spent his gap year garnishing a CV that would open doors to politics and the City. He spent three months as a researcher for his godfather, Tim Rathbone (Eton), the Conservative MP for Lewes, and attended debates in the House of Commons. Through his father he was handed a six-month spell working for Jardine Matheson, a Bermuda-registered trading conglomerate, in Hong Kong. The company was run by an old family friend, Sir Henry Keswick (Eton), who offered Cameron a place on the company's training scheme after he graduated. Keswick later donated £100,000 to the Conservative & Unionist Party in the 2017 general election.

Cameron showed little interest in politics at Oxford but he did throw himself into the traditional public displays of privilege, joining the Bullingdon and Piers Gaveston clubs whose memberships are exclusively taken from the public schools, especially Eton. The rituals, which include smashing up restaurants and running riot through the city streets, are largely based on the behaviour of the pupil-run societies that dominated the ungoverned public schools of the eighteenth and nineteenth centuries. Today, it is said that a prospective Bullingdon Club member must burn a fifty pound note in front of a homeless person.

Hooliganism and vandalism are part of the club's *raison d'être*. In 1894, after dinner, Bullingdon members smashed the lights and 468 windows in Peckwater Quad of Christ Church, along with the blinds and doors of the building. This was repeated in 1927. In 1987 Cameron and Boris Johnson were part of a group of 'Bullers' who broke off their dinner in an Oxford restaurant to throw a pot through one of its windows. According to Cameron biographers Francis Elliott and James Hanning, Johnson was one of the members subsequently arrested and detained overnight by the police. More recently, in 2004 drunken 'Bullers' took to smashing crockery and wine bottles in a local pub. An attempt to pay for the damage with a cheque was rebuffed by the landlord and instead four of the group were arrested and slapped with penalty notices after a night in the cells.

In response to the 2011 London riots, Cameron had made much political play of saying that the offenders must be dealt with firmly. Asked by Evan Davis on the *Today* programme whether he could see any likeness between the rioters and members of the Bullingdon Club, Cameron said: 'We all do stupid things when we're young. And I think that's clear. But I think what we saw in terms of the riots was actually very well organised, in many cases, looting and stealing and thieving.'[23] Both events resulted in criminal damage and people put in fear for their personal safety. If anything, the Oxford rioting was better organised, and the offenders' private wealth presumably meant theft wasn't a priority.

There are many more societies and unofficial groupings that are governed by the rituals, argot and traditions of the public schools which continue to flourish at university. For example, the Stoics, an Oxford club, observes such a high degree of secrecy that public school undergraduates have to swear an oath never to admit to being a member. Nearly all of these clubs exclude women and many revolve around deeply antisocial behaviour. Piers Gaveston is best known today for a particularly sordid incident allegedly featuring David Cameron and a dead pig's head.[24] For state-educated boys and girls who only encounter the privately educated at university, this behaviour can be both intimidating and unfathomable. But far more harm is caused by behaviour that is simply imperceptible to the uninitiated.

★

After graduating from Oxford with a first-class honours degree Cameron faced an enviable career choice – wealth or power. Within a few weeks he was interviewed by Alistair Cooke (Framlingham), then deputy director of the Conservatives' research department. According to a number of reports, shortly before the interview took place Cooke received a phone call from Buckingham Palace. The male caller stated: 'I understand you are to see David Cameron. I've tried everything I can to dissuade him from wasting his time on politics but I have failed. I am ringing to tell you that you are about to meet a truly remarkable young man.'[25]

Whether he needed a leg-up in this way is debatable. Cameron was already well connected in the party through his cousin Ferdinand Mount. He had also transferred his allegiance from school and university societies to the gentlemen's clubs of London, which help to keep public schoolboys in touch with each other after university. Cameron's father was chairman of the most exclusive of them all, White's. Founded in 1693, its members include Prince Charles, Prince William, the disgraced media mogul Conrad Black, Geordie Greig (Eton), editor of the *Mail on Sunday*, and Norman Lamont (Loretto). Churchill's imposter friend Brendan Bracken, who tricked his way into high society, was also a member, as was Oswald Mosley (Winchester). Membership is exclusively male and public school. To become a member of White's, your proposer must write your name in a leather-bound book. Thirty-five other members must sign to secure your place; those who oppose may scrawl 'never'.[26]

Cameron was offered a researcher's post on the paltry starting salary of £10,000. But his private means meant he was able to move into an apartment in the exclusive Harrington Gardens in Kensington with his old friend, the film producer Peter Czernin, an heir to the Howard de Walden fortune.[27] It was in the Conservatives research department that he met George Osborne (St Paul's), who would go on to be his chancellor and closest political ally.

Other colleagues, who collectively became known as the 'brat pack', were Steve Hilton (Christ's Hospital), one of Cameron's closest strategy advisers during his early days in Downing Street, and Hilton's future wife Rachel Whetstone (Benenden) who later left the UK to run Google's communications unit. But it was Cameron's Eton friend Ed Llewellyn, two years above him and in the same year as Boris Johnson, whom the future prime minister relied on as his closest confidant and subsequently made his chief of staff. Osborne also opted for an OE as his chief of staff, former head boy Rupert Harrison.

This clique of Young Turk Tories worked and played together. They even holidayed together. Among their number were Michael Gove (Robert Gordon's), Chris Lockwood (St Paul's) as well as journalists and PR gurus including Robert Hardman and Matthew D'Ancona (St Dunstan's).[28] They met whenever the occasion allowed, including hunt meets in Devon and then near Chipping Norton, where the Camerons later moved.[29] Most of the group were invited to Cameron's wedding to Samantha (St Helen and St Katharine, and Marlborough College).[30]

This band of policy researchers and advisers secured a velvet revolution in the leadership and direction of the new Conservative Party. Many of their seniors had either attended the same schools and clubs or knew people who had. Some may have been part of the Masonic societies organised by most famous public schools under the aegis of the Public School Lodges' Council. Cameron's own career was boosted when he became adviser to the chancellor of the exchequer, fellow White's member Norman Lamont.

It was around this time Cameron committed himself to entering Parliament, but was told that he first needed experience outside of politics. Once again family and school contacts came to the rescue. Cameron's mother-in-law, Annabel Astor, regularly entertained guests at her remote holiday home in Jura. One guest, the self-made millionaire Michael Green, who ran Carlton Communications, liked to arrive by helicopter.[31] When she heard her son-in-law was looking for a plumb job out of politics she called Green, who quickly ended Cameron's short search for employment.[32]

In 1994 Cameron took up an £80,000-a-year job working as Green's right-hand man. He thrived at Carlton and used his new-found influence to help his network by bringing in people like Rachel Whetstone to high-powered positions. When Baron Beaverbrook (Charterhouse), for whom he had written speeches, asked if his daughter could do some work experience at Carlton he arranged that too.[33]

Although he prospered at Carlton, Cameron kept his eye firmly on the main prize – a parliamentary seat. So, to the dismay of Green, he left the company to begin a round of applications for Tory seats. For the first time in his career he found his Eton background worked against him as Conservative Party associations found he came over too much as a Tory toff. He was rebuffed in Ashford, Reading and Epsom.[34] It was the only time his Eton education stood in his way.

He was finally successful in Stafford. In the general election of 1997 Cameron called in some favours and persuaded a number of Tory big guns, including Michael Heseltine, to visit the constituency. But he still lost the seat to Labour by more than 4,000 votes.

Undaunted, he returned to Carlton while continuing to look for another winnable seat. He eventually found it in Witney, where the oratory skills he'd developed at Eton set him apart from the other candidates and saw him win the Oxfordshire seat in the general election of 2001.

★

In the aftermath of a second Labour victory the Conservative leader, William Hague, resigned. As old Tory hands including Kenneth Clarke and Michael Portillo jostled for the Conservative crown, Cameron even contemplated throwing his own hat into the ring. It was of course an absurd idea as he had been in parliament for less than six months, but Cameron's ambition knew no bounds.[35] Cameron bided his time and primed his powerbase. As the party floundered under Iain Duncan Smith and then Michael Howard, Cameron formed a strong partnership with George Osborne, who had joined him among the 2001 Commons intake. Their schooling and family background (Osborne's father was a baronet) made them perfect bedfellows.

Since many of the Cameron and Osborne group had substantial homes among the leafy Georgian terraces of west London, they became known as the Notting Hill set. All of them were privately educated and most had gone to Oxford. Cameron's network of supporters and advisers who had access to plenty of cash (David Feldman stomped up £20,000 for a sumptuous launch event) worked closely with his friends in the media, the *Independent*'s Bruce Anderson (Campbell College, Northern Ireland's most prestigious public school) and *The Times*' Daniel Finkelstein (University College School), who talked up Cameron's chances. He went on to win the 2005 Tory leadership election, a turn of events which some described as an Etonian putsch.

Going into the 2010 election the Tories lagged behind Labour in the polls. There were many in the Tory Party who thought it impossible that Britain would elect an OE as its next prime minister. To win over the electorate and end Labour's thirteen years in power he would need to broaden his appeal. Crucial to his success would be the Tory press and the most influential media moguls in the country: Rupert Murdoch (Geelong Grammar School, Australia's most expensive boarding school), Paul Dacre (state scholarship at University College School), and his much younger boss and owner of the *Mail* titles, Lord Rothermere (Gordonstoun).

Cameron, of course, already had the right contacts in place. The editor of *The Sun*, Rebekah Wade, was married to Charlie Brooks, an Old Etonian friend of Cameron's brother Alex. In 2009 the Brooks had moved close to Cameron's constituency home in Oxfordshire and they became frequent guests at each other's parties.[36] Soon, according to evidence given by Kenneth Clarke to the media select committee in 2017, Cameron and Osborne had the ear of Murdoch, his media executive son James (Horace Mann, the most exclusive school in New York) and PR tycoon Matthew Freud (Westminster). Before the 2010 election was called, Cameron could count on *The Sun, News of the World* and to a lesser extent *The Times*.

The wooing of Dacre proved more challenging as the long-standing editor is renowned for maintaining a cordial distance between his paper and the politicians he may end up stabbing in the front and back. But Dacre, who was by no means ill-disposed to Cameron's Etonian background, having sent his own sons there, eventually came round. *The Telegraph*, a natural Cameron cheer-leader, fell into line.

The 2010 election result was not enough to beat Labour outright but Cameron managed to seize the initiative by wooing Liberal Democrat leader Nick Clegg (Westminster) to form a coalition. The politicos were astonished: the Lib Dems had spent their whole careers opposing the Tories. A Lib Dem–Labour coalition had seemed inevitable. How did Cameron pull it off?

The natural chemistry between the Clegg and Cameron teams may have stemmed from a shared background. In the Clegg corner there was Chris Huhne (also Westminster), Danny Alexander (Lochaber High School, where former Lib Dem leader Charles Kennedy was also educated) and David Laws (St George's College, Weybridge) while Cameron wheeled out Osborne (St Paul's), Ed Llewellyn (Eton, and a family friend of the Cleggs) and Oliver Letwin (Eton). For the first time in their political lives these men were in touching distance of power, which would mark the end of their quest from playground to high office. They almost fell over each other in the rush to shake hands.

There are many who believe that Cameron, Osborne and Clegg were only interested in power for power's sake. Say Ashcroft and Oakeshott: 'Within [Cameron's] own party, a narrative was emerging that, having got the top job, he had achieved all he wanted.' Later on, one of Osborne's favourite responses to political trouble was reportedly: 'Oh look, it's all a game.'[37] For those who have been educated at Eton or St Paul's, that rings true. The trouble is the stakes are so much higher when you are playing with people's jobs and families.

★

Inside Downing Street, Cameron wasted no time gathering around him a clique of old school friends and members of his tight network of supporters. Some were elected, some not. Soon, key government decisions were being taken in the marble-topped kitchens of west London and rubber-stamped as an afterthought by the cabinet. Ministers and civil servants, who felt excluded from government, suspected that it was unhealthy to run Britain in such a narrow echo chamber.[38]

Helen Ghosh, a former Home Office permanent secretary, said that women were conspicuous by their absence from Cameron's executive decision-making club, which she described as an 'Etonian clique'. There were plenty of promoted OEs to support Ghosh's claim. Boris Johnson's brother Jo Johnson was appointed head of Cameron's Downing Street Policy Unit, while Oliver Letwin was put in charge of developing cabinet policy. There were also key appointments outside government in Cameron's gift to OEs. The Etonian son of his old headmaster, Eric Anderson, was made the independent reviewer of terrorism laws.[39] By 2014, concern over the number of Etonians at the heart of government had become so serious that Cameron's ally, Michael Gove, told the *Financial Times* that the numbers of Eton-educated advisers was 'ridiculous and preposterous'.[40]

Gove, godfather to one of Cameron's children, was the first Conservative education minister to send his child to a state secondary school and publicly argues that twenty-first-century prime ministers should be choosing from a much wider talent pool. Unfortunately, when, as education secretary, he came under pressure to introduce a free school meal policy for poor children, instead of commissioning a report from someone who'd already worked on the issue, he gave the job to Henry Dimbleby (Eton), son of veteran broadcaster David, whom he had bumped into on holiday in Marrakech.

In the run-up to the 2015 general election David Cameron agreed to be interviewed by the BBC in his Cotswold kitchen. The whole Cameron family was present and the idea was that it should be less formal than some of the other set-piece interviews he had done with the broadcast media. Cameron and his advisers hoped it would soften his image and show the prime minister to be more ordinary, portraying him as a loyal husband and devoted father.

The choice of who should conduct the interview was crucial. The man selected for the job was James Landale, the then deputy political editor of the BBC. The two men had met many times when Landale was reporting on politics. But there was also something much deeper about their acquaintance. Both men were near contemporaries at Eton. They also shared an interest in the Hong Kong-based trading conglomerate Jardine Matheson: Landale's ancestor was the 13th Tai-pan of Jardine Matheson & Co. and member of the Executive Council and Legislative Council of Hong Kong.

A BBC film crew had spent a relaxed week filming Cameron cheering on his son Elwen's football team, shopping in the local butcher's shop and preparing food in the kitchen of his Oxfordshire home. It was while Cameron was at home with Samantha and his children that Landale had popped him that now famous fatal question and asked him how long he was planning to serve as prime minister.

It was a question that a politician as street savvy as Cameron should have been able to bat away with ease. Instead he answered honestly that, should he win the election he had no intention of serving a third term. It may have been said to honour a pledge he had made to his wife, and her presence during the interview made the question difficult to avoid. Or he may have thought that he was unlikely to win a second term and was planning to stand down shortly anyway.

Whatever the reason for this apparently off-the-cuff remark it was to alter the course of British history. Its most immediate impact was to make Cameron vulnerable to a leadership challenge from an emboldened Boris Johnson. It kick-started a fourteen-month Tory leadership race which turned the Referendum campaign into a beauty contest to choose his successor. Cameron had gambled that he would win the EU referendum, like he had successfully gambled on the Scottish referendum, and Boris, in so many ways a europhile, had gambled that he stood a much better chance of succeeding his school friend as prime minister if he threw his weight behind Brexit. It was all part of the game, not just within politics, but in the Conservative Party, and the public school clique within it.

★

After the Tories won an outright majority in the 2015 general election, 53 per cent of Cameron's reshuffled cabinet had been educated at an independent school at some point in their life.[41] Under Cameron's leadership, the country appeared to be run as an extension of his old school.[42] This may not have been what Cameron or his advisers, partners and hangers-on intended or believed they were doing. Nevertheless, this was the widely held perception, one which was predicated on some uncomfortable truths.

In late 2015, Boris Johnson, then London mayor, drew up proposals that would have helped the city's black-cab drivers fight back against the growing number of private-hire cars using Uber. But three months later he dropped several of the most controversial ideas, including forcing customers to wait for five minutes between requesting a car and beginning a journey. The London cabbies claimed that Johnson had been leaned on by Cameron and his advisers, one of whom was then working for Uber. The saga left a bad taste and raised questions about whether Cameron's close-knit circle of friends was acting in the best interests of the country.[43] Worse still, Cameron was also accused of trying to cover up allegations of serious crime among his friends.

Patrick Rock, who was a close friend of both David Cameron and Ed Llewellyn long before he became a key Number 10 adviser, resigned as deputy director of the Downing Street Policy Unit in February 2014 as a result of a police investigation into child pornography allegations. Rock was given a two-year conditional discharge after downloading indecent pictures of scantily clad girls as young as ten in sexual poses. Before his arrest, he had been responsible for developing government policy to require internet companies to fit anti-porn filters as standard.[44]

It later emerged that the police investigation into Rock had been kept quiet by Downing Street, who were keen to keep Rock's name out of the public eye. The situation was made worse when it was revealed that he had previously been the subject of a complaint of harassment – an allegation that had been investigated by his friend Llewellyn. Downing Street denied any cover-up but the perception that Cameron was guilty of favourable treatment for his friends persisted throughout his premiership.

When Cameron resigned in the wake of the EU referendum the scale of this protection, patronage and preferment was laid bare. Almost all those featured in his list of resignation honours had begun their journey at public school. Some are very conscious of this unseen advantage and try to hide their private education – the CVs and LinkedIn profiles of Cameron's special advisers often leave out the name of their school.

While many of these were names already in the public domain and had led to claims that Cameron ran his government as a 'chumocracy', there were others who weren't.[45] By scratching the backs of so many of his network, Cameron had inadvertently exposed the incestuousness of public school associates.[46]

One of the most revealing was the patronage bestowed on Nicholas Howard, Cameron's assistant private secretary, given an OBE. His name or position is hardly known outside Westminster. He is the son of Michael Howard, who'd mentored Cameron when he was home secretary. In 1993, Howard, a grammar schoolboy, provoked a wave of criticism when he sent his son to Eton after saying he did not think a Pimlico school near where the Howards lived would be good enough.[47]

The most brazen appointment of all was that of Laura Wyld, who was given a peerage by herself as head of the prime minister's Appointments Unit. Such a blatant round of self-serving patronage and advancement to a very narrow group of friends and advisers prompted bitter criticism. The then Lib Dem leader Tim Farron said Cameron's resignation honours list was 'so full of cronies it would embarrass a medieval court'.[48] But the most damaging criticism came from inside Cameron's circle: Steve Hilton called the awards a symptom of 'our corrupt and decaying democracy'.[49]

Cameron was able to walk away from Downing Street knowing that he had honoured the long-held Etonian tradition of looking after friends in need. They could now cash in on their time in government. Some set up consultancies to advise companies they'd been introduced to while in power; others joined multi-national businesses with the implicit intention of opening doors to Whitehall. There were even examples of former advisers now being paid to advise each other.

As for George Osborne, less than a year after being sacked as chancellor he was parliament's highest-earning member, receiving £650,000 a year working one day a week for City investment firm BlackRock, where his friend and adviser Rupert Harrison had already secured a well-paid berth. He has also earned £800,000 from delivering speeches to bankers and executives and was paid £120,000 a year for a research role at a university in the USA. All this on top of his job as MP. In February 2017 he was made editor of London's *Evening Standard* on an estimated £250,000 a year, prompting calls for him to resign his seat, which he did at his leisure.[50]

The meteoric rise and padded fall of David Cameron is a story that can only be told because of the public school system. His privileged education gave him the training and access that hugely increased his chances of winning. By charting his rise to power it is possible to show how easy it is for a tight coterie of people to play the system. Some of them come from wealthy families, some are aristocrats. Others may be the sons and daughters of entrepreneurs or oligarchs. But the single most important thing they have in common is that they received a private education in England. Not to put too fine a point on it, they bought their success. And in Britain that's how the system works, as Vladimir Putin well knows. Betting on an Etonian successor to Cameron and Johnson, the Kremlin in 2018 appeared to have ordered its cyber army to get behind the #Moggmentum hashtag and support Tory leader hopeful, Jacob Rees-Mogg.[51]

11

BOYS' OWN BREXIT

In 1993, the UK Independence Party (UKIP) was established with the single political goal of taking Britain out of Europe. It didn't look like it was going to last long. Within a few years its founder, Professor Alan Sked, a former Liberal Party candidate who'd attended the fee-paying Allan Glen's School in Glasgow, had left the party over concerns about far-right infiltration.[1]

Further in-fighting and a poor showing in the 1994 European Parliamentary elections left the party vulnerable to a better-funded and better-organised rival group of eurosceptics. Capitalising on UKIP's weakness, multi-millionaire James Goldsmith founded his Referendum Party in the same year and quickly attracted the rump of UKIP's eurosceptic support.

The Goldsmiths, formerly the German Goldschmidts, were a wealthy family who had been involved in international merchant banking since the 1500s. Goldsmith's great-grandfather had been financier and consul to the Grand Duke of Tuscany and his grandfather a multi-millionaire, but by the time James himself inherited the family titles there was little left of the Goldsmith fortune. There was, however, enough family cash to send James to Millfield School and then Eton College. He left Eton in 1949 aged sixteen after winning £8,000 on the horses (about a quarter of a million pounds today). He told the rest of his Eton boarding house, 'A man of my means should not remain a schoolboy.'

During a business career characterised by high risk and asset stripping he accumulated a fortune rivalling anything held by his forebears. He used part of it to fund his pet project the Referendum Party and pursue his long-held belief that Britain's interests were incompatible with a Europe dominated by Germany. The party's public profile was greatly enhanced by endorsements from a clique of celebrities and politicians, among them the actor Edward Fox (Harrow), and the millionaire gambler and zookeeper John Aspinall (Rugby), whose stepfather, Sir George Osborne, was the grandfather of our recent chancellor.

In the 1997 general election Goldsmith's party spent three times as much as the Conservatives on press advertisements and five times as much as Labour, but won only 2.6 per cent of the vote. Months later Goldsmith, who had lost his deposit, died of cancer. Following his death, the party disbanded, clearing the way for the return of UKIP and Nigel Farage.

★

Farage was in the same maverick mould as Goldsmith and his backer Aspinall. He was educated at Dulwich College, one of Britain's oldest public schools with a proud, if distant, tradition of educating local poor scholars.[2] During his time there, the school was visited by Enoch Powell (King Edward's, Birmingham) and the politician credited with creating Thatcherism, Keith Joseph (Harrow). Powell was famous for his 'rivers of blood' speech in 1968, in which he attacked immigration and new anti-discrimination laws. It made him extremely popular but later led to claims of racism.

In his autobiography, *Fighting Bull*, Farage described how on meeting Powell as a teenager, the MP 'dazzled me for once into an awestruck silence'. In fact, Farage was so impressed by Powell that he tried on several occasions to get the former Tory minister to endorse his UKIP parliamentary candidacy. On each occasion Powell politely demurred.

Farage's time at Dulwich and the politicians he met there clearly left a deep impression on the teenage schoolboy and his political development.[3] However, in 2013 it emerged that some teachers had thought Farage's views on immigration and ethnic minorities were racist and a cause for concern. In June 1981, Chloe Deakin, a young English teacher at Dulwich, wrote a letter begging the master of the college, David Emms, to reconsider his decision to make Farage a prefect. Deakin did not know Farage personally but her letter includes an account of what was said by staff at their annual meeting, held a few days earlier, to discuss new prefects. One teacher had said Farage was 'a fascist, but that was no reason why he would not make a good prefect... Another colleague, who teaches the boy, described his publicly professed racist and neo-fascist views; and he cited a particular incident in which Farage was so offensive to a boy in his set, that he had to be removed from the lesson. This master stated his view that Farage's behaviour was precisely why the boy should not be made a prefect. Yet another colleague described how, at a Combined Cadet Force camp organised by the college, Farage and others had marched through a quiet Sussex village very late at night shouting Hitler-youth songs.'[4]

At the time, far-right groups were stirring up racist hatred against Britain's immigrant communities. The National Front held marches in south London which had sparked violent clashes, and during the 1981 Brixton riots, not far away from the school, part of the grounds of Dulwich College were used as an operational base by the police. Emms later said he didn't remember receiving Deakin's letter: 'I didn't probe too closely into that naughtiness, but the staff were fed up with his cheekiness and rudeness. They wanted me to expel him, but I saw his potential, made him a prefect, and I was proved right.'[5] Others were far from convinced.

In August 2016, as Farage was championing Britain's exit from Europe, a former school friend wrote an anonymous letter to the *Independent*, voicing concerns:

> I haven't chosen to write before, but I simply have to now. I now wonder if there is a connection between you at 16 and you at 52. I don't believe you have fascist sympathies now, but there are things that tell me your views might not have changed that much despite the many years.
>
> I think there comes a time – however difficult it may be – when enough is enough. I remember those school days in the UK. As you know, teachers were concerned…
>
> For I vividly recall the keen interest you had in two initials of your name written together as a signature and the bigoted symbol that represents from the many doodles over your school books. Nigel Farage, NF, National Front. I remember watching you draw it. Just a laugh, eh, Nigel?
>
> As the son of an immigrant family, your frequent cry of 'Send em home' and mention of the name Oswald Mosley didn't mean much to me either until much later when I learned of the British Fascists… But I also remember something altogether more alarming: the songs you chanted at school. In her letter Chloe Deakin mentioned reports of you singing Hitler Youth songs, and when you were confronted by that, you denied it.
>
> But I do remember you singing the song starting with the words 'gas them all, gas 'em all, gas them all'. I can't forget the words. I can't bring myself to write the rest of it for it is more vile than anything the teachers at Dulwich would ever have been aware of.
>
> I too think that things can be in the past and that people grow up from being naughty schoolchildren. Heaven help us if they didn't, let's face it, but heaven help us if we believe all children do.[6]

Farage was quick to defend the general thrust of the claims made against him: 'To say that this is going over old ground is an understatement. The period during which I was at Dulwich was highly politically charged with the rise of Thatcherism and the Brixton riots just down the road. There were many people of that time who were attracted to extreme groups on both sides of the debate.' He told the *Independent*: 'Whoever sent you this [letter] must be a little [out] of touch to say that I supported Oswald Mosley as he believed in a United States of Europe. Some people need to get over Brexit.'[7]

At the time Dulwich College did not comment on any of the allegations.

But the school's new headmaster, Dr Joseph Spence, told me that had Farage been at Dulwich today his extreme views would have been challenged.[8] Indeed Farage has returned to speak to the Dulwich boys several times. 'Farage is a dedicated old boy... [but] it would be inflammatory for us to deal closely with him. I personally, and we institutionally, have been deeply disappointed by some of the things he has said. But we have invited him to speak to the boys because we want to encourage free speech.'

To illustrate the point Spence refers to an incident involving alt-right polemicist and former Breitbart News editor Milo Yiannopoulos, who he describes as 'a YouTube phenomenon who has built his reputation on deeply misogynistic views'. Spence recalls: '[He] was asked by the boys running the Economics Society to give a talk here on the myth of the gender pay gap. For the first time in my career as headmaster I said, "He's not coming." I thought his presence would be incendiary and not help sensible debate at a time when we had just created an equality society [looking seriously and sensitively at questions of gender and at gender politics] – the boys understood my decision.'

Milos Yiannopoulos, educated at a Kent grammar school, was less understanding, firing back an email in which he accused the college of closing down free speech: 'I do enjoy winding up professional grievance mongers with the truth. This should not preclude me from speaking at your college... True I'm just a tabloid journalist who likes to swear and mock the excesses of modern feminism. But if we don't defend the free speech we find distasteful, what's the point of it?'[9]

Spence says: 'In the 2016 general election Dulwich College alumni were candidates for five political parties. That tells you where we are – rather than our most prominent old boy formerly being the leader of UKIP. The co-leader of the Green Party is an old boy, too... If Nigel Farage was at Dulwich today and expressing the views he does then he would be challenged. There is a code of conduct which we comply with. A boy who arrived as a boarder a few years ago had deeply misogynistic, racist and homophobic views. Something he said was leaked to the press. He was challenged here, but not expelled or vilified, and he spent two years in a boarding community with boys from all sorts of different nationalities and left here a very different person to the one who arrived.'

In his book *The Purple Revolution: The Year That Changed Everything*, Farage said he owed Dulwich a 'great debt' and that his education was much better than the one on offer today because it had more boys from poorer backgrounds whose fees were met by the local authorities.

After leaving school Farage entered the City where he amassed a fortune working as a commodities broker for a succession of French and American traders and banks. With his future secure, Farage began building a political career as the anti-establishment candidate, the little man against the big corporate stitch-up. He also used his money to send his eldest son to Dulwich too so that he could also secure a top job in the City.[10] Rather than opposing the establishment, Farage had embraced it and through his son's schooling become the very embodiment of privilege and advantage while posing as a political underdog.

But Farage was not the only politician who was building a career out of taking Britain out of Europe. Indeed, there were many politicians working for Brexit behind the scenes, almost all of them privately educated, and a striking number born abroad – perhaps overcompensating in their extravagant championing of British values and antagonism to Europe. Daniel Hannan was educated at Marlborough College in Wiltshire, where he met another leading figure in the Brexit movement, Mark Reckless. The school describes him as 'a proud Old Marlburian deeply conscious of the great tradition of writers'. Farage also shared sympathies with Tory backbenchers like John Redwood (Kent College), Bill Cash (Stonyhurst) and Jacob Rees-Mogg (Eton), and even managed to woo Douglas Carswell (Charterhouse) over to UKIP – a high-profile defection that forced the Tories to think hard about the restless right wing of their party. There was even a Labour Leave faction led by Kate Hoey (Belfast Royal Academy).

On 20 February 2016 Vote Leave and Leave.EU/Grassroots Out received the news they had been waiting for. David Cameron announced there would be an EU referendum to be held on 23 June 2016.

*

Almost immediately five cabinet ministers publicly declared their support for Vote Leave: Michael Gove, the lord chancellor and justice secretary; Chris Grayling (Royal Grammar School, High Wycombe), leader of the House of Commons; Iain Duncan Smith (St Peter's RC Secondary School), the secretary of state for work and pensions; John Whittingdale (Winchester), the culture secretary; Theresa Villiers (Francis Holland School), the secretary of state for Northern Ireland; as well as cabinet-attending minister Priti Patel (Watford Grammar School for Girls), the minister of state for employment. The referendum had now become a proxy war for the soul of Conservatism, and for four months the British people were treated to the most dishonest campaign in British electoral history. At the start, Boris Johnson wrote an article comparing the EU to the Nazis while David Cameron claimed that leaving the EU would lead to war.

Looking back, the *Financial Times* columnist Simon Kupar wrote: 'The public schoolboys focused the Brexit campaign on an issue many ordinary Britons do care about: immigration. To people like Johnson, the campaign was an Oxford Union debate writ large. Once again, their chief weapons were rhetoric and humour.'[11]

But there was also a sinister and dangerous side to the war of disinformation. The Vote Leave poster that stated that after Brexit the NHS should receive 'the £350 million the EU takes every week' was so toxic that it was disowned by Farage. His own anti-migrant poster, featuring a queue of migrants at the Croatia–Slovenia border accompanied by the words 'BREAKING POINT', was reminiscent of stills from a Nazi propaganda video, and was reported to the police with a complaint that it incited racial hatred and breached UK race laws.

On the Remain side, George Osborne was heavily criticised for a series of bleak Treasury assessments about Britain's prospects outside the EU, which became known as 'project fear'. They claimed that every household would be £4,300 worse off per year and that house prices would fall by 19 per cent in the event of Britain leaving Europe.[12]

Funding for all this misinformation came from a very small group of secretive and mostly privately educated financiers and fund managers. Organisations that backed Leave during the EU referendum campaign received a total of £24.1 million in donations and loans between 1 February and 23 June 2016, according to the *Sunday Times*, 61 per cent of which came from just five businessmen. The biggest Brexit donor was Arron Banks, born in South Africa, educated at Crookham Court Manor School, now closed down following a paedophile teacher scandal. Banks gave a £6 million loan to Leave.EU and then donated a further £2.1 million to Grassroots Out through his Better For The Country Ltd campaigning firm. The other four were Peter Hargreaves (Clitheroe Grammar School), co-founder of financial advice company Hargreaves Lansdown (£3.2 million); Jeremy Hosking, financier and co-owner of Crystal Palace Football Club (£1.69 million); Lord Edmiston, state-educated Christian philanthropist (£1 million); and Crispin Odey (Harrow),[13] founding partner of Odey Asset Management (£873,328).[14]

The lead donor for the Stronger in Europe campaign was the businessman David Sainsbury (Eton), who gave £4,223,234. Another significant Remain funder was Mark Coombs (Dulwich), who donated £750,000. Billionaire hedge-fund owner and former futures trader David Harding (Pangbourne) donated £3.5 million to the same campaign.

Before the country went to the polls, the Leave campaigners had one more card to play in the battle to persuade the British people to support Brexit. Some believe it may have even been a decisive factor. In the summer of 2015, US billionaire Robert Mercer, a close friend of Donald Trump and an investor in alt-right media company Breitbart News, introduced Farage to a data company set up by two Old Etonian brothers who had cut their teeth on controversial military style 'psy-ops' which they ran in election campaigns in the developing world.[15]

Nigel and Alex Oakes were colourful businessmen with a special interest in psychological profiling. Alex Oakes was a close school contemporary of David Cameron, while his older brother was an ex-boyfriend of Lady Helen Windsor and a former executive of the Tories' favourite advertising agency, Saatchi & Saatchi.

In the late 1990s, Nigel Oakes established a business, Strategic Communication Laboratories (SCL) Group, that specialised in influencing behaviour by identifying key audiences and using social media to connect with them.

Big data was big business and politicians and companies were paying SCL to influence elections and behaviour all over the world. The company had even undertaken counter-terror operations on behalf of Britain's Ministry of Defence and in 2015 secured a $750,000 contract to help NATO states in the Baltic counter Russian propaganda.[16]

At the height of their success the Oakes brothers decided to set up another company, Cambridge Analytica (CA), which would specialise in winning elections. The brothers teamed up with a third Etonian, Alexander Nix, who became CA's chief executive. (It was the smooth-talking Nix who was later caught in a Channel 4 undercover reporting sting where he was recorded offering a range of dirty tricks to discredit a political candidate.) Then, in 2016, CA took its social media campaigning to America.

The firm first worked on Ted Cruz's campaign to become the Republican presidential candidate. Mercer was so impressed with CA he became a major shareholder while Trump's then chief strategist, Steve Bannon, joined the company board. Perhaps inevitably, given these connections, the Trump campaign ended up paying almost £5 million to the company to help it target swing voters.

Buoyed by their initial success in the US presidential primaries, the firm had also turned its attention to the EU referendum. Nix wrote an article claiming CA had 'supercharged' the Leave.EU campaign, headed by Farage and bankrolled by Aaron Banks. The company established a reputation for crafting messages that play on people's anxieties. For Leave.EU this meant targeting voters' fears of immigration. Later the firm was accused of harvesting the data of 50 million, mostly American but some British, Facebook users to help target voters.[17]

CA forcefully rejected the claims it had undertaken work that was not declared by the Leave campaigns, and when Nix came to give evidence to MPs in February 2018 he flatly denied undertaking any paid work for Leave.EU. Aaron Banks also said Leave.EU did not receive any data or work from CA.[18] But CA's alleged role in the EU referendum later became the subject of three investigations by the Electoral Commission, the Information Commissioner and the Commons culture committee. And that was not all.

The players behind CA also appeared to have links to the mainstream Brexit group, Vote Leave, which had employed two Westminster public school PR whizz kids with a proven track record in influencing national opinion. Matthew Elliott, educated at Leeds Grammar school, was a founder of the TaxPayers' Alliance, Big Brother Watch and Business for Britain. He was joined by the Svengali figure of Dominic Cummings (Durham School), a close political adviser of Michael Gove. A third member of the Vote Leave team was Tom Borwick (Stowe), the son of a Tory MP. Borwick had been a consultant for CA before he joined Vote Leave as its chief technology officer, responsible for 'creating and integrating the development roadmap and tools for the EU referendum campaign'.

Although Cummings and Vote Leave denied using CA it later emerged that the Vote Leave campaign had paid £2.7 million (nearly half its spending budget) to a tiny Canadian data profiling company called AggregateIQ (AIQ) which was alleged to be linked to CA.[19] In 2018, as the furore broke around Facebook's failure to protect its users' data, CA whistle-blowers claimed the Brexit campaigners had broken the referendum spending rules and misused personal data. Whatever the truth of the allegations one man was certain that the money spent on data analytics had been put to good use. Cummings explained: 'Rational discussion accomplishes almost nothing in politics, particularly with people better educated than average.' Instead, he said, 'we were the first campaign in the UK to put almost all [98%] our money into digital communication... Without a doubt, the Vote Leave campaign owes a great deal of its success to the work of AggregateIQ. We couldn't have done it without them.'[20]

One *FT* columnist wrote: 'Cummings' decision to hire data experts instead of the usual politicos, combined with a cynical understanding that it did not matter if what the campaign said was factually correct, made Vote Leave unlike any other political operation.'

Political parties of all stripes have now woken up to how social media targeting can win elections. But there are only a few companies who promise to deliver it, and the Eton-educated founders of CA were a long way ahead of the pack.

★

On 23 June 2016, Britain voted Leave.

At the outset, Cameron had believed he could win the vote with ease and his advisers assured him that UKIP on its own could not organise a successful counter-campaign. But when Johnson and Gove became the leading figures of the 'mainstream' Leave campaign, Cameron was guilty of complacency by refusing to sanction attacks on his old friends. Adopting an overly chivalrous position, no doubt informed by Eton's fair-play rules, he treated the two men as friends first and political adversaries second. Cameron, who hadn't really countenanced the prospect of defeat, didn't want any bad feeling between him and the Brexit ministers after the referendum and so refused to fight fiercely for Remain. He later told George Osborne 'it was like fighting with one arm tied behind our backs'.

But it was Cameron who shouldered the brunt of the blame for the unexpected vote in favour of leaving the EU. Even his loyal

Etonian supporters turned on him. Nicholas Soames said afterwards: 'If you were to ask me, do I wish David Cameron, that he hadn't said that he would have a referendum, yes, I bloody well do!' In a similar vein, Michael Heseltine said he thought he had 'lost the plot'. Similarly, Johnson's backing of the Leave campaign was seen by many as a self-interested manoeuvring for position within the party. This characterisation was compounded by two draft articles Johnson had penned for the *Telegraph* – one in favour of Brexit and one opposed. In a BBC documentary about Brexit, Alan Duncan (Merchant Taylors'), the Conservative minister for Europe, said: 'I've always thought that Boris's wish was to lose by one so that he could be the heir apparent without having to have all the S-H-I-T of clearing up the mess. That's always been my view of Boris.'[21] Vince Cable, who as business secretary in the coalition government had witnessed the origins of the referendum vote at very close quarters, characterised the Brexit debate as 'two groups of silly public schoolboys reliving their dormitory pillow fights'.

Farage and Johnson were, of course, the obvious political winners. But the public school financiers also did very well out of Brexit. Crispin Odey had commissioned several polls on the possible outcome to make money and get ahead of the market. His gamble that the markets would crash on news of a vote to leave the EU made him £220 million overnight. Odey, who manages more than £8 billion and has an estimated personal fortune of £900 million, revealed that in the run-up to the vote he had invested heavily in gold, a safe haven amid market turmoil, and bet on the pound falling against the dollar. The Old Harrovian told a BBC documentary on the morning of the referendum result: 'There's that Italian expression, *il mattino ha l'oro in bocca*, "the morning has gold in its mouth", and never has one felt so much that idea as this morning, really.'

He wasn't alone. Billionaire Sir Paul Marshall (Merchant Taylors') donated £100,000 to Vote Leave. He, too, was reported to have made at least $10 million for his Global Opportunities fund at Marshall Wace after shorting stocks.

Even losing Remain donors made money. David Harding donated £3.5 million to the Britain Stronger In Europe campaign but was still one of the big winners on referendum day. Harding lost the vote but may have consoled himself with a significant windfall at his Hammersmith-based trading firm Winton Capital Management. One of its largest products, the Diversified fund, gained 3.1 per cent on the Friday while flagship fund Winton Futures surged by 2 per cent.[22]

As soon as the vote was secured, Johnson and Vote Leave told the public that most of what they said during the campaign wasn't true. In particular, immigration was impossible to control – the majority of immigrants were from outside the EU – and the £350 million refund for the NHS was probably rubbish. Then Johnson went to play cricket with Lord Althorp (Eton).

As the value of the pound tumbled, Gove and Johnson, supported by a host of close advisers, began burnishing their leadership credentials for what they clearly saw as the real contest. For dozens of other political advisers on both sides of the Brexit debate it was also time to cash in on the referendum result. Ameet Gill, Cameron's former strategy chief, teamed up with Paul Stephenson, the director of communications for Vote Leave, to found a consultancy, Hanbury Strategy, a lobbying firm that was to focus on Brexit. Daniel Korski (educated at a private school in Copenhagen), the deputy director of the highly influential Downing Street Policy Unit, set up a new company, Public, with his OE friend Alexander de Carvalho. De Carvalho is an extraordinarily rich aristocrat, the son of the Heineken brewing company heiress and married to Countess Stephanie von und zu Eltz, of Vienna.[23] His new business venture with Korski, incorporated at Companies House on 5 July, just days[24] after the EU referendum, offers companies post-Brexit consultancy advice. The firm specifically helps start-up technology companies that want to work closely with the government. 'There's an opportunity now [with the Brexit vote] rarely afforded to a fully functioning Western democracy to rethink the entire underwiring of the state,' Korski told the media.

Portland Communications, run by serial networker and former Tony Blair adviser Tim Allan, immediately saw how important it was to offer big salaries to former government advisers who had all the right Brexit connections. Portland recruited Victoria Dean (International School of Geneva where fees are £26,000 a year), a former British diplomat with experience in Brussels, to head up its Brexit team. They also brought in Henry Cook, a former aide to Michael Gove; James Starkie, the network manager of Vote Leave; and Amy Richards, a former press office manager for the Remain camp.

Cameron signed an £800,000 deal for his memoirs, joined the board of the global electronic payments firm First Data, was appointed to head Britain's billion-dollar investment initiative with China and embarked on a corporate speaking tour reported to be worth £200,000 a speech. He has also quietly rejoined his father's London club, White's, taken up shooting grouse and begun the search for appropriate suitable private schools for his children who, as prime minister, he was forced to have educated by the state.

There is a certain type of politician who has built a career out of bashing Europe. Figures like Nigel Farage have made it their lifelong mission to extricate Britain from the EU, while more opportunistic star-seekers, like Boris Johnson, and even David Cameron once upon a time, demonised Brussels in order to advance their own standing within the Tory Party. In the absence of an empire and with the public opposed to almost any military action, Europe is the only (safe) jingoistic game in town. By rallying the faithful and calling on the British Bulldog spirit, politicians can sound Churchillian without actually having to do anything.

The British public have been more or less oblivious or unbothered about whether they are ruled by an elite in Westminster or one in Brussels. Occasional arguments about farming subsidies or fishing quotas have exercised vested interests in the UK but there has never been a mass movement to get out of Europe. Those who led and funded the charge against Europe came from a narrow social class. They claimed to be anti-establishment representatives of the people yet they were anything but. They were sent to a small number of privileged schools, met at university and mixed in the same circles. Their shared educations instilled in them a drive which put personal ambition before national interest and they were prepared to say absolutely anything that might achieve the intended result.

The public school-educated politicians and advisers who stood against the Brexiteers contributed to their own devastating defeat by taking the British people for granted. Some compared Cameron to Lord North who lost the American colonies while others saw it as a modern-day Suez.[25] Cameron and his coalition of 'no-changers' had failed to grasp that Brexit was not just about Europe, it was also a protest vote against the out-of-touch Westminster coterie whose privileged lives are now so different from those led by the electorate.

The whole story of Brexit can be told without reference to anyone educated in the state sector, from the eurosceptics building their movement, to the prime minister who promised a referendum to stave off rebels in his own party, to both the Remain and the two Leave campaigns. Even the phrase 'take back control' was formulated by a canny privately educated strategist. It begs the question: who was wresting control, and from whom?

12

FOR THE FEW, NOT THE MANY

The rise of Jeremy Corbyn and his brand of left-wing politics has confounded political wisdom, defeated moderate opposition within the Labour Party and dealt a serious blow to the right-wing press. Corbyn's election as Labour leader and the party's surprising showing in the 2017 general election have been characterised as a victory for grassroots democracy and the party's working-class membership – a people's revolution. But a closer look at the key figures behind Corbyn's campaign reveals a by-now familiar list of public school-educated fixers and donors who have profited from the division and disintegration of the Labour Party.

The disconnect between a working-class movement and the privileged backgrounds and education of those who led it begins with the Labour Party leader himself. Corbyn's middle-class back-ground and his parents' willingness to throw money at his private education present a discordant picture of a man who claims to represent ordinary voters.

In fact, there is nothing ordinary about Jeremy Corbyn's upbringing. His parents David and Naomi met in the 1930s at a meeting in London for supporters of Spain's Republicans in the fight against Franco's fascists. David, born in 1915, was a solicitor's son who grew up in west London and became a skilled electrical engineer working for the war effort. Naomi was that rare thing in those days, a female scientist, who later became a maths teacher.

Her father was a successful surveyor who disapproved of her romance with the far less wealthy David. Jeremy was the youngest of four boys, born in Chippenham in Wiltshire four years after the end of the war. The Corbyns set up home in the pretty, ancient village of Kington St Michael in a large detached house.[1] In the 1950s his father was headhunted for a better-paid job in engineering and the family could afford to move to a much grander residence. They chose a seven-bedroom manor house which had once belonged to the Duke of Sutherland. The Corbyns moved into Yew Tree Manor just outside Newport in Shropshire and sent their four boys to expensive fee-paying schools.

Jeremy went to Castle House Preparatory School where annual fees today are nearly £10,000. Despite having a very good local primary school nearby, the Corbyns were determined to ensure their sons got the best possible advantages in life. Fees for four children would have been out of the reach of most families in the community but the Corbyns would have been able to benefit from a sibling discount.[2] Castle House is a Grade II-listed building located down the high street from the local primary. When the Corbyn brothers were there pupils wore distinctive smart, blue uniforms so that they stood out walking through the town. A pupil who attended the local state primary school remembers: 'We were too young to be aware of a class thing, but everyone knew Castle House was a cut above the rest.'[3]

The school was a feeder for the prestigious Adams' Grammar School in Newport where all the Corbyn boys were later sent. Adams' had been established in 1656 with a very generous foundation which provided for the education of local boys, though by the time the Corbyn boys arrived it was a hybrid grammar school, heavily reliant on fee-paying boarders, many of them from overseas.[4] In all but name it was a public school. A former pupil who attended Adams' with the Corbyns recalls that 'it was a fairly brutal place. Prefects were entitled to flog children and I remember they would make you bend your head down under the table, so that when they hit you, you would hurt yourself by involuntarily banging your head on the underside of the table.' Another former pupil says boys were flogged for as minor an offence as 'having your cap at a rakish angle'.[5]

Jeremy Corbyn, the youngest of the four brothers, joined Clive House, named after Clive of India, and quickly established himself as a rebel, campaigning against nuclear weapons and the Vietnam War. The school maintained a lively debating society, where Corbyn cut his teeth as a public speaker. However, he would have nothing to do with another public school institution, the Combined Cadet Force, which was a staging post for Adams' pupils who went on to Sandhurst or signed up to the Royal Navy and Royal Air Force colleges. Corbyn later said: 'I was again in a minority of one and refused to join this thing, so I was put on gardening duties.'

Instead he devoted his energies to school politics. In the wake of the Profumo scandal the country went to the polls in 1964, electing the first Labour government for thirteen years. Adams' held a mock election in which Corbyn stood as the Labour candidate. His brother Piers, now a well-known weather forecaster, represented the Communist Party.[6] Jeremy Corbyn's friend and campaign manager Bob Mallett remembered: 'At a middle-class boarding grammar school in leafy Shropshire, there weren't many socialists. We were trounced.'[7] Corbyn left with just two E grade A-levels and a warning from his headmaster that 'you'll never make anything of yourself'.[8]

Yet his academic failings did nothing to dim his self-confidence and belief that his voice should be heard. At twenty-one he was appointed a union official for the National Union of Tailors and Garment Workers. In 1974 he left the parochial confines of Shropshire for London where at the age of twenty-four he was elected to Haringey Council in South Hornsey ward, becoming one of the country's youngest local politicians.

Apart from a profile of his 'posh provenance' in *Tatler*, very little has been made of how Jeremy Corbyn's education shaped his political career, gathering around him the tactical nous and expertise of a number of public school-educated party strategists. Corbyn's great ally John McDonnell, the shadow chancellor, had enjoyed similar exposure to the public school ethos when he too attended a fee-paying boarding school. McDonnell spent two years at the £33,000-a-year (2017 figures) St Joseph's College in Ipswich in the late 1960s.[9] He even appears in the school's prospectus as a star alumnus.[10] In the run-up to the 2017 general election, McDonnell made no public reference to this part of his schooling, so when *The Sun* published the revelation shortly before polling day he tried to kill the story. His official CV only says he attended Great Yarmouth Grammar School, leaving at the age of seventeen, and boasts of him working in a series of unskilled jobs while he studied for his A-levels at night school at Burnley Technical College. In reality, he left his grammar school to train as a priest and spent two years at the exclusive St Joseph's College, where his fees were paid by a church grant.

After the *Sun* story appeared McDonnell tweeted: 'No way could they [his parents] afford fees. They were proud I tried for the Catholic priesthood and equally supportive when I returned to local school. I returned to Grammar after I decided I did not have a vocation to Catholic priesthood. My Dad was bus driver and Mum a shop worker.'[11] Yet for two years McDonnell led a very privileged life indeed.

McDonnell's friendship with Corbyn goes back decades and was built around their support for Labour's most famous left-winger, Tony Benn. It was McDonnell who, having unsuccessfully sought to fight the left's corner in the leadership contests in 2007 and 2010, persuaded Corbyn to stand in the first Labour leadership ballot in 2015. He told *The Guardian*: 'I said I wouldn't do it... I have done it twice already and had a heart attack a couple of years ago. We turned to Jeremy and said: "Come on, it is your turn, you have a go." "All right, all right," he said, "I'll do it. I'll have a go." A sacrificial lamb. But once we got on the ballot paper, well, it is just incredible. It really is incredible.'[12]

Corbyn's biggest hurdle was securing enough votes from the Parliamentary Labour Party to get his name on the national ballot in the first place. Once he'd scraped through with the minimum number of MPs (he got the thirty-fifth minutes before the 2015 ballot closed) Corbyn could appeal directly to the party membership. It was another privately educated Bennite to whom Corbyn and McDonnell now turned.

The socialist activist group credited with Corbyn's eventual victory is Momentum, a well-organised and hierarchical political machine which has kept Corbyn in the leadership and rallied support to his cause. Since 2015 Momentum has grown nationally to over 150 local groups, 23,000 members and 200,000 supporters who all share a radical Labour agenda that includes the redistribution of wealth and power.[13] Its founder is Jon Lansman. A charismatic and influential campaigner barely known outside the Labour Party, Lansman is a hard-line left-winger who was a key figure in Tony Benn's bid to be deputy Labour leader in 1981, when Benn was narrowly defeated by Denis Healey. Lansman's background is far removed from the hundreds of thousands of working-class Labour supporters who Momentum claims to represent. He was educated at Highgate School. Originally a free charity school for local boys, it became during the nineteenth century one of England's top public schools and is today a member of the prestigious Eton Group.

It's not clear how much money Lansman has ploughed into Momentum, but the Lansman family (Lansman's brother and son) look after a network of more than twenty property and investment companies, one with reported links to Luxembourg, and hold assets well into the millions. Given the Labour Party's vociferous opposition to tax havens and the companies that use them to avoid tax, the Lansmans' links to Luxembourg could leave the Momentum founder open to charges of hypocrisy.

Many privately educated members of the Labour Party, including Tony Benn, have been attracted to far-left politics. No one doubts Benn's beliefs were honestly held. Benn and his wife famously took their children out of private education so they could be schooled at the local comprehensive. Lansman has also made sure his three children are state educated in Hertfordshire. For him, life has been one grand project to deliver a truly socialist government of Britain, forever placing him in the annals of Labour history. He has toyed with standing for office himself and still harbours political ambitions of his own – he worked behind the scenes for Benn and Michael Meacher and in 2015 was forced to deny claims he was planning to stand at a by-election after Meacher's death. But two years later Lansman stood for membership of the Labour Party's ruling body, the National Executive Committee, and in January 2018 he was successfully elected.

Since Tony Benn's campaign, lessons have been learned which have been put to good use in the service of the new hard-left pretender, Jeremy Corbyn. Crucial to the Benn campaign was a group Lansman helped run, the Rank and File Mobilising Committee. Its tactics were unprecedented: sending senior left-wing politicians to rallies across the country, launching verbal attacks on 'right-wing' Labour MPs, criticising the Parliamentary Labour Party on issues like nuclear weapons, and rapidly forming a new core of united hard-left supporters. Lansman was even accused by Denis Healey of orchestrating barracking to shout down dissent at Labour meetings, though he was later exonerated with an apology from Healey.

Momentum has been accused of using similar tactics in cementing Corbyn's power base. It owes its effectiveness and reach among the grassroots to another, much younger public school activist. In 2015 James Schneider, a twenty-eight-year-old Wykehamist, was one of only four full-time Momentum staffers. Yet he played a key role in mobilising an army of 17,000 volunteers during the first Corbyn leadership campaign. After Corbyn was safely ensconced, Schneider helped turn Momentum into a mass social movement engaged with community organisations. Schneider's telegenic sangfroid and public-speaking skills have been attributed to his expensive education. His promotion to Corbyn's team was recognised in the school magazine with an official notice congratulating him on his appointment. The item appeared above a report on a clay pigeon shooting event: 'JGH Schneider (F, 00–05), the National Organiser of Momentum, is joining the Labour Party Leader Jeremy Corbyn's office in a strategic communications role, where he will be working alongside SPC Milne (Coll, 71–74).'

SPC Milne is better known as Seamus Milne, director of strategy and communications, and perhaps Corbyn's most important appointment. The youngest son of former BBC director general Alasdair Milne, his journey in radical politics began at school in 1974 when he stood in a mock election as a Maoist Party candidate. These early links to communism were exposed by another Wykehamist, Tory minister John Whittingdale, who was in the same year as Milne. In March 2016, when Whittingdale was culture minister under David Cameron, he tried to embarrass Milne, now his political opponent, by digging up Milne's election posters and manifesto.[14] This attempt to damage him by making out that he secretly held unreconstructed socialist views was undermined by Milne's own public and undisguised displays of affection for Marxism. In May 2015 Milne told a political rally in Glasgow that 'resistance and the unity of the working class is what will progress our movement'.

Shortly before the 2017 general election, Corbyn called on the services of another Marxist public schoolboy, one of the most extreme left-wing figures in the country. Andrew Murray comes from a wealthy banking family and went to Worth School, a Benedictine independent boarding school in West Sussex. It was only in 2016 that he officially severed his ties with the Communist Party of Great Britain and in the past he has voiced support for both Joseph Stalin and North Korea. As chair of Stop the War, Murray also played a crucial role in the largest political demonstration in British history, the 2003 rally against the war in Iraq. He stood down in June 2011 to be succeeded by Corbyn.

After Labour's surprising showing in the 2017 general election, when Corbyn clawed back Theresa May's parliamentary majority, Murray, who was seconded from the Unite trade union, was described as the 'hard-left's Steve Bannon'. Both men are regarded as keepers of the flame of their respective ideologies who are able to rally great numbers to the cause. Murray's daughter Laura was also an important figure in Momentum, building close links with Schneider and Corbyn's sons Ben and Sebastian. Following a stint as a Labour political adviser covering the communities brief, she was made Corbyn's 'stakeholder manager' in June 2017, giving her a key role connecting with groups linked to the Labour leadership.[15] Lansman's eldest son Max, a barrister, was also reported to have a key role with Momentum.[16] Corbyn's second son, Sebastian, worked on his father's leadership campaign before becoming John McDonnell's chief of staff.

Corbyn, McDonnell, Murray, Milne and Lansman have been close friends for many years and are part of a network of hard-left, partly public school-educated activists. Together, they and their children have brought the hard-left to the brink of power. They have used Momentum to wrestle the levers of control of the party and have even tried to depose hostile MPs within the Parliamentary Labour Party, as in July 2017, when a local Momentum group in South Tyneside published a list of New Labour MPs, including Chuka Ummuna and Chris Leslie, saying they should 'join the Liberals'. It has also been alleged that abusive online campaigns targeting Blairites have been linked to Momentum. And moderate Labour councillors in Haringey in north London complained that they have been victims of a 'purge' orchestrated by Momentum. By the close of 2017 Momentum-backed candidates, including Jon Lansman, were close to holding a majority on the National Executive Committee.

It has come at a political cost. In 2016 Momentum was accused by sections of the traditional left of carrying out a 'coup'.[17] After a meeting in October 2016, at which Lansman argued for changes to how policy was decided, he was accused of being anti-democratic. The Labour Party Marxists, a far-left group which opposed Lansman's plans, said in a statement on its website: 'This is worse than anything Tony Blair managed to foist on the Labour Party. How could we ever again gripe about the bowdlerising of Labour Party conference democracy if we acquiesce to the travesty that Jon Lansman and his cohorts at [sic] attempting to finagle us into?… This is an anti-democratic coup.'[18]

In response, a Momentum spokeswoman said: 'Momentum is made up of activists from several political and organisational traditions. [This] pluralist approach ultimately strengthens Momentum.'[19] But Labour now looks like a divided party with the Blairite and more moderate MPs being led by a much smaller group of hard-left socialists. The 2017 election result was a disaster for the dominant moderate Parliamentary Labour Party, who having failed to oust Corbyn themselves were relying on the British people to do the job for them. Corbyn's surprise success in 2017 and his strengthening hold over the executive of the party have temporarily quietened some of his critics. But there is a moderate wing within the parliamentary party who are exploring ideas for a new political grouping or even breaking from the party altogether.

★

For more than one hundred years Labour's troubled relation-ship with the public schools has presented it with political and individual challenges. It is, after all, a movement that was brought into being by the Fabian Society, a socialist group dominated by the Victorian elite. While many of Labour's politicians have roots among the working classes, from Keir Hardie and Ramsay Macdonald to Harold Wilson and Neil Kinnock, plenty do not. After the war a clutch of public school-educated men, including Clement Attlee, Hugh Gaitskell and Hugh Dalton, held high office in Labour governments. Aristocrats like Anthony Wedgwood Benn (who renounced his title, 2nd Viscount Stansgate, to become an MP known simpy as Tony Benn) and Frank Pakenham, the 7th Earl of Longford, also became pioneering social reformers in the Labour Party. Even Michael Foot, the party leader to whom Corbyn is routinely compared, was the privately educated son of a solicitor. He attended Plymouth College Preparatory School, Forres School in Swanage and Leighton Park School in Reading.

A privileged education did not count against Tony Blair either. In recent years it has not been the educational background of a Labour Party politician that has been important, rather where they decide to send their children to school. While previous Labour prime ministers Harold Wilson and Jim Callaghan both had their offspring educated at prestigious public schools, Blair came to power at a more sensitive time where the electorate expected pol-iticians to practise what they preached.

As it was, the Blairs neatly dodged the flak by sending their children to the London Oratory, a not so 'bog-standard' comprehensive, as Alastair Campbell had described the only Labour-sanctioned option for the party's children. A strictly Catholic day school in west London, the London Oratory is over-subscribed seven times over and takes 160 pupils each year from across London. Its academic results make it one of the top schools in the capital. Nick Clegg, an atheist married to a devout Catholic whose own party's policy was to end faith-based admissions, faced accusations of hypocrisy when he sent his own child there. Harriet Harman, who was educated at St Paul's Girls' School in west London, went even further, sending one of her sons to the Oratory and the other to a Kent grammar school.[20] She only held on to her place in government because Blair publicly defended her decision.

In 2003 Diane Abbott committed a more grievous offence against Labour education policy by placing her son at the then £10,000-a-year City of London School. Although she was not a minister she was bitterly attacked by her own party. Her position was made worse by the fact that she had criticised Blair for sending his son to the Oratory, saying Labour voters believed in equality. Not only that, but on Harman's decision to send her son to a grammar school she had complained: 'She made the Labour Party look as if we do one thing and say another.'

Abbott tried to defend her decision by telling the BBC: 'Private schools prop up the class system in society. It is inconsistent, to put it mildly, for someone who believes in a fairer and more egalitarian society to send their child to a fee-paying school.' But, she added: 'I had to choose between my reputation as a politician and my son,'[21] giving perhaps one of the clearest reasons for the persistence of the current system.[22] In 2016, Corbyn's shadow attorney-general, Shami Chakrabarti,[23] faced the same dilemma. After her appointment to the House of Lords it emerged that Chakrabarti, a human rights campaigner, was sending her son to Dulwich College. The story broke shortly after Labour had condemned Conservative plans to bring back grammar schools. Appearing on ITV's *Peston on Sunday*, Chakrabarti condemned the grammar school plan. Then when Robert Peston questioned her about her decision to privately educate her son she responded by saying: 'I live in a nice big house and eat nice food and my neighbours are homeless and go to food banks.' The implication was clear: if we start accusing people of being hypocrites for sending their kids to public school then we must critically examine all aspects of our lives.

Given Chakrabarti's long history advocating on behalf of the underprivileged this explanation didn't really do her justice. In January 2016, just before her plans for her son's education became public, she accepted a public-speaking invitation from another leading public school, Bedales in Hampshire, where she gave a lecture on human rights and afterwards granted a select group of pupils an exclusive Q and A. It was during this session, recorded by the school's cameras, that one of the pupils asked her for her opinion on the justice of private education. In the cosy and private environment of a public school, Chakrabarti provided a much more open insight into how she and perhaps many other senior Labour supporters view fee-paying education.

'I would like everybody in the country to enjoy the advantages that you have,' she said. 'And the advantages that I had at a comprehensive school in the 1980s. I am really worried by the fact that when I went through my comprehensive school to the LSE [I had] tuition fees and full maintenance grants, and that's pretty much why I am sitting here talking to you now. Because everything that followed couldn't have happened but for that degree and that opportunity. I'm worried that so many people of your generation don't have that option and I'm a bit embarrassed that it's my generation of middle-aged people who have enjoyed that privilege and then denied it to so many in your generation… My view about education is not that I want to deny it to anybody in particular but I want it to be extended. It's a bit like the debate about human rights, civil rights and political rights. Everybody believes in a great education system for their own children but they're just not so convinced that other people's children are either up to it or deserve it, and that's how people believe in human rights… The trick is wanting to extend that offering, that protection, to other people's children as well.'[24]

Chakrabarti appears to be arguing in favour of extending private education, so that more people can afford it, but a school like Bedales charges boarders over £35,000 a year. Universal private education is hardly the direction of travel in the Labour Party, which in the run-up to the 2017 general election was promising to impose VAT on private school fees. Yet Chakrabarti's decision to use private education has hardly damaged her.[25]

The Labour leadership is ideologically opposed to a fee-paying, privileged education, but can do nothing to stop its own membership sending their children to public schools. The picture is complicated by those Labour MPs and advisers who owe their own positions to a privileged grammar school system. Labour is also opposed to extending grammar schools but it can't deny that the education experiment of the 1960s and '70s boosted social mobility, helping a small number of bright kids from disadvantaged backgrounds into good jobs and positions of influence.

A key Labour strategist to benefit from the grammar school system is Steve Howell who in 2017 was called upon to bolster the Corbyn team. After working closely in the background with the leadership, Howell was made deputy director of strategy and communications in the run-up to the election. Howell, a PR guru and lobbyist who heads his own agency, Freshwater, went to Hendon County Grammar School with Peter Mandelson in the late 1970s. Hendon had been a fee-paying school, but when Howell and Mandelson were there it was a fully maintained state school.

Its pretensions and ethos were very similar to Adams' Grammar School and it was run along public school lines. The 11-plus selection meant schools like Hendon and Adams' were hugely popular with the sharp-elbowed middle classes who regarded the grammars as a cheaper route into the professions and better-paid jobs than the expensive and out-of-reach public schools.

In a memoir of his schooldays, Howell describes how the teachers marched around 'in gowns and run the school like we were all destined for Oxbridge and great things beyond'. It's a description that could have been borrowed from the pages of Alan Bennett's play, *The History Boys*, which so humorously satirises the pretensions of the 1960s grammar schools. Howell recalled:

The architect of this quasi-public school atmosphere was E.W. Maynard Potts MA MSc, as he liked to sign himself. Potts had been running the school in an elitist way for three decades and his resistance to change matched the stubbornness of the council. The local primary schools were feeder factories for Potts' delusions of grandeur. I had attended the nearby St Mary's Church of England School where at the end of the second year (Year 4 in new money), the children were divided between two classes deemed to have the potential to pass the 11-plus and a third for the 'no hopers' who were put in the temporary classroom in the playground. By what cruel thinking nine-years-olds could be dumped on the rubbish heap like that is beyond me, but this was an era when there were still children's books about 'Little Black Sambo' and our school uniforms were supplied by an outfitter who was renowned for squeezing the backside of every boy who ventured into his changing room.

While he was at the school Howell strongly objected to the way it was run, but he also realised the greater damage selective grammar schools were doing to the community:

The St Mary's 11-plus treadmill duly discharged most of the chosen ones into Hendon County and other nearby grammar schools, and the social divide between peers from the same area became entrenched. I cannot recall having any friends from secondary modern schools, not – I like to think – because I was a snob but simply because that was the way it was. Yet Hendon County was by no means at the top of the social tree: above us were the private 'direct grant' schools such as Haberdashers and UCS [University College School] and beyond them were public schools we viewed mainly through the lens of Jennings and Billy Bunter novels.[26]

The long-term problem for Labour is that while the Tories have seen a reduction in the number of privately educated MPs in recent years the influence of public school elites on the Labour Party has hardly changed, and by some measurements it has even increased. At the end of the 1950s, 19 per cent of Labour MPs had private school backgrounds. In 1992 it had fallen to 14 per cent, but in the 2017 election it was back up to 17 per cent. On the other side, although half of today's Tory MPs are from public school, it was nearly three-quarters at the close of the 1950s.[27]

Labour MP Justin Madders, chair of the all-party parliamentary committee on social mobility, thinks the reason Labour has been unable to be more radical in its reform of private education is that it has been distracted by fighting on other education battlefronts, namely free schools and the Tory proposal for more grammars. Fiona Millar is an education campaigner who was a special adviser to Cherie Blair in the early years of the New Labour government. She says that if Labour is to tackle education reform properly it must be much more robust in tackling the private school links of its leadership and front bench: 'Personally, I would say that anyone who had paid to educate their children should not be allowed to influence Labour policy on education. Their own personal choices

may colour their judgement and will inevitably lead to allegations of hypocrisy.' According to Millar, private school conflicts
also exposed the Labour Party to 'allegations of hypocrisy' being
splashed across the front page of the *Daily Mail*. 'This, I'm afraid,
has been the history of education reform on the left where people
are fearful of allegations of hypocrisy and therefore do nothing.
From what I can see the people around Corbyn are no different
and Labour is still too afraid to have that kind of battle.'[28]

Had the Wilson or Attlee governments delivered on their
promises to properly tackle private education, Corbyn may not
be where he is today. Denied the crucial services of public school
advisers like Milne, Schneider, Lansman and Murray, Corbyn may
not have been able to capitalise on his shock leadership victory.
But Corbyn and, to a lesser extent, McDonnell, directly benefited
from a private education system that gave them the self-confidence and ambition to drive forward the radical Labour project.

It would be easy to see fee-paying education as a historic issue
that has little bearing on the future of the Labour Party. But the
disproportionately high number of privately educated Labour
politicians continues to seriously undermine Corbyn's claim that
his MPs are for the 'many not the few'. This was brought into
sharp relief in the 2017 contest for the leadership of the Scottish
Labour Party when the membership was offered the choice of
two privately educated candidates: Anas Sawar, who sent his son
to the same public school he had attended (Hutchesons' Grammar
School in Glasgow), or the eventual winner, Richard Leonard,
educated at a public school (Pocklington School) in Yorkshire.

It is hard to blame a politician for the school their parents chose
for them, but when the same politician compounds that unfair
advantage by sending their own children to a private school it
gives the impression that Labour values don't apply to the people
who espouse them.

13

THE CLASS LADDER

The prosperity and gaiety of Eton town is almost entirely dependent on its ancient juxtaposition to the local school, though very few boys from the immediate community have been schooled at Eton College in the last one hundred years. During term time the town is decorated with boys in their three-piece tailsuits and striped trousers parading up and down the medieval high street. Other public schools have banned boys and girls from wearing uniforms which advertise their privilege and attract the grievances of the real locals who resent being reminded of their place in society. But at Eton, which has had its fair share of unsavoury incidents (including a savage attack on the son of former Conservative Party leader Michael Howard), there is no such rule. The school feels it has nothing to apologise for and, after all, its students are the cash cows from which almost every commercial premises on the high street derives a living.

Each year in mid-July, well before induction day at the start of the Michaelmas term, the good burghers of Eton are treated to a school pageant when the house Dames escort the parents and pupils to the high-street banks so that each boy can be issued with a personal debit card linked to the school. Using these cards the boys are free to pour hundreds of thousands of pounds into the town's coffers. This new arrangement was introduced after local traders complained that it was taking too long for them to be paid under the old chit system, where each purchase was written down in a boy's personal account.

Being schooled at Eton is an expensive business. Induction day continues with visits to the tailors, sports outfitters, stationers and even furniture shops, where parents buy desks, chairs and ornamental rugs for their son's bedroom. Non-refundable registration fees and start-up costs for a child attending Eton can easily run to £2,000, supplemented throughout the year by up to a further £1,500 of sundry charges and purchases. Then there are the extra tuition fees and overseas trips which can set parents back £6,000.[1] Pupils are also encouraged to carry loose change so they can tip the school's butlers, chambermaids and tradesmen – the etiquette of which is carefully explained before the start of school.

Then there are the hidden costs. The *Good Schools Guide* warns parents to watch out for the charges which can get added onto the public school bill, including 'donations' for school building funds or medical and personal property 'insurance' fees. 'Scrutinise your bill carefully. We have noticed an increasing tendency to pop in items with a footnote saying that "unless you notify the school and deduct the amounts mentioned, it will automatically be charged to you". For example, the Old Boys/Girls Society or your "contribution" to charities. Do not be shy about deducting these sums from your cheque.'[2]

So even before parents have stumped up the annual fees, which at Eton in 2017 were running at £12,910 per 'half' (a confusing name for a term), there is an additional overall £10,000 to be found. This brings the first year's fees to around £47,000. Parents sending a child to Eton in 2017 would have needed to have £70,000-plus in spare change before tax.[3] Anyone not confident of comfortably clearing this level of disposable income on top of their ordinary earnings would be well advised to read the Eton smallprint carefully: 'A boy whose account has not been paid in full by the start of the half (or in the case of payment by instalments, where any instalment has not been paid by the due date) may be excluded from the school until it is paid.' There are additional penalty charges for pupils who are removed from the school without proper notice. In 2017–18 they stood at £9,883 a term.

Gone are the days when the school bursar was prepared to waive a term's fees because a family was minor aristocracy and had fallen on hard times. Eton College is not that sort of charity. The school is now run as a corporate enterprise with charitable status. In 2016 it collected £47 million in fees, up from £45 million from the year before. In addition, it charges pupils £4 million in extras on such things as music lessons and school trips. But it spends more than this (£58.7 million) on maintaining the school and the employment of 981 staff, of whom only 188 are teachers. The school also runs three commercial enterprises focusing on hospitality, commercial education and property development which together generate a healthy profit. Appropriately for a high-flying business, the headmaster receives an annual salary of between £190,000 and £199,000, commensurate with the base pay of a FTSE 100 chief executive.

Yet these headline figures belie the true scale of Eton's vast wealth. The school retains endowment funds, securities and investment property portfolios worth nearly £500 million. By way of comparison, the Queen's Duchy of Lancaster Estate, from which the monarch draws an income, was valued at £472 million in 2015.

The Eton estates include 398 buildings and historic colleges, many of them listed and dotted about Eton town. Over the years, the school has also accumulated a treasure trove of 175,000 works of art and antiques, including a collection of Egyptian antiquities bequeathed by former pupil Major William Joseph Myers, a veteran of the Anglo-Zulu War of 1879.[4] Many of the artefacts are priceless. None have been sold.

Up until 2002 a place at Eton could be secured by simply putting a boy's name down for one of the school houses as soon as he was born.[5] The names of David Cameron and Boris Johnson were added to the Eton list in this way. Today competition for places means admissions are not so straightforward. All entrants must pass a bespoke psychometric test and then dazzle during an interview with a master. This gives the school, which says it is looking for evidence of creative and original thinking, plenty of flexibility for deciding who gets in and who does not.

Parents have complained that scoring highly in the test does not guarantee an offer, but Tony Little, headmaster of Eton between 2002 and 2015, insists the school goes to extraordinary lengths to make objective decisions. He cites one case where the school told the family of a child, who would have been the seventh generation to go to Eton, that they would have to look for an alternative school: 'We thought the kid would struggle in the modern Eton,' said Little. 'There was psychometric testing, a school report and an interview and each had equal weight. There were five people separately who would review the information about every child. And I was one. We had to do it completely blind. For example, the test score might be mitigated because the interview was so good. We spent a huge amount of time trying to get it right for the children.'[6]

Eton College's principal activity remains the education of the British and, increasingly, world elites. It has been doing it for centuries. Of the 260 boys who left Eton in 2015, sixty-eight (almost one in four) attained places at either Oxford or Cambridge universities. The remainder went to other leading British or international universities.[7] But this is, of course, only part of the Eton success story. The list of world leaders, politicians, billionaires and pupils from the crème de la crème of the English aristocracy has given the school top status among the great public schools. A place at Eton buys a seat at the top table of British society – an entry to the world's wealthiest and most influential families.

★

The pecking order of the English public school is inscrutable to those who have never been educated at one, but in terms of wealth and prestige Eton, Harrow, Winchester, St Paul's, Westminster and Charterhouse form a magic circle of top schools. Another twenty or so schools are part of an outer circle, although each would claim they have certain qualities that set them apart from the rest. The girls' schools have a similar social hierarchy. Ostensibly, parents say that the academic quality of a private school is what really counts, but snob value and popular perception make the name and reputation of an institution the most important criterion when choosing a public school. At £40,000, parents don't just believe they are buying a better education. The added value is a cachet and a networking opportunity that can propel an entire family into another social stratum.

The Middletons used the public school system to fast-track their daughters to the top of English society and in Kate's case marriage to the heir to the throne. State-educated Carole came from humble beginnings in Southall, west London, but by the time Kate was four the family could afford to send her to St Andrew's School in Pangbourne from 1986 until 1995. Later she boarded at Marlborough College. At St Andrews University in Scotland, much favoured by public schools, she met Prince William where their relationship blossomed.

Wayne and Coleen Rooney are trying to do the same with their two boys who have been enrolled at a Cheshire prep school and Manchester Grammar School.

The Rooneys, of course, have the cash to get their sons into the most exclusive public schools. But for the majority of modestly rich families with high ambitions, such epic social climbing is out of reach. Instead they settle for the contacts and society invitations granted by a basic (or minor) public school education that they hope will make a financial success of their children's lives.

Public schools invest heavily in very effective old-boy and old-girl networks that can put school and university leavers directly in touch with key people who have the power to hire or help new recruits. The Social Market Foundation's 2014 report, *Open Access*, put it like this: 'Independent schools in the UK are bastions of privilege, where a small proportion of predominantly affluent families pay high fees for an education that is associated with higher attainment, good social networks, and lucrative long-term employment outcomes for those attending. Extensive evidence indicates that the education and employment outcomes of those attending independent schools are, on average, much higher than those attending comprehensive state schools.'[8] In his own report on private education, Sir Anthony Seldon, former headmaster of Wellington College, noted: 'All schools can develop and maintain widely drawn address books and contacts of the school's alumni to help leavers to acquire internships and jobs.'[9]

In 1897 the Old Etonian Association (OEA) was founded to keep Old Etonians in touch with one another. Today its contacts and networks are so highly valuable, former pupils have to pay to access parts of the OE database, which boasts 16,000 members across the world. The OEA reminds its members: 'As an OE you may be interested in the School's Admission process for your son, grandson or nephew; if so, please see Entry to Eton. We are always delighted to welcome new generations of Etonians from OE families, subject to our Entry Procedure. Approximately 40 per cent of our boys have OE connections.'[10]

Most public schools have set up similar specialist networking groups. Dulwich College's Old Alleynian Global Network boasts 10,000 members. Marlborough College has an OM Banking & Finance Group which 'aims to create a network of OMs in finance who share the ethos, attitude and outlook on life gained at Marlborough', 'host interesting and unusual events that capture the interests of people in the finance sector' and 'provide a well thought out programme of mentoring for pupils and young OMs'. For those looking for a more secretive networking society with a proven track record in social advantage, the schools also run their own Masonic lodges: the Public School Lodges' Council represents thirty-five public schools, including Eton, Harrow, Winchester and Charterhouse.[11] According to the national Freemasons accounts for 2017, part of the £33 million it distributed in charitable donations went to Masons to pay for their children's education.[12]

The workings of these networks are oiled by the world's most famous and influential figures from the City, government and show business who regularly return to their alma mater to inject impetus, inspiration and a helping hand.[13] Eton's recent speakers include OE Justin Welby, otherwise known as the Archbishop of Canterbury. Harrow's recent list of visitors include former head boy Lord Butler, who chaired the inquiry into the Iraq intelligence failure, Old Harrovian and hedge-fund manager Crispin Odey, and OE Jacob Rees-Mogg MP who seems happy to cross schools.[14]

★

Small class sizes, selective admissions policies and specialist tutoring mean many public schools achieve excellent exam results. Often the only difference between one good school and another is the add-ons – the sporting facilities, the theatre, the food, the laundry and taxi service and the luxury accommodation.

Today, education is only part of their product. Schools also have to sell themselves as hotels, leisure centres and travel agents. Instead of dormitories pupils have large bedrooms with en-suite bathrooms and views of the grounds. Half of the Independent Schools Council schools now showcase concert halls and swimming pools while almost a third boast a dance studio; 6 per cent can offer pupils school rowing facilities.[15] Some even market their 'stabling' facilities. All this requires a small army of chefs, matrons, butlers and chambermaids. Most schools even have a complaints book so that 'guests' are made to feel that their parents' cash is properly respected.

Tony Little says the 'competition for fees' means schools are having to invest in more and better facilities to win business. 'The additional costs didn't come with getting more teachers, it came from the back office costs – huge numbers of non-teaching staff. When I was at Chigwell School in the 1990s, I had a full-time secretary, a lady to come in to do admissions, and that was it. At Eton we had an entire HR department. We had to have a full-time counsellor and a part-time adolescent psychiatrist. It all comes at a cost.'[16]

The libertarian writer and author Ross Clark describes the accompanying rise in fees as an arms race, but he warns: 'Private schools have got away – so far – with charging what they do partly as a result of fortunes falling into the hands of some middle-class families courtesy of inheritance and the house-price boom.'[17] Tony Little is also concerned that this level of luxury and commensurate fees is unsustainable: 'The monumental rise in independent school fees in the UK has far outstripped inflation. They charge because they've been able to.'

Some fear that private schools might be making the same mistakes as the big banks before the financial crash in 2008. 'We've been inflating a fees bubble. In the end, all bubbles burst,' says Andrew Halls, headmaster of King's College School, south-west London. 'It would be mad to build a business model on the assumption that things are likely to stay the same or get better forever. History shows that never happens.'[18] Even if the bubble does not burst soon and fees carry on rising, there are risks that Britain's richest independent schools will simply price themselves out of their national market and become merely finishing schools for the children of oligarchs.

A school's reliance on fees puts considerable strain on the relationship between the governors, head and the parents. A customer who pays for a service that they don't believe is value for money is in a much stronger position than parents of a child at a state school. So when expectations are not met or things go wrong parents are quick to complain. For the public schools, complaints about anything from the quality of the food to the standard of teaching must be taken seriously. Taxpayers might pay state teachers' wages, but only indirectly, and so parent pressure tends to have less impact in state schools.

Should relations between the private school and the parent break down there are often serious reputational or even financial consequences. When Gary Lineker's eighteen-year-old son George failed to obtain the three B grades he needed for a place at Manchester University in 2010, the former England football team captain appeared to lay the blame at the door of his son's prestigious public school, Charterhouse, which at the time was charging annual fees of £25,000.[19] He complained that the school had treated his son as a 'guinea pig' by ditching A-levels in favour of a new exam system, the Cambridge Pre-U, which seemed 'to have been marked much harder than the A-level papers... At the moment his university place has been withdrawn, but we are hoping we might be able to find a way round this. We are all very disappointed.'

His son was less diplomatic in his own criticism, posting on Facebook: 'didn't get into a uni... cheers school u massive knobbers!' It later emerged that Lineker junior had been spotted on a week-long holiday to Tenerife just weeks before his exams as well as being pictured on nights out with ex-*Big Brother* contestant Sophie Reade.

The Rev. John Witheridge, the school's then head, defended the school's exam results and said they refused to comment on the performance of individual pupils.

In 2014 Witheridge voluntarily left the school to be replaced by a new headmaster, Richard Pleming, who the school had head-hunted from Wrekin College in Shropshire. Pleming lasted just three years in the role, resigning after a prolonged and particularly nasty campaign to remove him, which was allegedly orchestrated by parents and ex-pupils who objected to his over-authoritarian methods.[20] Pleming later suggested to *The Times* that the trouble started when he tried to get Charterhouse to play a greater role in the community and work more closely with the state schools.[21] He now teaches at a London inner-city academy.

International students do seem to be a growing part of the schools' backup plan, though not all parents are happy with the way things are done in England. International banker Arnold Holle, who moved his family from Dusseldorf to London and sent his children to Sevenoaks and Westminster, was so disappointed by the English public school system that he cautioned his fellow countrymen against it. In an article for the *Frankfurter Allgemeine Zeitung*, he observed students at the UK's top boarding schools fare little better, if at all, than those receiving a free education in Germany: 'Learning less and paying a lot is one thing. Much worse, however, is that even a short stay in an English boarding school will lead to children losing any respect for money. How many chauffeurs are waiting today at parents' evenings in Germany in dark limousines at the school gate?... There are virtually no scholarship recipients at English boarding schools... All in all, no other Western country makes it more difficult for its underclass to rise upwards. The social injustice here in London cries out to the heavens. The school system is one of the main reasons that not only social mobility persists at a low level, but continues to decline every year.'[22]

Nevertheless, the allure of the English public school education has always attracted children from the world's ruling dynasties and society elites. Eton has schooled three kings of Nepal, the prime minister of Thailand and many of the crown heads of Europe. Harrow's international royal roll call is even more impressive, including the first prime minister of India, Jawaharlal Nehru, and ruling monarchs like the Emir of Qatar. Ahmed Abdel Hadi Chalabi, the prime minister of Iraq in 2006, was educated at Seaford College, West Sussex, a minor public school. The wife of Syrian dictator Bashar al-Assad was also privately educated, at Queen's College, a private girls' school on London's Harley Street, whose alumnae include Gertrude Bell, Anna Wintour and Peaches Geldof.

Today the super-rich tend to shop around the world for their children's education in the same way they look for property investment abroad. English public schools are favoured by Russian oligarchs, Chinese tycoons and Gulf State oil barons. All seven of Roman Abromovich's children have attended or are attending English public schools. His oldest daughter Anna said her morning journey to £15,000-a-year Godolphin & Latymer in west London usually began with a helicopter ride to Battersea helipad. Figures published by the Independent Schools Council (whose 1,331 schools educate 522,879 pupils out of the 625,000 children privately educated in the UK) show that one new pupil in every twenty now comes from abroad, with 50,473 foreign pupils educated in the UK at ISC schools.[23]

Brexit is stimulating even greater interest in British private education. Public schools have reported a rush of applicants from the world's richest families since the fall in sterling following the Brexit vote. Ed Richardson, director of education at Keystone Tutors, says that although the US, Switzerland and Australia are popular with Asian families, the UK's private boarding schools are still seen as the 'gold standard'. He says that 'currency, quality of life and access to the best universities are the key trends boosting demand for a British education. Ambitious families in Singapore have traditionally sent their children to schools in the US, not necessarily because they think they are better, but because of the cost. Now, they are telling me that the fall in the value of the pound is making the UK look much better value. That sentiment will be echoed in many other places.'[24]

Nowhere is interest in Britain's top public schools more intense than China, which is the largest single foreign contributor to British private schools. Despite a recent crackdown on ostentatious displays of wealth, the Chinese elite continue to be transfixed with English brands and this is no different when it comes to Western education. Eton, Harrow and Winchester are ranked alongside

Burberry and Wedgwood. Wang Sicong, the twenty-eight-year-old son of China's richest man, was educated at Winchester College and is already worth £430 million.[25] That the disgraced Chinese politician Bo Xilai sent his son to Harrow has done little to dampen Chinese enthusiasm for top-flight British schools. One reason is that the schools pride themselves on discretion and privacy. Oligarchs and African princes don't like publicity and neither do English public schools. In 2017 Eton quietly recruited one of the UK's most senior counterterrorism policemen as head of its security. Brendan O'Dowda, who had been in charge of the South East Regional Organised Crime Unit, now has the job of protecting the children of some of the richest and most politically sensitive families in the world.

Individual public schools are coy about saying exactly how many foreign pupils they take each year. According to Tony Little, the former Eton headmaster, 'Parents want a school to be fundamentally British. I have heard of schools with 50 per cent Chinese and so there does come a tipping point on nationality which is a problem. Most foreign parents buying a private education are buying a British education. So what you don't want if you're Chinese is to turn up and get a whole load of Chinese, speaking Mandarin exclusively. There are two types of independent schools – recruiting and competitive entry schools. We had informal quotas at Eton – I had in mind a rough number – roughly speaking we worked on the principle that no more than 10 per cent of the school population were non-British.'[26] Such a significant influx of foreign students has helped give the schools a healthy ethnic-minority profile, mirroring the state sector's, of around 30 per cent. Academics at University College London have called this 'fake diversity'.[27]

Not all parents are happy with the changing demographics. At least one parent at Eton reported surprise when they were told (perhaps wrongly) that Patel and Kim were now the most common surnames at the school's twenty-four boarding houses. The promotion of the Eton brand, considerably boosted by the publicity surrounding the 'unofficial' 2016 meeting with President Putin, has made the Berkshire school the first port of call for foreign families looking to buy an education. There is a perception that all that is required to secure a place is a big enough cheque or a sizeable donation to the school's endowment fund.

But Little says that on a number of occasions he had to be robust, especially when approached by high-rolling Russians: 'We had that with a big-set Slavic guy, Russian... what was his name, one of Putin's enemies... Boris Berezovsky. We changed the admissions system at the beginning of my time at Eton. There was a good reason for doing so but you had to register your child at the age of ten and a half. You did the test at thirteen. The reasons we did that was because the school was so oversubscribed it was giving people ample notice. The reason for mentioning this was your typical oligarch rolled up with a thirteen-year-old – actually, genuinely, there were no places. Whatever else, the integrity of the admission process was huge.' In the end, Berezovsky junior found Harrow more accommodating.

It wasn't only oligarchs who tried to 'push' Little around when it came to accepting certain pupils: 'I remember on two occasions getting letters from government ministers on government headed paper telling me it was "in the national interest" to take a particular boy. A foreign boy. We made damn sure we didn't. "In the national interest" I read as "in the interests of that minister". So we had to make sure we didn't get pushed around.'

In the twenty-first century, the public schools have become heavily financially dependent on the fees from overseas students who can comfortably meet the increasing costs of a private education in the UK. The big public schools have even set up testing stations outside the UK to process the admission of these overseas students. Winchester runs centres in Prague for its Russian applicants and Hong Kong for those applying from China. Today a multi-million-pound industry of international agents and super-tutors has grown up to service the global trade in private education. It is an unregulated marketplace where competition for pupils means many schools will pay commissions to agents for bringing in high-paying students. Naturally, parents are not always told about the commissions or why students are shepherded to the schools that cost the most. There have also been cases of agents writing admissions essays or colluding with families to misuse UK visa regulations.

In December 2016 the scandal of foreign families allegedly paying cash for places hit the headlines. Reporters from the *Daily Telegraph* had spent months undercover, posing as representatives of a Russian businessman who wanted his son to study in England. They met several educational consultants and school representatives, including the then registrar at Stowe School, David Fletcher, who was secretly filmed saying a six-figure payment would be helpful when there was a 'marginal decision' over whether a pupil should be admitted. He even suggested that one overseas family had recently given £100,000 towards a project at the school to help secure a place for their child. They always 'have to be able to pass [the entrance exams]', but payments would be looked upon favourably.

The *Telegraph* investigation also found that educational consultants were prepared to facilitate payments of up to £5 million to high-profile public schools on behalf of families hoping to win places for overseas children. Two agents in London told undercover reporters that donations would help to secure places. One suggested that any link between a payment and an offer of a school place could be downplayed by ensuring that the money was not donated until after the child had started. Schools' agent Ekaterina Ametistova, a partner at educational consultants Bruton Lloyd, was reported to have said she was aware of pupils being placed at top public schools in exchange for donations of at least £1 million. 'But the boy has to be good,' she said. 'It has to be both.'

After the story broke, Fletcher resigned from Stowe, having admitted to making 'inaccurate and inappropriate statements' and stating that the school has 'no reason to believe' that a donation has ever influenced a decision to award a place.[28] No independent inquiry into the alleged practice of cash for places has been instigated. But the scandal has raised other, even more unsettling questions about the provenance of so much cash sloshing about in public school coffers at the start of each academic year.

Hundreds of millions of pounds' worth of foreign fees paying for pupils from Russia, China and the Middle East makes private schools vulnerable to money laundering. Yet the education sector made only nine out of the 382,000 reports received by the UK authorities of possible money-laundering incidents in 2014–15. Such a low level of reporting is out of step with the number of cases where convicted criminals have been shown to have used their illegal wealth to pay for their children's private education. Nigerian businessman James Ibori was jailed for thirteen years in 2014 after being convicted of a £157 million fraud and money laundering relating to his time in Africa. At his trial it emerged that he had used part of the cash to pay for his luxury lifestyle, including boarding his children at a private school in Dorset. Three years later it emerged that a couple, Hong Chin and Li Wei Gao, used the proceeds of their sex-trafficking racket to send their daughter to a private school in Surrey.[29] In the same month a Manchester businessman who swindled almost half a million pounds from three companies admitted spending part of the money on private school fees.[30]

Anti-corruption campaigners say that the loophole by which schools and colleges are not compelled to make 'suspicious activity reports' to the National Crime Agency must be closed. Transparency International, the anti–money-laundering organisation, is investigating whether more should be done by British schools and universities to carry out checks on the provenance of their fees, especially from countries with reputations for corruption.

Its executive director, Robert Barrington, says: 'Independent schools' income from foreign students has greatly increased in the last decade. Most are legitimate, but we suspect a lot is not. And whose job is it to check? Schools may not be expected to know which are legitimate bank accounts, but some of their pupils come from parts of the world with high levels of corruption. While the money being used for fees is small by money-laundering standards, we are laundering the reputations of the families by opening the door of respectability to the next generation.'

The lack of mandatory checks on the provenance of school fees means it is difficult to gauge how much might be linked to dirty money. I have seen evidence of how a Syrian businessman and supporter of President Bashar al-Assad has been able to send his children to public schools in Dorset despite being on a UK Treasury sanctions list. But Barrington warns that English school and university fees have also been used as bribes to foreign officials. Private schools and universities 'should accept there is a problem, sit down around the table with experts and address it. Most independent schools have charitable status. Surely if it is a sector that is in any way compliant with money laundering they put their charitable status under threat.'[31] In March 2018 the chemical attack on two Russian citizens in Salisbury led to calls by both Russian and British politicians for oligarchs linked to Putin to be stopped from sending their children to private schools in the UK.[32]

★

The relentless quest for more and more fees has forced some of the best-known English public schools to cash in on the overseas markets by establishing off-shore franchises in countries like China, Russia and even Kazakhstan. Here they are well placed to market their brands directly to a middle-class client base who may not be able to afford the expense of sending children to the UK.

Harrow led the way in 1998 by setting up a school in Bangkok, where its famous straw boaters helped promote its brand of quintessential English education. It now has schools in Beijing and Hong Kong, too. But it is Nigel Farage's old school, Dulwich College, which is capitalising most on the education of foreign students. Through an exclusive worldwide charter agreement with Dulwich College Management International, the UK school has established a number of overseas schools as part of a franchise, all taking the Dulwich name. Six thousand students are benefiting from a Dulwich education overseas. Four Dulwich Colleges have been established in China (two in Shanghai, and one each in Beijing and Suzhou), one in Seoul, South Korea, and one in Singapore. The latest addition to the family, Dulwich College Yangon, has started accepting students in Myanmar. These seven schools are all co-educational and principally cater to the expatriate community. In addition to the international schools, Dulwich has established two high schools in Suzhou and Zhuhai in conjunction with prestigious Chinese schools, to teach the IGCSE and A-level curriculum to Chinese pupils who are aiming for top universities in the UK, USA and elsewhere.[33]

The number of pupils attending English public schools abroad in 2017 was 31,773, the majority children from rich and influential families. It is an important expression of Britain's own soft power. Most among the new breed of schools are run by local management companies. Some are even considering franchising entire regions to education providers, including American chains. At that point, the link to the playing fields of England becomes rather stretched.[34]

In the clamour for foreign cash, the education product is not always as English as the schools would like. Dulwich, despite a strong Christian tradition, accepts that it cannot teach religion in its Chinese schools, while King's School in Canterbury pulled out of a partnership there, concluding that the constraint was inappropriate given its association with the cathedral, the historic seat of the Church of England. Dulwich's head, Joe Spence, says that the schools are not 'missionaries' and must respect the cultural norms of the host country. But he insists this does not affect the quality of the International Baccalaureate or GCSE being taught.[35]

As demand continues to grow, promising new markets are opening up in South America, notably Chile and Mexico.[36] For its part, Eton has chosen to eschew the foreign franchise market. Its governors believe such a move would damage the brand. Instead, it has set up an online business which provides internet-based schooling for the children of the Chinese middle classes with one-to-one online teaching from tutors in the UK. The cost, about £700 per pupil, will be paid by Chinese parents as an optional extra, like a music lesson. The revenues from the new business are funnelled back into the school coffers.

In December 2017 Westminster School announced it too was joining the gold rush for overseas pupils by setting up six schools in China. It said this was to help fund bursaries for 'disadvantaged' students in London. It is perhaps a sign of more sceptical times that this news was not universally welcomed. Andrew Adonis, the former education minister, said Westminster's foreign enterprise was all about helping the 'non-super-rich' rather than the genuinely poor.[37]

Latest figures show there are fifty-nine overseas campuses run by English public schools.[38] But the high cost of a private education has left the English public schools vulnerable to competition from chains of fee-charging schools run by foreign enterprises. The best-known is Dubai-based GEMS Education. As we saw in

Chapter 9, Gordonstoun sold a Hampshire girls' school to GEMS in 2004 when the company was making its first forays into the British private schools market. Today the company has three schools in the UK and is reporting record profits internationally. GEMS is not a charity and because of its economy of scale (it has 250 private schools all over the world)[39] it can undercut English public school fees.

It also boasts some key personnel from the British establishment and public school sector. Sir Michael Peat (Eton), the former private secretary to Prince Charles from 2002 to 2011, is independent chairman of GEMS' board of directors. GEMS has also recruited the former Ofsted chief inspector of schools, Sir Michael Wilshaw, to help with its education strategy in India. But perhaps the company's most eye-catching appointment is Tony Little as chief academic officer. The international schools, many of which are in UAE, are run like English public schools and teach the British curriculum.

In May 2017 Little told the Headmasters' and Headmistresses' Conference in London that private schools could no longer rest on their laurels: 'There are school systems now aiming at achieving, on paper at least, neutral fees. That is to say, the amount of benefits they [parents] can derive – for example, reduced [fares for] flights on a particular airline – match or exceed the fee that they are paying in the first place.'[40]

According to Little, GEMS is set apart from many other for-profit educational groups by its social access ethos: 'You do have the high fee-paying premium schools but also midmarket schools down to the affordable schools – for example, there are 180 of these in India where the average annual fee is $200 and these are being rolled into Africa. And in a new role GEMS has started managing schools for governments by setting up public–private partnership schemes. India is the prime focus but talks about South-East Asia and Africa are in early stages. So that's what really interested me as

did the stated ambition of the company – to give a quality education for every child in the world... The immediate targets are that
there should be five million children at bricks and mortar schools
and five hundred million benefiting from other means – online or
teacher training.'

Little believes the future for private education is selling affordable schools for millions of children in developing parts of the
world: 'I think the future for parent-paid education is very strong
globally. But it could look very different from what we consider
it be in the UK. I think worldwide it is highly likely that we will
see a lot more private education because governments can't keep
pace with growing parental expectation.' In Britain he believes
the picture is much less rosy, though he argues that the 'majority
of parents would have their kids at an independent school if they
could. The sentiment is still there.'

Ultimately, wherever a child grows up in the world, it boils
down to this. If the family has enough money, they can afford to
pay to improve their child's life chances at the expense of other
families who cannot. In Britain, where those attending private
schools are already blessed with huge advantages, parents use their
wealth to multiply these gains over other children. The American
economist Alan Krueger, who developed the 'Great Gatsby curve'
correlating inequality with social immobility, has said that well-off
families use private schools in America to protect their assets and
pass them onto the next generation.[41] The English public school is
a much more complex and subtle institution but it too guarantees
that the advantage is seamlessly transferred from one generation to
another – and having failed to reform the system at home, we are
now exporting the model to the rest of the world.

14

DORMITORIES OF ABUSE

The history of public schools has shown that for long periods our boarding schools were breeding grounds for abuse. Predatory paedophiles and sadists roamed dormitories with impunity. In Georgian and Victorian times abuse was tolerated as part of the toughening up of the schoolboy on his journey to manhood. A succession of inquiries and reports into boarding schools, which began with the Clarendon Commission of 1867 and continued into the 1970s, marked a shift towards a culture which placed children's welfare at its heart. Gradually attitudes changed and overtly abusive practices and customs were curbed.

But private schools are by definition cloistered communities, and so they will always attract a small number of men who seek to take advantage of a position of trust beyond public scrutiny. Too many times complaints were made and children were either disbelieved or silenced. When cases could not be denied they were hushed up and the teacher quietly moved on. Everything was done in the utmost secrecy. A public school's reputation is worth millions of pounds in school fees and donations, and bad publicity can be a very costly business. Because public schools are under no obligation to inform the authorities about a case of abuse they have been getting away with it for years.

Now all this paranoia and cover-up is coming home to roost as schools face a deluge of litigation and criminal prosecutions relating to historic, and in some cases not so historic, child abuse. The scale of the claims means that only a very small number of the leading public schools will be untouched by the scandal.

David Greenwood, of Yorkshire-based Switalskis Solicitors, who has won substantial damages for pupils from schools across the country, says his firm is working on new cases involving about a dozen private schools. 'I've seen lots of cases where schools adopt a range of legal tactics, sometimes employing expensive lawyers, first trying to deny allegations because they simply don't want to face up to the problem,' he says. 'There is an institutional response that involves protecting the good name of the school. It means that the people who need to be protected and encouraged to come forward are discouraged.'[1]

Greenwood says because there are no mandatory reporting rules, the schools rely on the loyalty of teachers and governors to 'close ranks' and face down accusers. 'This pressure to band together is stronger in public schools, partly because it is easier to get sacked from a private school... then the [accused] teacher is moved on to other schools.' He says that increasingly schools are seeking 'confidentiality' agreements to protect their reputation. 'Whilst I understand that abuse cases can tarnish schools, keeping abuse cases under wraps is exactly the opposite of the openness demanded by all the [child safeguarding and welfare] guidance.'

But the private schools have found a way round the regulations. Astonishingly Greenwood says his investigations have shown that up to 40 per cent of schools do not have a written child safeguarding policy. 'Schools aren't doing anything more to protect children than they have done in the past. This is partly because they don't want to do anything that might raise the spectre of child abuse which might put off fee-paying pupils.'

The schools now implicated in child-abuse scandals are the alma maters of royalty, prime ministers, captains of industry and our favourite actors and entertainers.

In February 2017, three former masters at George Osborne's old school, St Paul's in Barnes, south-west London, were sentenced to a total of thirty-nine years for sexually assaulting boys. Patrick Marshall, a teacher before Osborne's time at the school, was jailed for eighteen years for sexually abusing ten boys in the 1960s and '70s while he was employed first at Windsor Grammar School and then at St Paul's. Marshall, seventy at the time of his conviction, a rowing coach and Geography teacher, used his position to gain the trust of the boys' families, before plying the youngsters with alcohol and presents and making them perform sexual acts. According to a Metropolitan Police report, Marshall abused one boy who was grieving the loss of his father.

The investigation into the St Paul's abuse was codenamed Operation Winthorpe and found that Marshall created a 'clique' of boys around him, targeting victims as young as eleven. He took some of his victims on trips across Europe, staying over at their homes. 'Child after child after child was groomed,' said prosecutor Rosina Cottage QC during the trial at Southwark Crown Court. 'He moved from one boy to the next boy to the next boy.' Two other former St Paul's teachers were also convicted and jailed as part of the child-abuse investigation.

Three months earlier another ex-teacher, David Sansom-Mallett, also seventy, was jailed for fourteen years and nine months for a catalogue of abuse at St Paul's prep school, Colet Court. Although the investigation was concerned mostly with historic abuse cases, one of the teachers convicted was still teaching at St Paul's in 2013. He was sentenced to four months' imprisonment, suspended for two years, at Kingston Crown Court in June 2015 after he pleaded guilty to ten counts of making indecent photographs of children and five counts of possessing indecent photographs of children.

Other schools linked to child-abuse investigations include Caldicott boarding prep school in Buckinghamshire, where Nick

Clegg was educated. In 2014 the former headmaster, Roland Peter Wright, then eighty-three, was sentenced to eight years for grooming and sexually assaulting five pupils between the age of eight and thirteen between 1959 and 1970. Wright had been due to be sentenced at Amersham Crown Court alongside another teacher, Hugh Henry, eighty-two, but Henry threw himself under a train before the hearing.[2] Another former teacher at the school, John Addison, fifty-four, from Slough in Berkshire, pleaded guilty to offences of indecent assault and indecency with a child and was sentenced to five years' imprisonment at Aylesbury Crown Court in November 2012.

Clegg, who was joint head boy at the school in 1980, told *The Times*: 'These reports will disturb everyone, but most especially those, like myself, who were pupils at the school and were entirely unaware that such abuse was taking place. I can only imagine the devastating impact that such abuse must have had on the young boys who were affected. My heart goes out to them.'[3] The school later issued a statement apologising to the victims of the abuse, adding: 'Thirty years on, Caldicott is now a very different school. We put the safety and welfare of our pupils at the heart of everything we do.'

The case led to calls for mandatory reporting of abuse by schools. Tom Perry, one of Wright's victims, waived his anonymity to tell *Channel 4 News*: 'Abuse of a child broke the bond between a child and his or her parents, because of the sense of complicity that the child often feels in the abuse, which meant they often felt they could not speak out.' He said mandatory reporting was particularly necessary in the independent sector, where 'fee-receiving institutions are presented with a conflict of interest over reporting, because it is discretionary'.

The true scale of child abuse in public schools, both violent and sexual, will only be made clear after the publication of the reports of the Independent Inquiry into Child Abuse and the

Scottish Child Abuse Inquiry. In Scotland claims have been made against Tony Blair's school, Fettes, and Prince Charles's school, Gordonstoun, while high-profile public schools named by lawyers in the Independent Inquiry into Child Abuse include City of London, Clifton College in Bristol and St George's School in Norfolk. The ambit of both these inquiries, whose final reports are not expected until 2020, extends to a number of religious education institutions as well as private choir schools linked to the church.

Church of England broadcaster Giles Fraser has claimed that what the church and the public schools have failed to acknowledge is that 'the problem [of violent abuse] was deep in the educational philosophy of the public school system, and the poisonous ideas it developed about the sort of men required to run the British Empire'. He says 'it is safe to assume that human beings have thrashed each other, and their children, throughout their history. But the popularity of beating children in the British educational system, and the idea that it had moral, character-forming proper-ties, cannot be understood without the rise of so-called muscular Christianity during the second half of the nineteenth century... The whole culture of public school beatings was dominated by [a] narrative of violent atonement – old men with beards thrashing young boys, apparently for their moral and spiritual edification.'[4] The historic and continuing close links between church and private schools mean these institutions, which often share priests and teachers, are closed off from the community, allowing child abusers to carry out their crimes in secret.

In recent years a series of child-abuse scandals has demonstrated that neither church nor school has had the will or the capacity to tackle the problem. Time and time again, crimes are covered up and the abuser is allowed to move on to a new school or church. Perhaps the most serious case linking the failures of church and school is that of the evangelical Christian–camp leader, John Smyth.

Smyth attended a leading private school in Canada before qualifying as a barrister and practising in London in the 1970s. One of his most high-profile cases involved the Christian morality campaigner Mary Whitehouse in her successful private prosecution for blasphemy at the Old Bailey against the newspaper *Gay News* and its editor, Denis Lemon, over the publication of James Kirkup's poem 'The Love that Dares to Speak its Name'. He also acted for Whitehouse in her failed prosecution of the National Theatre production of Howard Brenton's play *The Romans in Britain* in 1980.

Outside his legal career Smyth also played a voluntary role in the Church of England and between 1974 and 1981 was chairman of the Iwerne Trust, which funded religious holidays exclusively for public schoolboys. The trust was established by a cleric called Eric Nash (Maidenhead College), whose nickname was Bash. These so-called Bash camps were aimed at the top thirty British public schools, and began a camp ministry which by 1940 was based at Clayesmore School in the village of Iwerne Minster, Dorset. Attendance was by invitation only. The camps were hierarchical, using military terminology: Bash was commandant; his deputy, adjutant and the leaders were officers. The camp prayer was, 'Lord, we claim the leading public schools for your kingdom.' Additional camps were started at Lymington in Hampshire to cater for the second tier of public schools, and at Rushmore in Dorset for privately educated girls.

Many senior members of the privately educated clergy passed through the camps, among them the future Archbishop of Canterbury, Justin Welby, who had known Smyth there but does not recall any abuse taking place. The boys, who were very often charismatic, athletic or smart enough to go to Oxbridge, were supposed to be the flower of a public school Christian education. Winchester College, with its strong religious origins, was a leading contributor to the camps and sent dozens of boys, among them the future Bishop of Guildford, Andrew Watson. (Winchester has continued its commitment to an 'intensely male environment' and strict ecclesiastical ritual into the twenty-first century.)[5]

Smyth used the summer camps to befriend young boys and then groom them back at his Winchester home. Later, his victims claimed that Smyth arranged for Winchester boys to come to his house, where he would subject them to savage beatings in his garden shed. Exactly what access he enjoyed at the school or how closely he worked with the teachers and school clergy remains unclear.

In the 1980s, a number of the boys identified Smyth as their abuser. Winchester's then headmaster, John Thorn, said that he confronted Smyth in 1982 after he was told the barrister had allegedly groomed a group of boys over regular Sunday lunches at his home near the school and was physically abusing them. In his memoir, *The Road to Winchester*, published in 1989, he wrote: '[Smyth] had gained such personal control over a few of the senior boys in the group, and had kept it after they left the school, that he was claiming to direct their burgeoning relationships with girls, and was, with their consent, punishing them physically when they confessed to him they had sinned. Absurd and baseless rumours were circulated that he was an unhinged tyrant, the embodiment of Satan. He must be banished. And – quietly but efficiently – he was. He left the Winchester district and then the United Kingdom. He departed for Africa with his family.' But crucially, Thorn did not name Smyth at the time of publication.

The extent of the alleged abuse only publicly emerged in 2017 when Bishop Andrew Watson issued a statement saying he had been the victim of one of Smyth's beatings. Others followed. One boy told the *Daily Telegraph* that Smyth made the boys admit to 'sins of masturbation' and told them that they must 'bleed for Jesus'. They were then taken to Smyth's garden shed where they were made to pull down their trousers and say a prayer before being repeatedly beaten with a cane. The unnamed boy said that he received 8,000 strokes of the cane over a number of years.[6]

In an interview with the *Sunday Times* in 2017, Thorn said the scandal was informally discussed with one or two governors: 'Somehow it didn't occur to one at that point to bother the police. I think now in retrospect, in respect to this ghastly man, it probably would have been more sensible to do that, but people at the time... The boys on the whole didn't want that to happen. This was historically the case. They did not want any publicity at all and probably still don't.'

The Iwerne Trust also carried out its own internal inquiry into the abuse in 1982. The author of the subsequent report was Mark Ruston, vicar of the Round Church in Cambridge, with whom Justin Welby lodged during the late 1970s, in his final year at university. The report stated that boys were given beatings of 100 strokes as punishment for masturbation and 400 for the sin of pride.[7]

Yet despite all available evidence neither the school nor the trust reported Smyth to the police. Instead he was allowed to leave the UK and move to Zimbabwe, where he set up the Zambesi Ministries which ran similar summer camps. There, the barrister continued with his abusive practices and was accused of swimming naked with Zimbabwean teenagers, showering with them in the nude and encouraging them to talk about masturbation. One alleged victim told Channel 4 that Smyth administered savage beatings with wooden bats, echoing the allegations made against him in Britain.[8]

Another of the boys who alleged he was beaten by Smyth in Zimbabwe was Rocky Leanders. He told me: 'The summer camps were held at an exclusive boarding school just outside Harare, and catered for boys from the elite schools... My school was a day school – non-boarding. Smyth took particular interest in my group as it was the first time anyone from our school had attended his camps, and being non-boarding, seeing how we coped being thrown into that environment.'[9]

Smyth later faced charges in relation to the mysterious death of a sixteen-year-old boy at one of the camps in Ruzawi. The boy, Guide Nyachuru, was found in 1992 at the bottom of a swimming pool in the grounds of Ruzawi College, where the Zambesi camps were held. In 1997, Smyth was charged in connection with the killing and with the alleged abuse of five boys. But the case was dropped. Smyth left Zimbabwe in 2002 to move to South Africa, where he became a religious campaigner against gay rights.

In April 2017 the BBC claimed that one of Smyth's victims was now headmaster at a public school that has already been mentioned in this chapter. Simon Doggart, who was educated at Winchester College, was headmaster at Caldicott Preparatory School until 2017, standing down after the BBC report was broadcast. It was alleged that Doggart, when still a pupil at Winchester, was recruited by Smyth who asked him to administer further beatings to his friends. An alleged victim told the BBC: 'John Smyth beat me first, appallingly, with his usual force. Then Simon Doggart took over while John watched. I recall immediately the absolute brutality of his beating – far, far worse than Smyth. There was no discussion, no emotion that I recall, just a fit sportsman using all his force.'[10] There has been no suggestion that Doggart ever harmed any of his pupils at Caldicott.

When the Smyth scandal became public in 2017, the successor to the Iwerne Trust, the Titus Trust, distanced itself from the abuse, saying its board only became aware of the allegations in 2014 when it reported them to the police and the Charity Commission. The Titus Trust continues to run Christian holidays for young people which 'develop leadership qualities'.[11]

A number of commentators have tried to put the camps in historical context. Charles Moore, former editor of the *Telegraph*, wrote: 'One has always to remember that the past is another country. Nowadays an all-male camp, run on military lines to win boys from top public schools for the Lord might seem a bit rum. Then, it was the natural offshoot of a century where the ruling elites and the Christian faith itself had been severely tested in two world wars.'[12] It is difficult to discern any fundamental difference between the stated ethos of the 'Bash camps' of the 1970s and '80s and the ones run by Titus today – they are holiday camps exclusively for public school pupils led by Christian clergy and teachers.

Giles Fraser says that while Justin Welby bears no responsibility for the behaviour of those involved with Christian camps in the 1970s, his particular 'brand of Eton/Alpha Course Christianity is cut from the same cloth as the muscular Christianity of the 1850s'. He suggests that is why the Church of England hierarchy remains 'obsessed with maintaining the Anglican communion (i.e. what's left of the empire) – it is no coincidence that Smyth fled to Zimbabwe and South Africa – and why it can't get past an over-fascination with homosexuality. The archbishop is not to blame for Smyth's sins. But he is still too much a part of the world that made him.'[13]

Four months after the Smyth case came to light, the Church of England published findings into another equally disturbing scandal that this time revealed direct collusion between the public schools and a paedophile priest with connections to the royal family.

Bishop Peter Ball, an alumnus of Lancing College in West Sussex, was a confidant to Prince Charles and circulated among the highest echelons of English society. He was also a serial paedophile and in October 2015 was jailed for thirty-two months after admitting to a string of historical sex offences against teenage boys and young men between the 1970s and the 1990s. An investigation into the handling of the original complaints made about Ball in the 1990s revealed that Lambeth Palace had failed to pass on six letters of allegations of sex offences to the police and that the then Archbishop of Canterbury, Lord Carey, had played a key role in keeping the bishop out of court.

The report, *Abuse of Faith*, published in June 2017, found that Ball, then Bishop of Gloucester, used his connections 'on many occasions' by telling suspicious clergy and outside investigators that he 'enjoys the status of confidant of the Prince of Wales'. The report noted that when concerns were first raised about his molestation of boys, two public school headmasters, one former headmaster and senior staff members from another public school were among those who wrote supportive letters. None of the teachers or schools has been named. But an Old Etonian High Court judge, Lord Justice Lloyd, was identified as the author of a character reference, which he wrote after knowing that Ball had already accepted a caution for child molestation. This was described by one bishop at the time as an 'old boy arrangement' where a 'powerful group of friends [were] coming to Peter's aid'. [14]

Although Ball's links to Prince Charles and other well-known figures made headlines at the time, little has been said about his relationship with the public schools. The report by Dame Moira Gibb devotes a whole section to this subject. Gibb found that Ball was involved in 'ministry in seventeen public schools'. Ball was also a governor of at least one school for many years where he had 'unsupervised contact with pupils there after he had been cautioned'. Links with the unnamed school continued until as late as 2007.

The report said: 'Ball's connections with schools often arose from his personal relationships with the heads of those schools. Some of them championed his cause when he was under investigation in 1992–93, and continued to support him publicly following his resignation.'

Investigators working with Dame Moira contacted every school with which Ball is known to have had a connection but none of them reported any concerns about his conduct. Yet the report found instances where troubled teenagers from some of these schools were directed towards Ball for advice and help. That is what happened to one of the complainants whose letter to the church should have been, but was not, passed to police in 1992: 'This boy was subjected to an improper approach from Ball. We have heard directly from one man who, at the age of fifteen, was seen on school premises by Ball and asked to masturbate in front of him. That man had also contacted the Church about this in 1992. Another survivor, who was not identified until the most recent proceedings, told us graphically how "what happened in those little rooms [was] little boys being told to strip off and pressed against his erection". We now know of five public schools whose pupils were abused by Ball.'

Dame Moira said that after his 1992 caution, Ball used his links with the public schools to seek to 'restore his good standing'. More worryingly was that in 1996 the Church of England agreed to Ball 'carrying out priestly duties in schools'. The report added:

> There is evidence that Ball then sustained his connections with some public schools for many years – he himself claimed to have been involved with between twenty and twenty-five schools after he had been cautioned… The Church would do well to look at its own responsibilities in this area. There will, quite properly, be relationships between schools and the Church, and relationships between senior teachers and senior figures in the Church locally. There will be situations where troubled young people, perhaps living away from their families, may be assisted by contact with a priest or someone else from a church. The Church should routinely take account of the possibility that 'special' relationships can give opportunities for abuse or improper conduct. We believe that, at least where there are ongoing chaplaincy arrangements in schools, the Church should establish that all necessary checks have been carried out appropriately and that there are no

concerns on Church records which would preclude the priest from exercising a ministry with young people.

The Ball report and the case of John Smyth demonstrate that public schools have been vulnerable to sexual predators until very recently, and must stop pretending that child abuse is a problem consigned to the past. Yet some remain closed to the problem. David Hanson, chief executive of the Independent Association of Prep Schools, contentiously claimed after the Caldicott case that he thought it was 'almost impossible' for sexual abuse to take place in modern prep schools.

Few child-abuse experts would agree with Hanson's complacent assessment.[15] Indeed, in April 2018 the Charity Commission decided to strip Ampleforth, Britain's most prestigious Catholic boarding school, of its child safeguarding powers. David Greenwood does not think public schools have done enough to end the culture of abuse and cover-up. His caseload reflects an enduring problem. Although Greenwood's firm is regularly contacted by younger men seeking legal advice, these cases often don't come to court until much later. He says: 'I have twelve cases against private schools now and I expect more in the next few years. People (usually men in their forties) are reluctant to bring a case until many years after they have left school when they feel they are ready to handle it. There has not been some amazing cultural change in the schools' approach to pupil safeguarding... So we won't know until the late 2030s or even 2040s what is going on now.'

Greenwood's findings are borne out by data collected by Alex Renton, whose book on boarding school abuse details his own and many other accounts of abuse. After contacting police forces across the country he discovered that since 2012, 425 people have been accused of sex attacks at UK boarding schools. Of those at least 125 cases involve *recent* sex attacks.

One former senior police officer told Renton that her investigations into abuse at a prep school in Dorset in the 1990s were hampered by parents of victims of abuse. Ex-chief superintendent Gill Donnell said: 'I recall quite clearly one parent saying to me the most important thing for him and his son was that his son got into Eton. This was his future and nothing was going to stand in the way of that happening, and that included any investigation into child abuse.'[16]

Unless public schools are forced to comply with mandatory reporting rules that impose duties on staff to raise concerns with the authorities, vulnerable children will continue to be at risk.

15

BAD CHARITY

The story of England's public school charities is one of slow corrosion. Over a period of 600 years the intentions of the original benefactors of the great public schools appear to have been mislaid. The ancient charters and foundations have been torn to shreds by lawyerly revisions and reinterpretations of their philanthropic endowments. The promise of the best education for the poor has been given to the rich. The drive for profit over community engagement has made our schools some of the wealthiest institutions in the country. It has reached the point today that even when the more enlightened schools wish to honour their charitable origins they find themselves hamstrung by the self-interest of paying parents and the inflexible demands of running a multi million-pound business.

Few schools have struggled more with their own history than Eton College, the old charity school set up to provide free education to seventy 'poor and needy' boys who would then go on to King's College, Cambridge. To preserve its core education purpose King Henry VI granted Eton a large number of endowments, including much valuable land. Eton's 1440 letters patent were issued by the King for the constitution of a college of 'fellows, priests, clerks, choristers, poor scholars, and old poor men, with one master or governor, whose duty it shall be to instruct these scholars and any others who may resort hither from any part of

England in the knowledge of letters, and especially of grammar, without payment'.[1]

Four hundred years later these statutes were cynically rewritten. Under a radical revision in 1870, all references to the school's charitable objects were obliterated. In the new statute nothing is said about the scholars being poor or indigent. Indeed, no suggestion is made of any charitable intention on the part of the governing body. It was one of its own, one of Eton's most illustrious scholars, who first exposed the school's betrayal of its founding purpose. Sir Lionel Henry Cust was director of the National Portrait Gallery in London before joining the Royal Household as Surveyor of the King's Pictures in 1901. Cust was also a historian, and after reviewing the 1870 Eton statutes he drew this alarming conclusion: 'The pious and charitable intentions of the Founder were thereby not merely amended, but wholly frustrated. It is one thing to increase and throw open to the world at large an endowment like that of Eton College; it is another to thereby destroy, perhaps in favour of the rich, the few and rapidly diminishing privileges of the poor.'[2]

Eton's founding and once-defining purpose of educating seventy poor scholars was later reduced to one of its 'medium to long-term aims'. Its charitable object now promises 'further access to the education provided by the College by increasing over time the percentage of boys receiving financial help with fees to at least 25 per cent' and ensuring the number of boys paying no fees at all remains at least seventy.[3]

To give it due credit, in 2015 Eton achieved something it had not done for hundreds of years. Without fanfare, the school was able to note in its annual accounts that it now provided free education for seventy scholars. One reason for the absence of any publicity on reaching such a momentous milestone might be the attention such a claim would have drawn to the other 1,200-odd students who are still paying for their charitable education.

Questions might have been asked about who are the poor scholars of today? Are they the children of the local poor and infirm, as they were in the day of King Henry? Today, of course, the word 'poor' is very much a qualified term among public schools, with some offering financial assistance to families whose combined income is as high as £140,000 per year.

Around 1,000 of the Independent Schools Council's 1,330 schools have charitable status. The Charities Act 2006 stipulates that trustees of school charities have a responsibility to ensure that they are running the school for the public benefit. Trustees must take action to ensure that the school does not solely benefit those who pay full fees. But crucially, since the 2011 court ruling won by the ISC, it is up to the trustees, not the Charity Commission, to determine how this is achieved.

To justify their charitable status, the schools now provide a range of data to show the commissioners they are contributing to the public benefit and not solely serving the interests of wealthy families who keep them in business. But this has become an arbitrary exercise for institutions that operate in the multi-billion-pound luxury service industry. Today the public-benefit test amounts to a box-ticking exercise in which anything that might touch on the community is offered up as a charitable act. Desperate examples include the existence of public rights of way across land owned by the schools; school open days; pupils participating in village fetes.

Little has changed since Jeremy Paxman made this damning observation when he visited a leading public school in 1991: 'There is much talk of "service". This last, perhaps the finest Victorian value, is the most empty claim of all. On close examination, the social service advertised in the prospectus means only digging old ladies' gardens, or the occasional afternoon when, released from military training, the boys will help out for the educationally subnormal. The nineteenth-century ideal of self-denial in obedience to the needs of the less fortunate survives only in the platitudes of headmasters.'[4]

The key test for any school that claims charitable status should be how many poor pupils are educated for free. In 2017, 522,879 pupils attended ISC schools. Of those, only 5,742 pupils paid no fees at all. That means just 1 per cent of public school pupils are schooled for free, a statistic that would embarrass any self-respecting Victorian headmaster, and would have been considered treasonous at the time of King Edward VI's statutes for the poor.

In addition, the ISC says that a total of 168,025 pupils receive a reduction to their fees, representing 33 per cent of all pupils, worth £900 million. It's a good headline figure which gives the impression that the schools are helping many thousands of poor families. However, the smallprint shows this is not the case. A large proportion of these generous discounts are given to the so-called school family. In 2017, 61,957 public school teachers' children, siblings of older pupils, children of alumni and clergy children were awarded £205 million in mostly non-means-tested fee subsidies. (One of Eton's charitable foundations is still called the Old Etonian Trust and is worth £6.1 million. It was only recently that it was paying bursaries to OEs who couldn't afford to send their own sons to Eton.)[5] A further £174 million is spent by the ISC schools on scholarships for families too rich to benefit from a bursary. Only £22 million was paid out to poor, but bright, children who qualified for means-tested scholarships.

But the biggest surprise is that more than £200 million of the £900 million help in fee remission is paid by the taxpayer, who subsidises the fees of the children of army officers (£80 million) and diplomats (£15 million) as well as government-sponsored places (£65 million). The figure also includes £49 million from the government's early years funding scheme, originally billed as help for struggling families, and £31 million for state-funded pupils taking up places for dance and music. The Ministry of Defence spends £1 million a year alone on school fees for officers' kids to be boarded at Fettes, Eton and Marlborough.[6] And a significant share of the seventy-odd independent grammar schools in Northern Ireland are under the ISC umbrella and all are state funded.

In fact, it would be more accurate to say that 43,000, or 8 per cent of pupils, qualify for a means-tested reduction in fees. Of those, fewer than 6,000 get it for free. It appears that the order of priority runs: first, profit from the richest in society; second, help the old boys who are already in the club; third, allow a small number to ride on one's coat-tails.

Basic annual boarding school fees in Britain broke the £40,000 barrier for the first time in 2017, putting them out of reach to all but the ultra-rich. The most expensive public school in Britain is not a name most parents will recognise. Hurtwood House is tucked away in the Surrey Hills, between Guildford and Dorking, in an Area of Outstanding Natural Beauty. Its only claim to fame is that the actress Emily Blunt went there. But in 2017 Hurtwood House, which is not a charity but a limited liability partnership, smashed through the £40,000 annual boarding fee barrier with annual boarding fees of £42,267. Because it's a business it doesn't even have to offer bursaries to disadvantaged children.

The supersonic rise in fees over the past five years amounts to a 20 per cent hike, and over the past fourteen years has been more than 70 per cent. School fees jumped by 3.5 per cent between 2016 and 2017, outstripping increases in wages and prices, although this was the lowest rise since 1994.[7] It is now estimated that the average cost of educating a child from nursery to Year 13 (upper sixth) is £286,000 per child for a day school and £550,000 for a boarder.[8] For a child at a top public school like Eton or Harrow, families could end up paying £600,000 per child.

The public schools are now coming under increasing pressure from politicians, education reformers and the Charity Commission to take action to address the deficit between the education of the mega-rich and the subsidised schooling of poorer students. For years the schools had been saying that the free scholars attending public school are children whose families are the poorest of the poor.

So how many of the 5,742 free pupils come from genuinely socially disadvantaged backgrounds? Or to put it another way: how many of them qualify for a free school meal? The ISC told me: 'We do not know how many of these pupils qualify for a free school meal as we do not collect any information regarding free school meals and schools have different methods of means testing.'[9]

Families with assets and a good accountant can play the system by demonstrating to the school that they meet the income criteria for bursaries, even if they are living in a multi-million-pound home and run a number of tax-efficient businesses.

Tony Little, the former Eton headmaster who stepped down in 2015, has claimed that this was how some families managed to secure free education under the 'flawed' assisted-places scheme, which was abolished by Tony Blair in 1999, and which the private schools would like to see returned. In his book *An Intelligent Person's Guide to Education*, Little said: 'With assessments of financial need based on income and not wealth, it proved too easy to play the system. Self-employed business people could show that they had no income despite their assets. There were even examples of parents borrowing a tatty car to come to interview. The scheme worked well for some families, but too seldom did it reach out to those in most need of help.'[10]

This is the same challenge facing the fair distribution of bursaries today. Barnaby Lenon, head of the ISC, would also like to see more rigour in the assessment of a bursary family's income and wealth. He told me: 'You have to employ people whose job it is to do proper investigations and get parents to fill in a detailed questionnaire and see their tax returns. It's not enough to just dismiss them all as liars and cheats. I mean obviously there's going to be a certain amount of that so you step up the measures to minimise the chances of that happening.'[11] Eton already sends a financial assessor to the home of every family applying for a reduction in fees.

A key question is how much can a family own and earn and still qualify for a reduction in fees? St Paul's, which charges £23,500 for day pupils and more than £35,000 for its few boarders, offers bursaries to families with a joint income of up to £120,000, under a new scheme introduced in 2016. Headmaster Mark Bailey said: 'The part-bursaries are being offered in a far more generous way. You will be looking eventually at [families earning] £150,000, £170,000, £190,000 potentially benefiting.'[12] Tim Haynes, headmaster of Tonbridge School in Kent, told *The Times* that thresholds needed to be high because the fees took such a large proportion of even a high earner's salary. His school offers bursaries of more than 100 per cent, so that pupils from modest backgrounds can afford equipment and school uniform, as well as fees.

Even for the super-rich there are still loopholes that help to reduce the cost of their child's education. Eton proudly boasts that during 2015–16, the amount it spent on 'fee remission' will have totalled £6.4 million. However, not all fee remission is means tested. Bright students who qualify for the 148 scholarships at Eton are not means tested on application, so they could come from the wealthiest families in the land and still benefit from a 10 per cent discount in fees. A further 134 boys received a bursary, although more than half are sufficiently well off to have to pay a substantial part of their fees.

What difference have these bursaries and scholarships made to the social and demographic profile of pupils attending elite schools? A team of researchers at University College London has spent many years trying to answer this question. In 2018 they published their findings, concluding: 'We find no evidence of any diminution in the social exclusivity of private schools compared with pre-2001 years, nor of any change during the 21st century... Both before and after 2000, nearly a half of private school children came from families in the top 10 per cent of the income distribution.' They said that an 'obvious interpretation' was that the effect of increased fees and the rise in absolute wealth inequality had offset any impact from bursaries, scholarships and other attempts to open up to a wider public.

One reason for this is that the bursaries and scholarships end up subsidising the fees of middle-class kids from the professional classes. But of most concern was the report's final sentence, which read: 'In the absence of an unexpected substantial fall in the fees, an unprecedented huge rise in charitable donations, or a radical policy change affecting the sector, we would speculate that the sector will remain, as a whole, as socially exclusive in the foreseeable future as it is now.'[13]

How is it possible that schools receiving such enormous fees can't afford to take more students for free? First, it is important to realise that public schools cannot generally use the fees paid by other pupils to subsidise the education of children from less well-off families. Parents who are already paying inflation-busting fees don't want to pay more, no matter how noble the cause. Funds for bursaries must come from endowments and donations. Lenon says it would be 'quite dangerous to let too many unworthy parents through the net' because fee-paying parents would feel they were subsidising the pupils whose families had the more creative accountants.

This leaves many schools relying on donations, which have not been so generous in recent years. At Eton, annual donations have fallen by £600,000 in 2016–17, down to £5.2 million from £5.8 million. Many Old Etonians and public school alumni profess themselves fed up with the begging-bowl approach, feeling plagued by phone calls, emails and letters asking for cash to maintain buildings and subsidise pupils. Eton has had to turn to America to boost its fundraising enterprises. An American Friends of Eton College Gala Dinner in 2016, staged in the heart of Manhattan, raised over $200,000. One of the auction lots was lunch with the OE actor and American audience favourite Damian Lewis. Back in Berkshire, Eton has established something called the Henry VI Society, whose sole purpose is to encourage Old Etonians 'to make provision for Eton' in their wills. For a minimum fee of £10 a month OEs can join the 1440 Society which holds drinks and dinner events attended by Michael Grade, Henry Blofeld and Barry Davies.[14]

But schools with the biggest challenge in raising bursary funds are girls' schools, whose alumnae don't donate so much. Warns Lenon: 'It's harder for let's say a middle-size girls' school because female alumnae don't seem to have the money, they probably haven't had the same glittering careers as the men have had… So the worst position to be in [in terms of bursaries] is to be at a female boarding school without lots of wealthy alumnae.'

The wider distribution of bursaries is further hampered by the terms of the historic endowments, restricted to the terms set by the original benefactor, which can make them over-prescriptive and difficult to apply. At Winchester College, pupils benefit from a £2 million bursary fund for aspiring golfers.[15] South London's Eltham College will award a discount of 50 per cent to children whose parents are 'chemists, travelling salesmen and grocers'. The Godolphin School, near Salisbury, offers as much as 70 per cent of boarding or day fees to girls whose parents (one of whom must belong to the Church of England) have separated or divorced. At Lathallan School in Scotland, scholarships are available for children interested in 'bagpipes or marching drums'.[16]

Such restrictions grossly restrict the bursary system. While some esoteric endowments can be invested and grow to become massive funds over the years, they may not actually help to provide means-tested bursaries. In 2015, Eton governors were forced to approve its first private placement of debt, borrowing £45 million to help subsidise fees. Issuing a statement to explain the decision, bursar Janet Walker said: 'We would like to be needs-blind. Hence part of the rationale of borrowing money and reinvesting it and hoping to make a return on it is, we want to pay more in fee remission and we don't want to take that money from current parents.'[17]

When Tony Little was headmaster of Eton he set up a new bursary foundation in 2005 to help boost the number of awards: 'There was a worry when I was there that we needed to fundraise so we didn't have to take money just off oligarchs.'[18] Under Little, the number of full bursaries rose from twenty to seventy and a total of 280 boys received a fee reduction. Eton built up an endowment worth £300 million, which has more than doubled since 2002. This gave the school a draw-down of about £7.5 million, which roughly paid for the bursaries and the maintenance of the buildings. 'Which,' says Little, 'meant students were not paying for upkeep of the buildings.'

Anthony Seldon says: 'It is very hard and expensive for independent schools to offer free or subsidised places. To subsidise a free boarding place at a public school at, say, £35,000 per annum requires an endowment of perhaps £2 million. To have one hundred such spaces, i.e. twenty a year over the five-year life of the school, would require £200 million. Many independent schools are operating with very tight margins, which no one seems interested in or believes.'[19]

Winchester, the oldest of the public schools, is also facing the harsh reality of restrictive endowments. In 2016, only 18 of its 700 pupils were on full bursaries, although 130 received some kind of fee reduction. Yet in the same year Winchester had funds worth £348 million. Its endowments are broken down into twenty-eight separate funds with specific purposes set by their donors. The school remains bound by its original foundation and contributes 40 per cent of fees towards the education (at Pilgrims' School) of sixteen Quiristers who sing in the school chapel.

Like most of the big public schools, Winchester has made efforts to grow its bursaries in recent years, from just £205,000 in 2005 to £3 million in 2016. But such rapid growth has become unsustainable. Now the school tells parents that only 'extreme' cases will receive full bursaries and it is not in the business of 'subsidising parents' lifestyles'.[20]

Writing in the school magazine, Winchester's bursar Steven Little explained how the school had to halt the rate of increase in its bursary awards:

> Recently we have found ourselves in the unhappy position of having to limit the bursary awards we can make for the first time, as parents and their sons become increasingly aware of what is available and we become more practised at reaching those who need our help. Demand is growing more strongly than our ability to meet it… The simple truth is that the Bursary Fund is far from sufficient to meet the present demand and the school has to top it up from general funds… The discrepancy with the amounts actually being spent is clear and the recent rate of increase of expenditure on bursaries is unsustainable. The school cannot safely do more until the Bursary Fund becomes larger.

In 2016 the school tried to partly meet the shortfall by selling off its ancient lands at Barton Farm just outside Winchester to developers who had planning permission for the building of 2,000 homes. The first tranche of capital has already given Winchester a £12 million windfall. In the same year the college sold additional land for £14.5 million.[21] But even this extra cash won't solve Winchester's short-term difficulties. As Steven Little explained,

'Barton Farm and other investments will play their part over time but they will not remove the continuing need for fundraising. In the meantime, we are having to limit the number and value of the awards offered and make difficult choices in prioritising who can and who cannot be supported.'

In keeping with other public schools, the 2016 Winchester accounts show that income from fundraising had fallen significantly. Across the country, school fees are simply not meeting the combined costs of education, bursaries for poor children and the maintenance of the ancient buildings. The truth is public schools are uniquely caught between their charitable obligations and the business of selling education to the wealthy. Marlborough College in Wiltshire, where boarding costs £36,525 a year, receives rent from the Cornwall village of Trevalga through a 'trust' set up by former pupil Gerald Curgenven, the last Lord of Trevalga Manor. Under the terms of the trust, Curgenven wanted Trevalga 'preserved and improved and, as far as possible, not sold or broken up'. By selling the houses, Marlborough would have been able to bring in more money to meet the growing costs of the school and its charitable commitments, but the residents refused to go quietly. They contacted two leading lawyers who had the proposed sale of the property suspended.[22]

Still, in 2016 the value of Marlborough's bursaries and other awards made to pupils amounted to £2.1 million or 6.7 per cent of gross fee income. Marlborough, in common with other old public schools founded before the twentieth century, has built up a complex fund structure of eighty separate funds, and the school is in discussion with the Charity Commission to simplify this structure so that it can free up more cash. But in terms of providing for poorer students, Winchester, Eton, Harrow, Christ's Hospital and Marlborough are the success stories. They are big enough and rich enough to support limited subsidies. The picture across the rest of the sector is much less rosy.

Take Stowe School. In 2016 just 7 pupils out of 800 had all their fees paid, compared with 12 from the year before. As Stowe candidly acknowledges, 'Fulfilling the promise of Stowe's Scholarships and Bursaries programme will require significant commitment on behalf of donors. Stowe, founded in 1923, is a relatively young school, and its endowment fund (valued at £6 million) currently provides only a modest proportion of the funding that we would like to make available to Stoics and their families. The rest must be found from fee income.' On the face of it Stowe is a wealthy institution with unrestricted reserves of £40 million, up from £34 million in 2015. Yet Stowe is not free to spend all these on charitable causes. Its 2016 accounts state: 'The company's unrestricted reserves are substantially represented by tangible fixed assets and are not readily available for spending.' The school wants to build up minimum free reserves of around £3.8 million out of operating surpluses, which will take some time.[23]

Andrew Turner, the deputy headmaster at Charterhouse, says the school's founder, Thomas Sutton, would find Charterhouse unrecognisable today. To return to its original purpose of freely educating all its pupils (there are 816 today) would require a colossal donation. Could the school ever be fully funded so that no student paid any fees? 'Not fully, unless there is a sugar daddy out there who's prepared to re-endow a school. There are people out there with that kind of money but I have not heard of a Bill Gates spending his money in that sort of way.'[24]

The truth is that public schools are either unwilling or, in most cases, so financially hamstrung that they no longer honour their original purpose of providing free education for the poor. Because bursaries are so costly, the choice of recipient has become very important. A free scholar who happens to be a top-class rugby or cricket player will add PR value to the investment.

Says Lenon: 'At Harrow when I started increasing the amount of bursary boys, not only were they excellent academically, but they were also very good at sport, so I could point out the reason we beat Eton at cricket was because we had two cricketers, one of whom I'd recruited from South Africa and the other from Zimbabwe on full bursaries, and incidentally both of whom played for the England cricket team in the past year.'

Lenon also sought out two exceptional rugby talents in Australian-born Billy Vunipola and London-born Maro Itoje, both of whom now play rugby for England. 'I recruited both of those and we won all the rugby and so the parents were delighted. And so of course I was doing it partly for the benefit of my school but also those pupils got a very good education. Maro Itoje got three A grades and went to university.

'Where would we be as a nation,' Lenon argues, 'in terms of cricket, rugby and all of these other areas, if independent schools hadn't taken the trouble to trawl the world to find these students, raise the money, give them bursaries, employ a cricket coach that was worthy of the quality of these pupils, and which led them afterwards to going on to British university and then playing cricket for England? The point I'm making is, these bursary boys did a lot of good things for my school, and the fee-paying parents [would recognise that] even though they weren't contributing anything.' This is controversial territory.

Schools that go scouting for pupils abroad may be depriving poor African communities, for example, of raw talent who would be assets for their own national teams. And while of course it is arguably better that at least some poor black and ethnic minority students are also benefiting from a privileged education, is this really aiding social mobility? This is what Channel 4's Krishnan Guru-Murthy was reported to have said on the subject: 'Employing black, privately educated women who speak nicely doesn't equal diversity.'[25] Conversely, white working-class kids often find it difficult to fit into a public school environment. The rapper

Professor Green was offered a place at St Paul's but rejected the whole idea of going to a 'posh' school.

★

Tony Little warns that public schools are facing huge challenges from state schools and the economy. 'It's a question for all private schools – do you seek to reduce the headline fee for everyone or do you recognise the fact there still are those who can afford it so you go for a higher fee [and offer more] bursaries. The ultimate aim, in my view, and this might be my perspective because I was on a scholarship (I was the first person in my family to be educated over the age of fourteen), is to be needs blind – you have enough dosh to take any child who is a suitable standard and would benefit from an education at Eton.' This is exactly the target set by Eton's celebrated headmaster, Sir Eric Anderson, in 2008, when he first warned of the dangers of only educating oligarchs and hedge-fund managers.[26]

But nearly ten years later Eton has more modest ambitions. Writing in the school's fundraising magazine in 2017, its headmaster, Simon Henderson, said Eton was 'committed to doing more' for 'those middle-class professional families, including Old Etonian families, who can no longer afford our full fees. These families have been the bedrock of support for our school over generations – they have provided the voices that have helped make Eton what it is today – and we are determined not to disenfranchise them. We do not want Eton to become the preserve solely of the rich and the poor and it is important that those in the middle appreciate that bursary funding is also available to them.'[27]

Only an American college like Harvard, which can call upon an endowment fund of £27 billion, can operate a truly needs-blind policy.[28] For Eton to be truly needs blind is, of course, an impossible dream: it would require an endowment fund in excess of £1 billion.[29] But it has become a useful buzzword, trotted out to mollify critics of the public school system.

*

A public school's claim to charitable status, and the tax benefits associated with it, is not solely dependent on how many poor or disadvantaged children it educates.

The second part of the 'public-benefit test' which the schools must satisfy concerns the contribution private schools make to their communities' education. In 2017 the ISC reported that 1,140 of its schools were 'involved in partnership with state schools... benefiting 175,000 state pupils'. This is an impressive claim which suggests public schools are shouldering a huge community responsibility. But most of these 'partnerships' amount to little more than allowing the state school kids to use playing fields after school, or inviting groups of pupils to attend school events. Some schools go further and send teachers to neighbouring schools to advise comprehensive heads on how to prepare lessons, or let their governors sit on state school boards.

In this way state schools are being used to help the public schools comply with their charitable obligations. This can lead to resentment from state school heads, who feel they are being patronised or exploited for charitable purposes. One head of a Surrey comprehensive told me: 'I got a call from Charterhouse asking me whether I wanted his science teachers to speak to ours about how they could improve their classes. I thanked him but said what I really needed was a Physics teacher to teach some of the classes while we waited for a new appointment. I didn't hear from the school again.'

Given the wealth and resources at the private schools' disposal, the current sharing of time and facilities looks paltry. More than

800 private schools have tennis courts, 633 have Astroturf pitches and 595 have swimming pools, while others boast state-of-the-art theatres and science laboratories. Even when they offer limited use of these facilities, one state head told me: 'There is a cultural chasm between us and them which won't be breached by offering up their heated swimming pool on a Monday night.'

At boarding school Ampleforth in Yorkshire one of its best-known former pupils, the radio broadcaster James O'Brien, says that he and the other boys were discouraged from mixing with the local kids who visited the school to use the first class sporting facilities. 'My housemaster told us not to fraternise with the boys from the village even though I was friends with some of them (because they had sisters). Ampleforth pupils, like many other public schools, use a special name, "grockles", to pejoratively refer to the common village folk who make incursions on the school grounds. When I was at Ampleforth in the early 1980s it was perfectly acceptable to call people peasants and plebs, long before the word chav was invented… this was the worst offence you could commit in a public school, to be in any way common.'

Nearly thirty years later this public school contempt for the lower social order was exposed for all to see when Conservative chief whip Andrew Mitchell (he attended Rugby School where his nickname was 'Thrasher') referred to two police officers as 'plebs'. Mitchell's scorn is mimicked in the schools. In 2017 a rugby game between a top south London private school, Whitgift, which charges day fees of about £20,000 a year, and a local state school, which has taken place every year since the 1960s, was abandoned over fears it was descending into a class war, with scuffles and so-called chav chants. It was a sad indictment of relations between the two school sectors who rarely meet on the playing field. Private schools tend to treat sporting competition as a closed shop, choosing to compete against each other in their own leagues and for their own cups. It seems parents would rather travel hundreds of miles to cheer on their children playing another public school than have to share the touchline with supporters of the local comprehensive.

Only very few public schools have put their support for their community state school on a legal footing by sponsoring an academy or comprehensive. According to the ISC, 116 of its schools have entered into a sponsorship or 'federation' relationship with an academy school. A federation is a much looser arrangement than a sponsorship – only thirty-nine public schools are involved in the latter.

In 2011 education minister Michael Gove addressed Wellington College's Festival of Education where he accused major public schools of being too worried about their reputations to pledge support. His criticism drew a response that exposed the entrenched position of the independent schools on the issue as well as their instinctive antagonism to government pleas for help. According to a report, one teacher from Sevenoaks School stood up and said to Gove: 'You have issued a challenge upon successful schools in the independent sector to sponsor a school in the state sector, would you ask the same of successful schools in the state sector to sponsor a failing school in the independent sector?' The question received an amused ripple of applause.[30]

Part of this ingrained hostility is borne out of a misguided belief that it's the public schools which deserve state support. After all, it was not long ago that public funds seemed to be flowing from the state to the private sector, rather than in the other direction. In 1995, Eton College was awarded a £4.6 million grant from the National Lottery for a state-of-the-art sports complex and athletics stadium to add to its two swimming pools and fifty-odd football, rugby and cricket pitches. The stadium now takes pride of place in its offering to parents with athletically gifted children. And as recently as 2017 the government was funding some private schools to support their local state schools, which of course counts towards their charitable contribution. Over a three-year period between 2014 and 2017 the Department for Education invested £175,000 in a partnership scheme between private and state schools. Among the private schools taking part were Merchant Taylors', King's School Canterbury, Shrewsbury School and Thomas's Kensington, one of the group of London prep schools attended by Prince George which charge £6,000 a term. In a Freedom of Information response the Department for Education told me: 'The aim was to raise the standard of teaching and learning in key subject areas in state schools, and those schools were the beneficiaries of the funding. However, in most cases the funding itself was routed through the independent schools.'[31] In one case the money was used to buy a state-of-the-art laser cutter sited at a private prep school in Norfolk. Many will wonder why the state is paying wealthy private schools to do what they once did for free.

Perhaps the most salutary of sponsorship tales is that of Dulwich College, which pulled out of academy sponsorship in 2014 after recognising it was not equipped to help pupils at a state comprehensive. Ralph Mainard, a deputy master at Dulwich who was then chair of the Isle of Sheppey Academy in Kent, candidly admitted that his school was not up to the job of supporting a school whose pupils come from very different backgrounds. He accepted that Dulwich could not 'move the academy at the speed and depth that needs to be achieved', adding, 'You need people who have a lot of maintained sector experience to actually come and work on the Isle of Sheppey. If you look at teachers out of independent schools, particularly schools like Dulwich – a selective all-boys school in the south-east of London – our teachers are appointed to deal with that market.' Mainard concluded that 'the profile of the students on the Isle of Sheppey is very different and there are certain points when you need people who understand that profile and how to help that profile.' The subsequent Ofsted report came to the same conclusion when it reported in 2014.[32]

In 2016 Sir Michael Wilshaw, Ofsted's former chief inspector, took a side swipe at Dulwich, when he gave a speech which showed that he had finally lost patience with the slow progress in closing the inequality gap. He told a conference on social mobility: 'I get quite angry when I hear independent school heads saying "inequality is getting worse, we've got to do something" and wringing their hands. Well, we know that. So get stuck in and sponsor an academy. I think they should lose their tax subsidies and the reliefs they get from the Charity Commission unless they sponsor an academy and show that they really mean what they say.'

From a free-market perspective it makes little sense for public schools to invest resources into making competitor state schools better so that the parents will no longer need to educate their children privately. Indeed, this was exactly the position held by a senior member of the Independent Schools Bursars' Association, according to Wilshaw.[33]

Asked about the partnerships and scholarships that private schools currently offer, Wilshaw derided them as a sop. He said: 'It's a way of meeting the demands of the Charity Commission and not much else. I say this, really, in a sense of moral outrage, that they are opening up all these independent schools in Dubai and the Middle East and elsewhere – sucking in more of our teachers, who aren't going to Derby or Northampton or Grimsby or Hull, but going off to an independent school sponsored by the big public schools over here. It's a sense of moral outrage that they're not doing enough for our own poor children.' Wilshaw is now working for a chain of fee-paying schools based in the Middle East and India which also employ some British-trained teachers, while Dulwich's international chain of overseas schools goes from strength to strength.[34]

Andrew Adonis, a former education minister under Tony Blair, added his voice to the chorus of disapproval in December 2017 when he said schools like Dulwich and Westminster were 'seriously off the rails' in terms of working with state schools.[35]

But Joe Spence, the headmaster of Dulwich College, strongly believes that one way his school can effectively fulfil its community duties is by partnering with local schools.[36] He says he was naive to let the Isle of Sheppey venture pass without challenging the idea it was a failure: 'Perhaps the biggest mistake I have made at Dulwich College is letting go unchallenged a single unfounded lazy press comment which said, "Dulwich College pulled out of the Sheppey Academy because it realised it couldn't support a state school." But the truth was that we actually gave five years to establishing a school that wouldn't have been built had we not kept lobbying for it. That we established a quality of education on the Isle of Sheppey that it hadn't had. That we kept involved until it became apparent that we did not have the resources [teachers] to effect the social transformation rather than the educational intervention that was needed. It would have been ignorant and arrogant to believe that we could have carried on in that way. What we could do was go into partnership with one of the big academy chains that we believed had the ethos and the resources to make a difference. So we had a beauty parade of a number of the big academy chains and talked to them about whether they would take over as a sponsor and we would remain as education partner.'

Oasis Community Learning (which runs forty-nine academies all over the country) was chosen.

'All we did was say that Isle of Sheppey has a particular socio-economic need – we carried on providing support. There was an element of naivety in my engagement then, in believing that we could have worked in that sort of partnership with Oasis. They didn't need us as a partner, they did it the Oasis way. It wasn't a question of us failing; it was a question of us knowing that we could do better as we do in other work with our state school partners, including Southwark School Learning Partnership and

E-ACT's City Heights Academy in Tulse Hill where we have the advantage of geographic proximity and a less prescriptive model.'

Spence estimates the school directly spends over £200,000 on helping state schools in addition to the £3 million spent on bursaries.

Like all successful enterprises, sponsorships require hard cash and should be much more than the lending of facilities. Eton has invested £500,000 in Holyport College,[37] a state boarding school in Berkshire which gets very good GCSE and A-level results and is now heavily oversubscribed. But there is one public school whose financial investment dwarfs all others. The Wellington Academy was the first in the country to take its name from an independent school – the world-renowned Wellington College, founded as a national monument to the Duke of Wellington by Queen Victoria in 1859. Wellington College sunk a £2 million endowment into the foundation for the benefit of its state-sector pupils. Two years after it opened in 2009, the academy was given an 'Outstanding' verdict by Ofsted. The Wellington College master behind the sponsorship deal was Anthony Seldon.

He told me it is unfair to describe as 'glacial' efforts being made to broaden public school partnership.[38] 'Compared to twenty-five years ago we're at a vastly different scale but it needs to go far beyond the lending of tennis courts and halls for prize-givings.'

Wellington is the lucky exception which proves the rule: the track record of most independent schools on working with their state school neighbours is a familiar story of foot-dragging and over-claiming. Tricia Kelleher, principal at Stephen Perse Foundation in Cambridge, said that 'the reality is that many schools in the sector do not have the wherewithal to undertake such a project in any meaningful way,' adding that 'creating an academy with a "posh" brand does not in itself guarantee an improvement in the education offered by the school or the possible life chances of its students.'[39]

Public concern that private schools were bad neighbours to the state schools first gathered pace after the Second World War and sharpened with the public school inquiries commissioned by Harold Wilson. In the 1990s and throughout Blair's premiership, education ministers and public school leaders continued to skirmish over the issue, culminating in the defeat of the Charity Commission by the Independent Schools Council in 2011. But battle recommenced under Theresa May, who on the first day of her premiership in July 2016 identified private schools as fair game: 'If you're at a state school, you're less likely to reach the top professions than if you're educated privately... As we leave the European Union, we will forge a bold new positive role for ourselves in the world, and we will make Britain a country that works not for a privileged few, but for every one of us.'[40] When the Conservative manifesto appeared in May the following year, there were concrete plans in place to make at least one hundred public schools sponsor a state school or risk losing their charitable status.[41]

Given all the criticism and negative publicity public schools face when trying to live up to their charitable status, it begs the question: why do they bother? The reason simply boils down to money: the UK spends more on private education than any other country in the developed world.[42] £9 billion is generated in school fees, a further £760 million comes from endowments and donations and another £200 million is given by government.

By securing charitable status, schools can claim a host of tax advantages not available to schools which are run as businesses. And the savings are staggering. A report by the Fabian Society in 2010 suggested that introducing VAT on private school fees (estimated to be £9 billion) could raise around £1.5 billion annually.[43]

A 2017 report using data obtained under the Freedom of Information Act found that private schools could also have expected to pay £1.16 billion in business rates between 2017 and

2022. But because public schools are charities they will pay just £634.26 million, equating to a £525.74 million saving. Eton, for example, which educates prime ministers and members of the royal family, will save an estimated £4.1 million in business rates in those five years. Yet state schools, which are not charities and do not receive fee incomes, must pay the full rate. The company of business-rate specialists which conducted the research concluded: 'It cannot be right that state schools pay normal business rates but 56 per cent of private schools, using charitable status, receive 80 per cent discount. As the overall tax burden continues to rise, businesses – particularly small and medium-sized enterprises – must have the confidence that fairness is at the heart of the tax system.'[44]

A school charity is also exempt from UK tax on most types of investment income and of course does not have to pay corporation tax of 19 per cent, which means every penny of profit a public school makes is tax free. Accountants have conservatively estimated that the annual tax liability on profits and investments could be in the region of another £500 million, particularly since many of our public schools run multi-million-pound corporate and hospitality event businesses or rake in cash from overseas campuses or online learning enterprises.[45] These activities can all operate as a wholly owned trading subsidiary. The subsidiary then gives its profits to the parent charity under gift aid, and thus avoids paying any tax on these profits. This is not some elaborate avoidance scheme – it is standard practice, and is happily accepted by HM Revenue & Customs. Donations to charity schools also benefit from the gift-aid savings, allowing the school to increase the value of the donations by 20 per cent. So overall the annual tax saving for the public school charitable sector is well on the way to £2.5 billion, enough to build 100 state secondary schools.

*

It's not just the schools themselves that can exploit tax laws to reduce the cost of education. There is a whole industry of school fees advisers to help parents further reduce the cost of private education. One firm promises: 'Good advice may reduce the cost of education by 50 per cent or more and ensure that your child completes their independent education regardless of a change in circumstances.'[46]

Financial advice website This is Money has discovered a 'litany of tactics used by rich parents to shrink the tax bill' – all of which are perfectly legal. Its report says that: 'Most of these won't be used by those with middle incomes. They often require huge lump sums, rich relatives or expensive financial advice that could not be justified for those without considerable wealth. But, for the richest parents, there are myriad ways to bring down the costs of an exclusive education.' The authors add that 'although technically doing nothing wrong, some of the tactics will raise questions about why taxpayers are at times effectively helping to subsidise the school fees of the most elite.'[47]

Most schools offer a 'fees in advance scheme' which gives parents a discount on fees because the money paid up front is invested in a financial product that generates generous tax-free interest rates. This is Money says: 'They involve parents and schools collaborating so they both benefit from the school's charitable status – which comes with special tax breaks.' Another ploy tax advisers suggest is setting up a family business and naming the children as shareholders. This scheme works particularly well if there are wealthy grandparents who are willing to help with their grandchildren's education. The fees are paid out of the company's dividends. The scheme works because children are also entitled to a tax-free annual allowance worth nearly £10,000. Wealthy families can also invest in offshore bonds. Each bond is divided into several smaller policies which in turn funds the child's school fees for a single term. Because the children are the beneficiaries, the scheme is tax-free.

Wealthy families can also invest lump sums in offshore bonds. The parents name themselves as trustees and the children the beneficiaries. The parents then split the bond up into a number of different policies – enough to pay out for each term of school fees. By assigning the policies to the children, the tax on the gain will be payable by the child – and not by the parent. Since the gain will be within their personal allowance, it will be tax free.

Private school fees might be paid by a big company on behalf of its senior executives, so that the schooling of the chief executive's children becomes another perk, or benefit in kind, that escapes full taxation. And pension funds can be deployed to further cut the costs because parents can make use of their pension by taking a quarter tax free when they reach fifty-five. With all these charitable tax breaks and such creative accounting, rich families can hugely reduce the cost of their children's school fees. The schools still get paid and the only person to take a hit is the taxman. For decades some of Britain's wealthiest families have exploited these tax loopholes.

The issue was first publicly called into question in 1969 by the Newsom Commission on private education reform. Public schools are quick to point out that by paying for their children's education, parents and private schools are saving the state millions of pounds in education costs that would otherwise have to be picked up by the state. It is an old argument that curried little favour in the 1960s when Sir John Newsom was trying to establish the real purpose of public schools. The commissioners, many of whom were headmasters or governors of public schools, said: 'We are not impressed by the argument sometimes heard that parents paying school fees are paying twice for their children's education – once through fees and again through rates and taxes for the maintained schools which they are not using. Every taxpayer and ratepayer contributes towards public services, whether he or she uses them or not. Fee-paying parents are, in this respect, in no different situation from single people or married couples without children.' But public schools do also benefit greatly from state subsidies. Most teachers working at private schools have been trained by the state. The independent sector takes around 1,400 teachers from state schools every year. And of course teachers' pensions are subsidised by the state.[48]

Today reform is back on the agenda, not just popular with Labour, who introduced the VAT reform to its 2017 manifesto, but also with Tories like Michael Gove. The Conservative MP for Surrey Heath has questioned how prestigious independent schools can justify taking lucrative taxpayer-funded subsidies when they cater to the 'global super-rich'. Gove wrote in *The Times* on 25 February 2017: 'There is one group of highly successful enterprises that is pretty much insulated from the present row about business rates. Our private schools. Because charities get an 80 per cent exemption from the levy. And, to my continuing surprise, we still consider the education of the children of plutocrats and oligarchs to be a charitable activity.'

He argued that VAT exemption on school fees 'allows the wealthiest in this country, indeed the very wealthiest in the globe, to buy a prestige service that secures their children a permanent positional edge in society at an effective twenty per cent discount'. Questioning how this could be justified, Gove asked: 'Are the children of the rich intrinsically more talented and worthy, more gifted and more deserving of celebration than the rest? Of course not. But our state-subsidised private schools continue to give them every possible advantage. Private schools have facilities, and provide opportunities, most state school students could scarcely envisage. And which most five-star hotels would struggle to provide.' Gove cited Millfield School's facilities, including an equestrian centre and clay pigeon shooting, two recording studios and a 350-seat concert hall. Stowe has a golf course and its own school nightclub, 'kitted out from the remnants of Crazy Larry's in London'.

Gove's antagonism is mirrored by another Brexiteer. Nigel Farage had been particularly critical of his old school, Dulwich College, after he sent his eldest son Sam there. He wrote an article in the *Daily Telegraph* on 14 March 2015 declaring: 'When my son was there, the social mix was entirely different from my day. When Sam reached the sixth form, he was the boy who came from the poorest family by far. When I was at Dulwich, rich families had holiday homes in Salcombe or Cornwall. When Sam was there, rich families had holiday homes with yachts in St Lucia. The change reflected how the professional rich – the lawyers, fund managers and accountants – had become massively, massively richer over the last twenty-five years.'

Farage, an ex-City broker whose father was also a stockbroker, complained that 'there was no boy in Sam's year whose father was a coal merchant in Penge because successive governments, after I left, began to take away the local authority grants to pay for able, poor kids to go to Dulwich. The college did try to build its scholarship system up, but could not get the numbers to the previous scale because of the cost. In reality, Dulwich just could not match the sheer volume of money that was coming from the government. Now, the government spends the same amount of money to send kids to schools where they achieve far less of their true potential.[49]

Gove was more concerned with the uncaptured tax than local authority grants. 'The fees for these schools are all more than £30,000 per year, per pupil. Well above the average annual salary of most Britons. They are out of reach for all save the very wealthy, or most fortunate. And yet they are all registered charities with huge tax exemptions. Why provide such egregious state support to the already wealthy?' Gove said the money raised from ending these tax advantages 'could be redeployed to help the most vulnerable children of all – those taken into care'.

The Tory politician who chairs the influential House of Commons education committee also has private schools in his sights. Robert Halfon MP, who was educated at Highgate School, told me it's time to seriously consider ending the tax breaks for public schools. 'I am passionate about social justice and I do believe private schools should do more to give opportunities to the most deprived children.' He has proposed making them pay a levy which would go towards sending children from deprived backgrounds to private school, an idea supported by Andrew Adonis.

The definition of charitable purpose has hardly changed since Wykeham founded the first public school in 1382. Yet English public schools of today bear no resemblance to the institutions set up to train poor boys for the clergy. They either can't or won't take any great numbers of poor students, and their commitment to the local community often extends no further than allowing others to pass through their grounds without calling the police. Instead of teaching children of the local poor, our public schools now cater for the sons and daughters of oligarchs and princelings, who use the schools to launder their reputations by buying seats at the heart of the British establishment.

16

ALL THAT GLITTERS

James O'Brien is a successful radio show host and television presenter. His no-nonsense, straight-talking interviewing style has helped him build a base of hundreds of thousands of loyal fans. The Tory MP Nadine Dorries is not one of them.

In March 2017 she took to Twitter to complain that O'Brien had blocked her over their differing views on Brexit. She is an ardent Brexiteer – he isn't. Dorries became so incensed by O'Brien's refusal to engage that she launched a public attack on his private education, tweeting: 'Well James O'Brien the journalist has blocked me. Is that how supposedly impartial journalists operate at LBC by blocking MPs?', later adding, 'to be fair, I think the fact that O'Brien is a public school posh boy fuck wit, has more to do with it than his being a journo'.[1] In a further tweet she suggested that his public school contacts must have helped him get his job as a presenter on the BBC's *Newsnight*.

Dorries' assertion that O'Brien was privately educated is true. He attended the Catholic boarding school Ampleforth College, before following his father into journalism and landing a job as editor of the William Hickey gossip column on the *Daily Express*. And O'Brien, who has previously referred to himself on air as a 'champagne socialist', happily acknowledged his pedigree schooling. But he also made the observation that Dorries had chosen to send her own daughter to Ampleforth.

The charge against Dorries, who has also called out Cameron and Osborne as 'arrogant posh boys', was of rank hypocrisy. Yet Dorries refused to recognise the irony and instead fired off another tweet saying that she was proud to have sent *both* her daughters to Ampleforth, where she said they had learned very good manners.[2]

Dorries is, of course, not the first public figure to subconsciously distance themselves from the personal decisions they have made about their own children's education. David Dimbleby famously tried to embarrass Jacob Rees-Mogg over his schooling when they were discussing Rees-Mogg's support for the expansion of Heathrow Airport on the BBC's *Question Time* in December 2015. When Rees-Mogg said he had been to school in the area close to the airport, Dimbleby interrupted the Tory politician to tell the audience that the school he was referring to was Eton. But Rees-Mogg drew uproarious applause when he coolly reminded the veteran BBC presenter that he had attended Eton at the same time as Dimbleby's own son.[3]

Public schools have a mesmerising influence over British people. Parents recognise on one level that by paying up to £42,000 a year they are securing an unfair advantage for their children, but at the same time they do not believe they should be held personally responsible for that decision. Who doesn't want the best for their children?

Even the singer-songwriter Paul Weller, whose work includes 'Eton Rifles', an extraordinarily well-observed satire of how the rest of society views the public schoolboy, ended up sending his five children to public schools, although not to Eton. It's an odd decision for a man who was a voice of Red Wedge, the music and arts movement of the Labour Party, and once complained to *The Observer* about an 'invisible establishment' and 'the big money people elite'.[4] A much more relaxed Weller told *The Independent* in 2010: 'I guess you get what you pay for; my little lad's only four and the other day he was counting in French. It's hard for me to get my head round what is a nice school because I never experienced that.'[5]

Someone who has been much more coy about where their children were educated is Amanda Spielman, better known as the chief inspector of schools. Asked by *The Guardian* in 2018 where her two daughters went to school, Spielman chose to plead the fifth. However, a little light digging quickly establishes they both went to the same school as their mother – £24,000-a-year St Paul's Girls' School. If there's a job in the public sector where a commitment to state education is a prerequisite, surely it is the one where you go round the country telling state school heads how to run their schools.[6]

For those who have benefited from a public school education, it can sometimes overshadow their achievements, especially in left-leaning industries such as the performing arts. Harrow-educated actor Benedict Cumberbatch spent several years complaining that he was the victim of 'posh bashing' and was being 'castigated as a moaning, rich, public-school bastard, complaining about only getting posh roles'. Things got so bad that he even threatened to leave the UK for America.[7]

The most absorbing example of this apparent conflict between privilege and authenticity was played out by the actor Laurence Fox when he was threatened with legal action by Harrow after he spoke out about his bad experience at the school. Fox, whose family has attended Harrow for generations, was expelled shortly before his A-levels and vowed never to send his own children there. Yet when fellow thespians Julie Walters and Christopher Eccleston complained in 2016 that public school-educated actors were dominating the profession, Fox hit back.

He said: 'They should probably stop talking. I think people should keep pretty quiet about stuff like that especially given the money they earn…'

But Fox was also defensive about how the world saw him: 'I may sound posh because I went to public school but I don't feel particularly posh. I'm not married to someone who's posh, and our kids don't seem that posh to me. But you're always going to have posh people feeling superior and not posh people feeling inferior, so you want to be somewhere in the middle. So long as you get on with people when you meet them, that's what it's all about.'[8]

Appearing on *Saturday Live* on Radio 4 in February 2016, Fox revealed that his father, *The Remains of the Day* actor James Fox, was similarly kicked out of Harrow as a young man, saying: 'My dad had been expelled and his father had gone and been expelled. Most of us have been expelled from Harrow and yet we continue to send our children there. I didn't respond very well to the Harrow education, but I was a pain to them as well, so in the end we parted ways.'

In 2015 Fox and his then wife Billie Piper were still undecided whether to send their own children to a private school, even if they have ruled out Harrow. He told the *Daily Telegraph*: 'It's probably changed a lot since I was there,' recalling an era in which fagging, for instance, was still the norm. 'But I still think that public school wasn't designed for the modern world. Also, I wouldn't want Winston [his son] in a place where there are no girls. It took me about five years after leaving to have any real confidence around women.'[9]

This ambivalence reflects the feelings of many who have been to a public school. No matter how appalling an experience it was, former pupils find it difficult to break from tradition. So, while ex-public schoolboys and privately educated girls often complain about their own education it doesn't necessarily deter them from sending their own children to fee-paying schools. They may candidly acknowledge its flaws as a fair system of education, but their own children are the exception to the rule.

Even George Orwell and Alec Waugh, two of the fiercest critics of public schools, ensured their children received a private education. Orwell had reserved a place at Westminster for his adopted son, Richard, although after Orwell's death he instead ended up at Scotland's oldest public school, Loretto School, near Edinburgh. Waugh sent his two sons to his old school Sherborne, which he had so mercilessly savaged in his book *The Loom of Youth*. When it comes to the education of the posh, it sometimes seems a case of 'do as I say and not as I do'.[10]

Dillibe Onyeama, the author of *Nigger at Eton*, who suffered terribly from racist and sexual abuse in the 1960s, says he can find no reason that would stop him sending his own children to an English public school. 'Since private education is appreciated in Britain, I do not see that it should be faulted. If influence and monetary power represent the norm in a capitalist free-enterprise state, on what grounds should parents be prohibited from playing the game the way the cards fall? If I could afford it, I am not sure that I would say no.'[11]

The spell private education holds over British parents is difficult to break. When aristocratic families have a falling-out with the public school system they tend to send their own children to day rather than boarding schools. Gerald Grosvenor, 6th Duke of Westminster, had a terrible time at Harrow in the 1960s. His reaction was to send his own children first to state primaries. Yet by the time they reached secondary school age he had packed them off to public schools in Chester.[12]

The journalist and author Alex Renton has written very powerfully about the harm boarding schools does to children.[13] He was the victim of sexual abuse at Ashdown House prep school, whose former pupils include Boris Johnson. But although he has vowed not to make the same mistakes with his own children, he does not disavow private education, only boarding schools. All this shows is that private education is a hard habit to kick. When the disgraced Eton-educated Tory minister Jonathan Aitken faced ruin and imprisonment after losing his libel case against the *Guardian* in 1997, one of his first thoughts was how was he going to continue paying his children's expensive boarding school fees.[14]

Nick Hillman, a former adviser to ex-universities minister David Willetts and who now directs the Higher Education Policy Institute, thinks there might be a cultural fear of the unknown. 'If you have no family experience of state school education then it is easier to go with what you know.' And parents are fearful of rearing children who might turn out very different to themselves.

There are two notable exceptions to this rule, namely Anthony Crosland (Highgate) and Tony Benn (Westminster). All four of Benn's children started out in private schools but were removed so they could continue their education in the state system. Melissa Benn remembers how important the question of education was to her mother and father: 'At the beginning of our schooling, all four of us were in private schools. My two elder brothers were at Westminster and I was at Norland Place [where George Osborne went]. But then as my parents became more committed to the idea of comprehensive education, we were all moved to state schools – I went to Fox Primary and then Holland Park, my brothers went to Holland Park.'

Benn acknowledges the switch from private to state was difficult for her father and caused him some anxiety: 'I was put into the St Paul's entrance exams at eight and eleven and both times I passed, and the reason I was entered was because there must have been a residual anxiety within the wider family and perhaps my parents were checking that I was still developing intellectually. But I didn't go and I think I would have been a very different citizen had I gone there.'

Interestingly, she says her mother was unaffected by the destructive class attitudes of the time: 'My mother was an American, and she was tremendously influential, politically, in our family, and in her marriage, and she was a great supporter of the new comprehensive movement.' She adds: 'I'm very interested in the decision my parents made. They were morally courageous. I now know as a parent that the combination of adolescence and secondary school causes tremendous anxiety to parents. The year before last I went to speak to all the heads of Essex state secondary schools and I think the comment I made which had most resonance with them was when I pointed out that they not only have the pressures of running state schools but that they are dealing with young people during adolescence.' Benn spent many hours discussing education with her father, who she says hated his time at Westminster School. 'He was very interested in my daughters' primary school. They both went to the most ethnically mixed school, where we live, in the borough of Brent – and he was so interested in the idea of these seventy-seven different nationalities within the primary schools and he said it was extraordinary. And he would say he had a very limited education in comparison! And we would talk about the benefits of state education, and then I would say, "OK, so come on let's talk about the benefits of YOUR education". And he would say, "I didn't like Westminster", and I would say, "yeah but it clearly gave you the skills to do this and that", and so we did have honest conversations. I think he would have been quite pleased that I went to speak to Westminster students, which I did, but after he died.'

Tony Little, former headmaster of Eton and author of *An Intelligent Person's Guide to Education*, believes private education is the first choice for most parents. He says: 'Polls show that most parents would have their children at a private school if they could.'

I haven't been able to find concrete evidence to support this view. And it is a claim that is complicated by subjective and impressionistic reasoning. If the question is framed 'do you want your child to have the best start in life?' the answer is hardly surprising.

English public schools sell their £40,000-a-year places on the basis of their exam results and so huge pressure is placed on departments to top the exam league tables. Some of the teachers are leaders in their field and are involved in setting the exams (at Eton seven of its teachers set exams for courses taught to their own school pupils)[15] and so the potential for conflict of interest is considerable. But in one way the schools are already playing the system and not always within the rules.

Public school teachers play a key role in setting exams that are intended to be equivalent to GCSEs and A-levels, but which state school heads believe are easier than those on the national curriculum. One state school head, a former member of the Association of School and College Leaders, told me that the IGCSE was easier than the GCSE: 'When we realised this and realised why the private schools were taking it, we started getting our kids to sit it. But when the government cottoned on to how easy it was they stopped us doing it. Of course, they could do nothing about the private schools.'

In August 2017, three of the leading English public schools – Eton, Charterhouse and Winchester – were all caught up in an exam cheating scandal. Pupils had been granted access or had seen the questions before sitting exams equivalent to A-levels. A teacher at Winchester and one at Eton were removed from their posts, sparking investigations by Ofqual and the House of Commons education select committee.

If there is an element of double standards in those who decry public schools and yet privately educate their own children, it's also worth noting that, when it comes to scandals involving schools found to be helping their pupils cheat in exams, the reaction has been oddly favourable. Far from deterring parents from sending their children to these schools, it can actually reinforce the idea that parents are 'getting what they pay for'.

Mumsnet, the online discussion forum for parents, hosted a thread from 2013 to 2016 on the 'state vs public' debate. It reflected a wide gamut of motivations for sending children to public schools, but the overriding focus was on improving the chance of getting your children into a leading university and/or improving the child's life chances. There are other factors, such as childcare and added 'snob value', but these tended to be secondary. For wealthy families, where school fees attract tax breaks and are often part of a package of executive perks, the case for a public school education is hard to resist.

BoffinMum offered this advice: 'I've used both sectors for my kids, taught in both sectors and attended both sectors. I would say that in a lot of cases it's not really worth the kind of money schools are charging these days, unless there's a particular reason, such as the only other state option being completely unsuitable, needing extras such as boarding or extended days that you can't get locally, or a child being very musical or needing ballet training, and needing copious timetabled opportunities for practice. Otherwise I actually think the state sector currently has the edge for a lot of children.'[16]

One Mumsnet couple, who were both state educated, said they were well paid and could 'easily afford the fees'. Peanutbuttersarnies said: 'I've worked out that private education for both would be about £300k. With this money we could save and give them a deposit for a house. Or buy a property when they go to uni for them to share as their first property. So private education would need to be pretty amazing.'

As spokesman for the independent schools' movement, Barnaby Lenon is paid to advertise the advantages of a private school education. However, Lenon, the son of a vicar who grew up in a council estate in Sidcup and won a scholarship to a small public school called Eltham College, is passionate about how much a child can achieve at one of his schools.

He began his training at Holland Park comprehensive and after stepping down as headmaster of Harrow he helped establish a state-funded free school, the London Academy of Excellence in Stratford, east London, where he is chairman of the governors. It is an exceptionally successful sixth-form college which now enjoys the support of a number of public schools, including Brighton College, Caterham School, Eton College, City of London School, Forest School, Highgate School and University College School. The school has been dubbed the 'Eton of the East End'. Lenon has written about what makes successful schools in his book, *Much Promise: Successful Schools in England*, plugged by his former pupil David Cameron, who described it as a 'must read'.

Days before we meet at Paddington Station, Lenon informs me I'll be able to recognise him because he will be wearing red trousers. Lenon did not get to run one of the country's biggest and most famous public schools for twelve years without knowing what colour trousers he would be wearing seven days before a meeting. From the start, Lenon makes it clear that he considers 'public school' to be a pejorative term used by the media and 'socialists' to create an impression of elitism, top hats, 'fagging and buggery'. He prefers 'independent' or, at a push, 'private'. When we grapple with the etymology of 'public school' he says he can't be sure of what 'public' really meant at the time. The Victorians retained the word 'public' because it gave the impression they were still honouring the terms of the public endowments. Lenon accepts that most of the medieval foundations were established to teach the poor 'but they became successful, expanded rapidly, and their endowments were too small to educate all the other pupils', hence the introduction of fees.

For Lenon, the appeal of the 'independent' schools is stronger than it has ever been. He says that they offer 'first-class' education and high chances of access to good universities at a cost much more reasonable than many people think. 'The average annual fees for a day school are just £13,500… with pupils drawn from a wide variety of social backgrounds,' he says.

He argues that the choice of private education is so diverse in this country that it is almost impossible to compare institutions. The top selective public schools such as Eton, St Paul's and Westminster are a world apart from an establishment in the north of England with a total intake of 150 run by a husband and wife. Says Lenon: 'Most independent schools are not academically selecting. They will take whoever comes along, that's true of virtually all prep schools, and it's true of the majority of secondary schools. They're catering to those parents… who can just about afford to send their kids or can afford it with a bursary.'[17]

Lenon is keen to stress there are 'lots of myths' surrounding public schools which may deter some parents from sending their children. He says many ISC members run exceptional facilities equivalent to 'three-star hotels' where child welfare is at the centre of their service. Of course, state schools suffer from equal and opposite myths about teenage pregnancies and classroom stabbings. The main difference is that state schools, by definition, are more open institutions, accountable to the public via the government.

But as far as Lenon is concerned any political objection to private education has been rendered redundant by the introduction of university tuition fees: 'When you and I were eighteen, nobody paid to go to university, now they're paying £9,250 a year plus maintenance loans. Receiving, if they're lucky, five hours of tuition a week and so that is no more expensive than going to an average independent school where they're going to be getting thirty to fifty hours' tuition a week. In terms of the principle, which of course many socialists would understandably stick to, that principle has now been given away by Tony Blair and subsequent governments because now people over the age of eighteen in this country are paying for their education. So, I don't feel that there's any reason to apologise any more for paying for your education even if one felt inclined to do so.'

Anthony Seldon says that it is only people opposed to independent schools who think that parents chose them 'for snobby reasons'. He explains: 'In truth there is a whole variety [of reasons]. Most parents I meet want the very best for their children and if the independent school is the best in the area, the answer is fairly obvious.'[18]

For someone like the comedian Jim Davidson, who was brought up in a council estate in south-east London not far from where Barnaby Lenon grew up, the memories of state schooling in the 1960s are not good. He told me: 'I was the one Protestant boy in a 400-seater Catholic school. It was a secondary modern. They didn't have the 11-plus. It was horrible, all we cared about was playing football. It was just really rough. I mean the teachers were frightened to death. It was like the Bash Street Kids. They never did any homework and I didn't go to school a lot of the time. In the fourth year I hardly did anything – I went fishing most of the time. And I just sent them a letter with my dad's signature saying I was sick. Everything was geared not to learn. And I didn't get any exams.'[19]

After Davidson made it in show business he sent his first daughter to a state school. 'I got married and got money and then I sent my daughter to a normal school and she was as bad as me in a frock. She got expelled for blowing up the chemistry lab when she threw a match in the Bunsen burners. I got booted out of that relationship when my daughter was five months old but I kept in touch with her even until this day. And she lived with me for quite a bit. But she didn't learn anything at school.'

By the time his second child was born, private schools were a natural choice among the new social circles in which he was now mixing. His son went to 'Cheltenham school – which I believe he hated. And boarded there. I didn't want him to do that but I'd split with wife number two. I turned up to watch him play rugby but I didn't interfere. So he left there with various A-levels and then later on in life as a mature student – about five or six years after he left school – he went back to uni and got a degree in psychology. But now can't hold a job down, just does jobs to pay the rent. He wants to be a rock star, so he needn't have gone to school. He just needs to know C, F and G. He's very handsome and talented and he plays in a band – he doesn't make much money but I don't think he's bothered and he's very happy.'

Davidson now regrets sending his son to Cheltenham. 'If I'd had it my way he wouldn't have gone. I would have given him the opportunity but let him decide.' Davidson ended up paying for his second son to go to Hurstpierpoint College in West Sussex, although he later tried to bribe him into leaving. Davidson recalls exactly how he broached the subject: 'I said: "Freddie, go to a normal school that costs nothing and on your eighteenth birthday I'll buy you a Ferrari," and he said, "Actually Dad, as much as I'd like a Ferrari, I think a good education is probably more important." Now he manages a car sales department at Nissan.'

So why did he pay all that money on private education? 'Private schools just seemed the thing to do – if you didn't do it you were a bit of a lefty. All the people I knew sent their kids to private school. Even the lefty ones. Especially the lefty ones.' But he also wonders 'how many fathers that have split up with their wives are quite happy to pay for their kids to go to school because of guilt? And do they really think it's better? Because the wives want to punish the father – less money for the new blonde bimbo.'

Did Davidson think it would give his children a leg-up in life? 'I hoped it would. But it didn't turn out like that. I didn't know much about private schools – I didn't know much about schools at all, but you think you pay that money… What it did do is, they speak well, and they have good knowledge of things, and they're quite sensible, they're not "Jeremy Kyle" kids. So even if they're not the brightest (and I'm not saying my kids aren't the brightest), they're around kids who want to learn, and I think that's the difference. If you pay for kids to go to school, they tend to work harder because you say, "Look, I'm bloody paying for you to do this." I'm probably the last of the uneducated Davidsons in my family.'

He ends by saying proudly: 'Charlie is a lawyer, a member of the Carlton Club, and I'm meeting him on Thursday and we're both going to a Freemasons' lodge together.'

While one barely state-educated comedian has given three of his kids a private education, another highly educated public school comedian has kept his children in the state sector. David Baddiel went to Haberdashers' Aske's in north London, whose former pupils include comedy actors Matt Lucas and Sacha Baron Cohen, former Tory home secretary Leon Brittan, historian Simon Schama and F1 world champion Damon Hill. Afterwards Baddiel took a double first at Cambridge.

His daughter attended Camden School for Girls, where other well-known parents have chosen to educate their children, including the actor Emma Thompson and the education campaigner Fiona Millar. His son goes to the local comprehensive school. But for Baddiel the question of his own private education challenges assumptions people have about public schools.

When Baddiel started out at Haberdashers', his father, then forty-two, had been made redundant by Unilever. He told me: 'He eventually set up his own business selling Dinky Toys in an indoor market but he made very little money from that. So the only reason I could go to Haberdashers' was because of the direct-grant system. This meant most people there were richer than me, or rather their parents were. Having said that, Habs is a bourgeois school. We have in this country quite an outdated idea of our education system, which is that private schools are posh and everything else isn't. Whereas the truth is that, within the private sector, Eton and Harrow and Winchester and St Paul's are posh. Everything else is middle-class. Plus of course selective. So it's much more about middle-class aspiration than wealth or privilege in and of itself.'

Baddiel says that the public schools have helped immigrant families who may not have assimilated in mainstream society: 'I've noticed in going to read to schools with my kids' books now that some of the same kind of schools have a very large Asian intake. When I went to Habs, it was a very large Jewish intake (in fact I believe it had, unbelievably, a quota). The point about this is: if you come from an immigrant background, education isn't about class. Immigrant kids, whether Asian or Jewish, have families on their backs who come so recently from proper impoverishment and/or persecution that they are very very focused on their kids doing well. Indeed, assimilation itself gets channelled through education. If you can get a good education, you are British, and therefore, safe. And it's much more to do with that cultural need than a more simplistic one of wanting to rise in class ranks.'

He adds: 'Having said that, being Jewish has a particular spin here. Because people in the UK don't have much sense of what Jewish is, because I went to a private school, it is sometimes assumed that I come from a privileged background. I think that would not have been the assumption had I been from another ethnic minority. I was listed by Michael Gove, whilst he was education secretary, as being one of a bunch of people who went to private school and was now successful in the arts. The assumption therefore – especially as I went to Cambridge – is that I had been awarded advantages in life due to poshness.

'But I got into Habs and Cambridge because I was clever. It was nothing to do with money and still less to do with connections or position or anything else. But I think we have something of an ingrained binary simplicity as regards class in this country, and like to avoid complexity. Anyway, I don't think going to a private school helped me that much. The teaching was good, in some cases, and in others not. It was very focused on Oxbridge league tables, so a structure was in place to get you there which may not have been elsewhere (my wife, Morwenna Banks, who didn't go to private school in Cornwall, tells me that she basically had to get to Cambridge on her own). And from Cambridge I got into Footlights, which taught me how to be on stage and make people laugh for the first time. Although when I came out of Footlights in the mid-eighties everyone hated anyone from Footlights because alternative comics were kings. So I had to start again. But that's another story.'[20]

In raising his own family Baddiel is committed to state education and has helped raise funds for his children's schools. He told the *Sunday Times*: 'I give money to help things that otherwise would not happen,' adding that the gap between facilities in the private and state sectors was 'ridiculous... These schools do their best with not enough money.'[21]

Baddiel said he also helped pay for pupils to stage a musical and for eleven-year-olds at his son's north London secondary school to see a performance of *Macbeth*. And he has donated for basics such as Bunsen burners and whiteboards. 'If you do not have the basic things you need to teach the subjects available then the teaching will suffer. Inflation is getting higher and budgets are going down. It is getting harder and harder.'

Tom Utley, the wonderfully understated *Daily Mail* columnist, is more qualified than most to judge the pros and cons of the two kinds of education: Utley followed his father to Westminster School; he is a former prep school teacher; he sent one of his sons to a comprehensive, one to a grammar and the other two to Dulwich College.

He asked in one of his columns in 2007:

Won't the younger two resent me for making sacrifices for their elder brothers, which I didn't make for them? What can I say, except that when I embarked on this breeding business, I had no idea how much I would be earning as the boys grew up? All I've ever wanted for any of them – the fourth quite as much as the first – is the best education that my circumstances could provide at the time.

My left-wing friends (a lot of them privately educated) have also accused me of trying to 'buy privilege' for the two who went to Dulwich. But it's not privilege I'm seeking for any of my boys. All I want, like every parent reading this, is that our young should have the best chance we can give them to realise their potential, wherever it may lie. If that's a 'privilege' in the British education system, then it damn well shouldn't be.

As it happens, our second (privately educated) son is thinking of becoming a secondary-school teacher. That fills me with joy. If he values his education so much that he wants to pass on his enthusiasm to others, that's just brilliant by me – and to hell with Bentleys, flashy holidays or tickets to the Royal Enclosure at Ascot.'[22]

Jim Davidson has also had time to reflect on his decision: 'If I was a young man starting out again here's what I'd choose. If I lived in the country I'd like a nice, village school perhaps they can walk to – a good happy atmosphere. And then you start to plan for secondary school. And I'd bring them into it. I said to my granddaughter, "Would you like to go to a school that specialises in dancing?" She said, "No, because then that is all that I will have." But at least the conversation was had… But I wouldn't want them to leave school at fifteen.'

He can see no reason to stop parents sending their children to private schools: 'If you can pay for it, you're loosening the burden on the state schools that are overcrowded and speak fifteen different languages. The world has changed – if you go to a school in south London now, probably English is only just about the majority of people's language, so it's more difficult for people who speak English to be taught.'

Despite the financial cost, there remains a stubborn demand for fee-paying education in Britain, draining the state schools of willing and often very able students as well as highly resourced parental support. The public school industry benefits from cuts to state education, which have left many state schools forced to crowd-fund part of their pupils' education.

The ISC has been quick to take advantage of the state school funding crisis, saying that 'Conservative cuts' to state education have led to a 'dramatic rise' in the number of parents choosing private schools. And it warns that it will soon be 'essential' for parents to switch schools if they want a 'good education' for their children.[23] But how accurate is this claim? Do public schools really provide a better education than their state school equivalents? Or put another way, do they represent value for money? A number of academic studies show that bright students do well in exams whether they are sent to Eton or the local comprehensive.[24]

There is also plenty of evidence[25] to show that once you even out the playing field at university, state school pupils outperform their privately educated counterparts. This suggests that the quality of teaching isn't any better in the private sector. Parents are really paying for smaller classes, a nannying support service and a place in the privilege network. Private school parents recently complained that the hot-housing of pupils to achieve good exam marks left their children with 'knowledge gaps' because there was no time for reading around the subjects.[26] Recent school league tables have also seen private schools lose out to better-performing state schools.

The 2017 *Sunday Times* school league tables saw fifteen private schools, including famous names such as Cheltenham Ladies' College and London's Godolphin & Latymer 'crash' out of the elite table. The results prompted Professor Alan Smithers of Buckingham University to say: 'Parents will increasingly be wondering whether private education is worth it.'

Melissa Benn says parents should consider that: 'If I look at the people I know, one set of parents who have chosen state education and the other who have chosen for their kids to go private, their children pretty much end up at the same universities if their families are from the same social class. (Private schools might have the edge in terms of Oxbridge entry, given their smaller class sizes and other privileges.) And studies show that children from state school often do better than their private school equivalents when they go to university, but they also become very different kinds of people and citizens, they go into often very different kinds of work, because, often, they have been socialised in completely different ways. And so my human perception of why parents so often choose private schools is their wish to get them into the right set of networks.'

The appeal of private education is made more attractive by state and tax subsidies. Diane Reay has been a visiting professor in Finland for five years. She says the Nordic model of community education removes the temptation of elitist education where she says 'less than 2 per cent' of their schools are private and even those don't enjoy any higher status: 'They can't understand why the most powerful people in society would want to segregate themselves from everybody else. This is because they have a strong sense of collectivity and community.'[27]

In France, where private education is restricted to the Catholic schools whose teachers are paid by the state, their politicians and judges are almost exclusively drawn from representatives of the national state education system. The same is true of Germany,[28] where the constitution forbids the education of children on the basis of their socioeconomic status and so their private schools cannot educate only the very rich. In both countries private education tends to be reserved for the teaching of children with special needs.

Reay says: 'It's become normative, accepted, that we have a private school system for the best and for the brightest. Of course people talk about the iniquity of their [private schools'] tax status but no one really talks about the damage they are doing to social cohesion, because it is the establishment which is segregating itself. This goes back to what it means to be a citizen and how different it is here… A good citizen should want for all children what they want for their own child. We don't have that here. Nordic countries still believe that. But our private school system has undermined that whole basis.'

A succession of British governments have let private schools grow into the behemoths of power and influence that they are today. But in a post-Brexit, populist world, an education policy of inaction may no longer be an option.

17

THE ENTITLEMENT COMPLEX

Is there such a thing as a public school personality which encapsulates both Boris Johnson and Jeremy Corbyn? Or one which links Philip Green to Richard Branson? What about Nigel Farage and Tony Benn? On the face of it these high achievers would appear to be diametrically opposed personalities. But they are all products of the same system. They have each spent long spells inside institutions where it was impressed upon them that whatever else happens in the world they must make a success out of their own lives. They are the chosen ones, plucked from the people to perform great things.

A public school education is a carefully constructed process which turns boys and girls into leaders of armies, political parties, multinational corporations and cricket teams. Pupils leave school with inflated egos, unshakeable faith in their own abilities and a craving for success. But this system for the self-selection of our leaders, which may have served us well in times of Empire and war (although, as we have seen, with some mixed results), may be damaging to a nation that is trying to come to terms with a more modest place in world affairs.

In an article published in the *British Journal of Psychotherapy* in May 2011, acclaimed Jungian psychotherapist Joy Schaverien first introduced the term 'Boarding School Syndrome' to identify a set of lasting psychological problems that are observable in adults who, as children, went to boarding schools. She found that children sent away to school at an early age suffer the 'sudden and often irrevocable loss of their primary attachments', which can cause 'significant trauma'. She reported: 'Bullying and sexual abuse, by staff or other children, may follow and so new attachment figures may become unsafe. In order to adapt to the system, a defensive and protective encapsulation of the self may be acquired; the true identity of the person then remains hidden.'

Another psychotherapist, Nick Duffell, author of books *The Making of Them* and *Wounded Leaders*, strongly believes there may be a real problem with this kind of schooling when it comes to the hot-housing of our leaders. Duffell has been conducting psychotherapy with ex-boarders for twenty-five years and is a former boarding school teacher and boarder himself. His pioneering study of privileged abandonment showed that sending children to boarding school is poor training for leadership. He says the issue is a complex one but his studies show that children survive boarding by 'cutting off their feelings and constructing a defensively organised self that severely limits their later lives'. He says that 'socially privileged children are forced into a deal not of their choosing, where a normal family-based childhood is traded for the hot housing of entitlement. Prematurely separated from home and family, from love and touch, they must speedily reinvent themselves as self-reliant pseudo-adults.' He calls the condition the 'entitlement illusion'.

Duffell argues that public schoolboys making their way in the real world are already damaged. He describes David Cameron, Boris Johnson, Jeremy Hunt, Andrew Mitchell, Oliver Letwin all as boarding school survivors.[1] 'Paradoxically, they then struggle to properly mature, since the child who was not allowed to grow up organically gets stranded, as it were, inside them. In consequence, an abandoned child complex within such adults ends up running the show. This is why many British politicians appear so boyish.

They are also reluctant to open their ranks to women, who are strangers to them and unconsciously held responsible for their abandonment by their mothers.'

Outside the confines of an all-male environment the public schoolboy can end up regarding women as trophies or exploiting them to achieve their greater goals. In 1988 Boris Johnson wrote a guide for aspiring Oxford University politicians in which he explained the best way to utilise female students. In *The Oxford Myth*, edited by his sister, he said:

> The Tory Reform Group [TFG] has the most social cachet of the OUCA [Oxford Union Conservative Association] machines, and its sherry party, laid on by its entertainment bureau, 'the Disraeli', presents rich pickings for the proto-hack. Lonely girls from the women's colleges, very often scientists, find themselves there and suddenly discover their own worth. Under assiduous courting, they become the TFG rep for St Hilda's or Somerville. Within a few weeks they are well on the way to becoming figures recognisable from English political life. With their fresh complexions and flowery frocks, they are the prototypes of local Conservative Party workers. Brisk, stern, running to fat, but backing their largely male candidates with a porky decisiveness they are vital people for the new TRG candidate to cultivate. For these young women in their structured world of molecules and quarks, machine politics offers human friction and warmth. The strongholds of this earnest middle-class Tory politics are in the women's colleges, Worcester and Christ Church. It would not have much chance of flowering in somnolent New College or the prickly bed of Balliol. It relies on discipline, loyalty and an unappreciated amount of political fervour.[2]

Duffell warns that with so many senior members of the cabinet from such backgrounds, the 'political implications of this syndrome are huge – because it's the children inside the men running the country who are effectively in charge.'

Duffell believes ex-boarders develop tactics for 'strategic survival'. He says: 'bullying is one; others include keeping your head down, becoming a charming bumbler, or keeping an incongruently unruffled smile in place, like health secretary Jeremy Hunt, former head boy at Charterhouse.'

Politicians like Cameron, Johnson, Gove, Osborne and Farage share an insatiable thirst for power and influence. In Victorian times such desire was tempered by the moral code of muscular Christianity. Today there is no brake. Jeremy Paxman, in his book *Friends in High Places*, came close to concluding that the modern public school is devoid of a code of morality and that boys are simply out for themselves. 'There is plenty of talk of Christian values but few have any idea what they mean in practice,' Paxman wrote in 1990, adding that it was 'scarcely surprising that there is widespread agreement that the current generation of public school pupils suffers from an inner spiritual emptiness and a lack of curiosity.'[3]

Three years earlier the headmaster of Wellington College, David Newsome, put it more candidly: 'When I observe the shallow materialism of some of the homes from which our boys come, and the glib expectation that a school such as mine will provide the culture, sensitivity and spirituality that are so flagrantly inconspicuous in the domestic mise-en-scene, I feel a twinge of despair.'[4]

But Paxman pointed out: 'It is quite different training young people for the old role of "serving society" and training them to make a lot of money.' One bishop whose pastoral role included visiting a number of well-known public schools had confided in Paxman that the idea of 'vocation' had almost disappeared. 'It's quite frightening,' he told the journalist, 'how selfish the pupils have become. They are overwhelmingly out for themselves.'

And John Rae confirmed this idea of an education devoid of moral responsibility when he wrote in *The Times* on 31 July 1987: 'Whatever their private misgivings, the schools endorse the priorities of the age: every man for himself in the competition for good A levels, a good university, a well paid job and red Porsche to roar up the school drive, scattering former teachers like nature's rejects in the race of life.'

This lack of moral vocation is clearly demonstrated by Cameron's class of 1984. As we saw in Chapter 10, only one of the forty-five Old Etonians went on to perform a community service or vocation in their later career. The one who did, entering the state education system, ended up leaving and teaching at a private school.

Will Hutton observed of Cameron in 2011: 'For him, politics is not about statecraft in pursuit of a national vision that embraces all the British. It is an enjoyable game to be played for a few years, in which the task is to get his set in and look after them and hand the baton on to the next chap who will do the same. The overriding preoccupation was to manage his tribe, now in thrall to the worst ancient Tory instincts which have been so consistently wrong.'[5]

Equally, George Osborne knew how to play his hand. It was a game that saw him become an MP before his thirtieth birthday, shadow chancellor at thirty-five and chancellor before turning forty. Achievements to make any housemaster proud. Having spruced up the CV, he picked up six more jobs in just a few weeks, including major conflicts of interest with his role as a member of parliament. There are rules that strictly regulate the movement of politicians from high office to big jobs outside government. But Osborne didn't bother waiting for permission from either the Cabinet Office or the Advisory Committee on Business Appointments (ACOBA).[6]

For Owen Jones, Osborne's seamless switch from Westminster to Fleet Street reflected the gulf between the unconnected working class and the wealthy elite.

Talented working-class aspiring journalists are discriminated against because they can't live off the Bank of Mum and Dad. With few exceptions, only the well-to-do can afford to do the unpaid internships and expensive journalism masters' degrees that increasingly must adorn the CVs of those with hopes of making it into journalism. Having parents with connections has helped multiple journalists, too. And yet a man with precious little experience in journalism – other than being rejected by the *Times*'s graduate scheme – can get parachuted into the editor's seat of a major newspaper because of who he is and who he knows. A cushy job for the ex-chancellor while the salaries of overworked *Evening Standard* employees are slashed.[7]

The extent to which Osborne's public school experience is responsible for his personal approach can be found in his blind belief in its product. He once told one of his special advisers at the Treasury that the quality of teaching at St Paul's was superior to that at Oxford.[8]

Osborne is, of course, not alone in trampling over the rules that govern public servants' behaviour. His friend and chief of staff, Old Etonian Rupert Harrison, left the government in 2015, also to join BlackRock, where he helped develop its retirement proposition. Given that Harrison was the one who drove forward the pension freedom reforms ushered in by the Tories, he was accused of a major conflict of interest. Although ACOBA waived through both Harrison and Osborne's appointments, others cried foul, including Labour MP John Mann who said: 'There is far too much cosying up to banks. It is as if BlackRock had taken shares in the Treasury.'[9]

Why do Harrison, Osborne, Johnson and Cameron find it so easy to help themselves to top jobs? The truth is a public school education not only gives a student a solid academic foundation, a burning ambition and a stellar contacts book – it also equips them with a range of non-cognitive skills which allow them to capitalise on their privilege and advantage. A 2014 study by the Social Market Foundation identified these non-cognitive skills as confidence, communication and resilience. The report concluded that such trained skills were thirty-three times more important in determining employment outcomes between cohorts born in 1958 and 1970 (the years when Cameron, Johnson and Osborne were at school). The authors said: 'A leading explanation for this is that jobs moved away from manufacturing to services, which require stronger non-cognitive skills. Other work has shown that social and communications skills, as well as physical and psychological characteristics, are becoming as important as formal educational attainment in determining later success.'[10]

But despite old boys appearing to embody stereotypical leadership traits, neuroscience experts say that the boarding school education is a poor training for leadership because leaders cannot make good decisions without emotional information. American neuroscientist Professor Antonio Damasio has conducted trials which show cold rational thought is less important in conducting negotiations than well-formed emotional calculation.[11]

Duffell suggests part of the public school temperament is a 'display of pseudo-adult seriousness' which he says is evident in the 'theatrical concern' of Cameron as it was in Tony Blair.

'It displays the strategic duplicity learned in childhood; it is hard to get rid of, and, disastrously, deceives even its creator. The social privilege of boarding is psychologically double-edged: it both creates shame that prevents sufferers from acknowledging their problems, as well as unconscious entitlement that explains why ex-boarder leaders are brittle and defensive while still projecting confidence.' Duffell says this is very noticeable in someone like Boris Johnson who is so supremely confident that he 'needs neither surname nor adult haircut' and who uses his 'buffoonery to distract the public from what the former media mogul, Conrad Black, called "a sly fox disguised as a teddy bear"'.

Johnson is not afraid of brandishing his elitism to enhance his leadership credentials. He exploits his training in classics and rhetoric to convey an aura of a divine right to rule. Duffell recalls one occasion which brought all this together in one act: 'On the steps of St Paul's, Boris commanded the Occupy [protest] movement: "In the name of God and Mammon, go!" Was it a lark – Boris doing Monty Python? Or a coded message, announcing someone who, for ten years, heard the King James Bible read in chapel at Eton? Those who don't recognise this language, it suggests, have no right to be here, so they should just clear off.'

This kind of language is not only out of step with a modern democracy but, in the wrong hands, it can also damage the national interest. Such was the case when Boris Johnson, now foreign secretary, arrived on a diplomatic mission to Myanmar. He recited the opening verse to Kipling's colonial poem 'The Road to Mandalay' while inside the Shwedagon Pagoda, a sacred Buddhist site. Kipling's poem captures the nostalgia of a retired serviceman looking back on his colonial service and a Burmese girl he kissed. Britain colonised Myanmar from 1824 to 1948 and fought three wars there in the nineteenth century, suppressing widespread resistance. Johnson's impromptu recital was so embarrassing that the UK ambassador to Myanmar, Andrew Patrick, was forced to stop him.[12]

To many of Johnson's political foes, his bumbling, erudite persona belies a steely ruthlessness. His former editor at the *Telegraph*, Max Hastings, had much worse to say about him after Johnson quit the race for the Tory leadership: 'Values, decency and honesty play a diminished part in modern politics – but the British people may be grateful that it is still a sufficient one to have halted the march on Downing Street of this dangerous charlatan.'[13]

Of course, not every public school pupil will succeed in the terms defined and recognised by their parents and peers. They will begin competing for places, prizes and scholarships from as young as seven years of age and spend an education acutely aware how much money is being spent on them.

Tony Little, in his valedictory interview before stepping down in 2015 as Eton head, warned that some parents wanted to live their lives through their children, creating pressures and expectations that may not be met. 'There has been a growth in some parents vicariously living their lives through their ambitions for their children,' he said. 'Some parents see where they want their child to be and when that doesn't happen, or the child doesn't want it to happen, it causes significant stresses.' His comments follow those of Clarissa Farr, who said in 2014 when she was head of St Paul's Girls' School that many parents showed 'frenzied anxiety' about success, leaving their children unable to cope with failure.[14]

For pupils from schools like Eton and Harrow, where every assembly and morning prayers includes a reminder of what their famous forebears have achieved, the fear of failing can be crushing. They will have failed because they aren't a cabinet minister, don't run a FTSE 100 company or will never act like Benedict Cumberbatch. In this way they are radicalised into holding what I would call extreme views about the nature of success and the extreme methods needed to achieve it. They leave school all pumped up, coiled springs of ego.

If they do not reach the very top, they will live 'wasted' lives. Tony Little concedes that 'disproportionately Eton kids don't tend to go into the public sector'. When Little was headmaster at Eton he noticed that the new generation of boys wanted to be 'entrepreneurs'. But, he says, 'in my generation it was much more linear than that, you train as a lawyer, become a judge. There was also a number who wanted to go into social entrepreneurship. Socially useful but running your own business. And that's a big change.'[15]

In terms of social contributions, Little says: 'It didn't matter whether they lived in a castle or a council house – being at Eton was a huge privilege for any boy. So they absolutely should give something back. I think they took that message and understood it. Quite a lot of twenty-year-olds would seek to do something well remunerated and the social bit kicked in later on. But if you looked at the ten boys in my house you'd be struck by how undistinguished they were. Maybe there's a public perception to push yourself that much higher now, maybe it ties into the Thatcher's children point – a general sense that there's a world out there to grab.'

The ambition of the top public schools for their pupils is impressive, but risks backfiring when those pupils encounter wider society. One Eton pupil in 2016 who had some of the best grades in his year experienced a grilling by a Cambridge admissions don that is becoming more familiar. As he sat down to his interview the tutor began by saying: 'Let's not ignore the elephant in the room... Eton has something of a reputation for breeding arrogant, posh young men. What do you think of this?'[16] This wariness of the stereotype may be already taking a toll on Eton's Oxbridge entrance numbers. Of the 260 boys who left Eton in 2015, almost one in four attained places at either Oxford or Cambridge universities. But these figures, while impressive compared to other schools, are the lowest since the school started keeping records.[17]

The ISC has begun to recognise that the pressure to succeed is sending pupils to university when they might not be best suited to academic life. Barnaby Lenon says schools must stop branding alternatives to university as failure and disgrace: 'I am sick of not particularly academic students saying they are going off to read English or Psychology – just because they have been told to. We need far better careers advice in schools that doesn't automatically tell you to read English at Exeter University.'[18]

★

Unfortunately, public school entitlement is a phenomenon not restricted to English public schools. Our former Empire is littered with establishments which have aped schools like Eton, Harrow and Rugby, instilling the 'public school personality' and forging dynastic links among the rich and powerful. This is particularly so in America.

The US private school system mirrors the English one in terms of paying for privilege. It's just a bit more open about it. American academics Jeanne Ballantine and Floyd M. Hammack have concluded: 'Those who can afford it go to elite private schools where they pay for the special "status rights" and social networks that allow for the "passage of privilege," and hope that this will maintain their children's privileged position or help them obtain a better job.'[19]

Donald Trump's private school is a legacy of the English public school system which exported a military system for educating elites.[20] Trump was born into a wealthy family. At thirteen years old his parents packed him off to the New York Military Academy (NYMA), spread across 120 acres in rural Cornwall, New York, located 60 miles north of Manhattan. It was founded in 1889 by Civil War veteran and former school teacher Charles Jefferson Wright when English public schools were in their pomp. At the heart of Wright's vision was a cadet-corps public school which combined the ethos of Eton with the military discipline of Sandhurst. Indeed, the military academy model has played a key role in the schooling of America's young society gentlemen. Central to its ethos is the building of leadership qualities. Today school fees at NYMA are equivalent to a leading public school in England, around £33,000 a year.[21] NYMA's famous alumni include the Hollywood director Francis Ford Coppola and composer and lyricist Stephen Sondheim.

When Trump was there in the 1960s it placed great emphasis on discipline and sporting achievement. According to Gwenda

Blair, author of *The Trumps: Three Generations That Built an Empire*, Donald Trump was 'in a place where winning really mattered, and he poured himself into doing better than everyone else at everything… He did his best to fit in, once even refusing to let his parents visit unless they left the chauffeur at home.'[22]

'He wasn't that tight with anyone,' said Ted Levine, Trump's roommate in their first year at NYMA. 'People liked him, but he didn't bond with anyone. I think it was because he was too competitive, and with a friend you don't always compete.' By the time Trump was preparing to leave, his senior year roommate, David Smith, said, 'Donald had a sense of how he wanted to be viewed. He really wanted to be a success. He was already focused on the future, thinking long-term more than present. He used to talk about his dad's business, how he would use him as a role model but go one step further.'[23]

Trump was educated at a school where many of the teachers were Second World War veterans and the discipline was tough. But the military Christian ethos of the school was merely perfunctory. Winning was everything and sometimes victory was achieved at all costs. Trump came out on top because he saw himself as a winner (he was 6 feet 2 inches tall and the baseball team captain by the time he left). Today when Trump looks back on his education he likes to focus on the quality of the teaching rather than the sports: 'I went to an Ivy League school,' Trump said at a 2016 campaign rally in St Augustine. 'I'm very highly educated. I know words, I have the best words.'[24] It's easy to recognise the 'thin-skinned, desperate-to-impress public schoolboy' in Trump the political leader who remains unable to let a single slight go unanswered. And it was NYMA which shaped his now-familiar attitude towards rules that govern the behaviour of everyone but Donald Trump.

But it seems even he recognises that so many years at a boarding school may have taken its emotional toll. 'I had very good marks. And I was a good student generally speaking,' Trump told the

Boston Globe of his decision to attend Fordham College for two years after NYMA. 'But I wanted to be home for a couple of years because I was away for five years. So I wanted to spend time home, get to know my family – when you're away, you're away right?'

The billionaire president has entrusted the same private schools with his own children's education, which he has used to groom the next generation in the Trump dynasty. For his daughter Ivanka, Trump chose the $56,000-a-year Choate Rosemary Hall School in Connecticut where President Kennedy was also educated. His son Barron has been sent to St Andrew's Episcopal School in Maryland, where fees are $40,000 per year. His two other children with Ivana, Donald Trump Junior (Buckley School, New York) and Eric (Trinity School, New York), and his daughter by second wife Marla, Tiffany (Viewpoint School, California), all received equally privileged and expensive educations.

The man most credited with influencing Trump the presidential candidate is the product of a very similar education. Steve Bannon, Trump's trusty campaign director and former Whitehouse chief of staff, spent his formative years at a military academy in Richmond, Virginia called the Benedict College Preparatory. The school mixed monastic life with a strict military prospectus that echoed the Christian morality of the Victorian English public school. Bannon continued his links with the school after leaving in 1971 and served on its board until 2012.[25] Both Trump and Bannon have built close links with Britain's public school Brexit brigade: Nigel Farage and Michael Gove were the first British politicians to be invited to Trump Tower in New York after the presidential election victory. When Bannon came to the UK at the end of November 2017 he held two key meetings: first with Farage; then Jacob Rees-Mogg.

Despite their privileged, private school backgrounds, Trump and Bannon have positioned themselves as outsiders, anti-establishment men of the people. It is the same tactic utilised by

Rupert Murdoch, the son of a wealthy colonial family, educated at Geelong Grammar School, the most expensive boarding school in Australia, according to Murdoch's own Australian newspaper. Geelong, close to Melbourne, was run along traditional public school lines, teaching classics, rowing and rugby. Its most famous alumni include Prince Charles who spent two terms in 1966 at its Timbertop campus in Victoria.

Murdoch has claimed that his sense of being outside the British establishment motivated him to tackle the vested interests of the country's ruling class. But the media mogul who now commands a dominant and influential position in UK affairs was himself a product of an elite education that drove him to surpass his own father's achievements in publishing. His anti-establishment credentials are critically undermined by his choice of further education, reading Philosophy, Politics and Economics at Worcester College, Oxford, where he stood for secretary of the Labour Club and managed Oxford Student Publications Ltd, the publishing house of the university's student newspaper *Cherwell*. And, like Trump, Rupert Murdoch has bolstered his own media empire by sending his own children to the world's top private schools.[26] But the arch-exponent of the art of attacking the establishment from within is Nigel Farage. When *The Times* investigated Farage over his EU allowances, the UKIP politician and his party (crammed full of privately educated MEPs and party officials) denounced the journalists as establishment figures by naming the public schools they attended.[27]

★

In his book *Learning Privilege*, the American academic Adam Howard explored the lessons students learn in elite schools about their place in the world, their relationship with others, and who they are. Howard argues that these lessons reinforce and regenerate privilege.[28] We have already seen how networks of public school-boys have a disproportionate influence on the government of this country and the generation of wealth in the City. Nick Duffell says: 'Since the major path to power in our society – via public school and the glories of Oxbridge – is still desirable and well-trodden, it has been easy for us to normalise this tradition and remain seamlessly accustomed to the entitlement it affords. For the most part our elite fail to recognise the degree and manner of their entitlement; some of today's politicians appear to believe they have got where they are by hard work alone.'

Do we want to continue with this system for choosing our leaders and those who mould our society and institutions? Nick Duffell doesn't think so. He argues that the institution of the public school is 'manifestly unfit for purpose'. Indeed, he believes that 'British elitism supports an outdated leadership style that is unable to rise above its own interests, perceive the bigger picture and go beyond a familiar, entrenched and unhealthy system of adversarial politics. Such a leadership style is not to be recommended. It may well be dangerous given the demands of the current world in which increasingly problems are communal – indeed global – and in which solutions urgently demand non-polarized cooperation and clear focus on the common good in order to take effect on a worldwide scale.'

This view is supported by Diane Reay, emeritus professor of education at Cambridge University. Reay comes from a working-class coal-mining community and taught at inner-city primary schools for twenty years. She told me: 'They are making decisions for the rest of us based on a very very slim knowledge base about what the rest of us are like: what our attitudes are, what our values are, what our needs are and how we live our lives. That is deeply problematic... because where you have people who have been segregated from the rest of the community there clearly is a lack of empathy and understanding.'

She says even her own students who had been privately educated betrayed a subconscious misunderstanding of families they had had no contact with. 'They would conclude that these parents were not caring adequately for their children and "needed to change" or were "bad parents". I think this comes from a background of where they have had very little experience of the working classes other than the people who service them. They are their cleaners, they are the people who empty their bins.'[29]

Many years on from serious accusations of amorality both in the curriculum and in the educators themselves, headteachers argue that the schools have evolved and are much more interested in educating the whole child in the context of moral responsibility. Even if this is true, it is little consolation to those of us who are being governed by the previous generation, especially where their unusual upbringing gives them little experience of the way the rest of the country lives, or, worse still, where the qualities that propelled them to leadership are not leadership qualities.

18

A CLASS APART

In the second year of the Second World War, the days of England's public schools appeared numbered. Britain was facing its darkest days, yet some politicians and reformers believed the malign dominance of the public schools was almost as serious a threat to society as the Nazi armies waiting on the other side of the Channel.

George Orwell declared that an entrenched system of private education was incompatible with a healthy democracy. He wrote in *The Lion and the Unicorn*: 'We could start by abolishing the autonomy of the public schools and the older universities and flooding them with State-aided pupils chosen simply on grounds of ability.' Even Winston Churchill conceded reform was inevitable and urged his ministers to find ways to flood the public schools with poor pupils chosen by local authorities.[1] But as we have discovered, this all came to nothing.

Britain is a very different place now. Rapid advancements in civil rights, communication, transport and technology would make our country unrecognisable to Orwell and the politicians of his day. But in one respect it is more familiar than ever: hugely disproportionate power is wielded by an elite group of citizens schooled at a select group of institutions. Indeed, there were more privately educated ministers in Theresa May's 2017 cabinet than Clement Attlee's in 1946.

In two decades of research the Sutton Trust has consistently demonstrated that the UK's top echelons of society are dominated by those educated at private schools. It bears repeating that public school alumni constitute 74 per cent of senior judges, 71 per cent of senior officers in the armed forces, 55 per cent of permanent secretaries in Whitehall, 53 per cent of senior diplomats, 50 per cent of members of the House of Lords and 45 per cent of public body chairs. So, too, 44 per cent of business leaders on the *Sunday Times* Rich List, 43 per cent of newspaper columnists, 33 per cent of MPs and half of BBC staff. A place at a public school increases the chances of picking up an Oscar or competing for Britain at the Olympics.

The public school system of preferment and privilege has evolved over hundreds of years and now operates as a parallel, stealth state. In 1969 this was how Harold Wilson's public school commission, itself dominated by privately educated heads, openly assessed the link between public school education and advantage: 'The public schools are not divisive simply because they are exclusive. An exclusive institution becomes divisive when it arbitrarily confers upon its members advantages and powers over the rest of society. The public schools confer such advantages on an arbitrarily selected membership, which already starts with an advantageous position in life. There is no sign that these divisions will disappear if the schools are left alone. They themselves deplore this. It is time we helped them to change a situation which was not of their making.'[2]

But successive governments, conflicted by their own links to public schools, have failed to tackle the problem. My research shows that since 1806 Edward Heath is the only elected British prime minister to have no personal involvement with the private education sector. Gordon Brown, who did not win a general election, is the only prime minister to both attend a state school and send his children to one.[3]

The public school business is booming like it has never boomed before. Latest figures show that more people than ever are benefiting from our apartheid education system. In the 1970s, after Harold Wilson's government had completed its investigation of public schools, only 311,000 children were educated at private schools (1.5 per cent at direct-grant schools and 5.5 per cent at fully independent public schools).[4] Today the equivalent figure has doubled. In numerical terms this amounts to 625,000 pupils and a further 32,000 students in countries as diverse as China, Kazakhstan, Russia, Singapore and Qatar.

The Independent Schools Council, the body which represents the vast majority of public schools in the UK, says that there are now more children being educated in its schools than at any time since records began. It means that roughly five million people living in the United Kingdom have been to a private school. Contrast this figure with the 2,708 pupils who were attending the nine leading public schools when concerns were first raised in Victorian Britain.[5] Then only 1 per cent of children of the relevant age group was educated privately.[6] Today the combined pupil population of those Clarendon schools is more than 8,000 (not including the foreign and expat students who are being taught by British teachers in overseas campuses). Which means that, 150 years after the zenith of the British Empire, almost three times as many boys (and an even greater increase for girls) are now receiving elite educations. In short, Britain has experienced a public school population explosion. To accommodate the record number of pupils the public schools are embarking on ambitious building programmes. Charterhouse (which is going fully co-ed in 2021), Roedean (a £9-million accommodation refurbishment) and Harrow (which is investing in a new sports complex) are good examples of schools that are increasing their capacity.

Two reports in 2017 highlighted the tight grip that the public schools still hold on the most influential roles in society. A study undertaken by the blue-blood society reference book *Debrett's* found that more than two-fifths of the 500 most powerful people in the country were privately educated.[7] This was followed in October 2017 by ground-breaking research undertaken by the London School of Economics, which discovered that the alumni of the nine Clarendon public schools are ninety-four times more likely to reach the most powerful positions in British society than those who attended any other school. This unique historical analysis of *Who's Who* found that these schools educate roughly 0.15 per cent of all students aged thirteen to eighteen but account for nearly 10 per cent of all *Who's Who* entrants. The report concluded that these 'public schools remain extraordinarily powerful, and any decline in their power has stalled completely over the past sixteen years'.[8]

★

In 1990, when Boris Johnson's Etonian friend Darius Guppy took a dislike to a reporter from the *News of the World* who had been investigating his business dealings he called up his old school friend for help. Guppy, who knew Johnson also worked in the media (*Daily Telegraph*), asked Johnson for the man's address so he could arrange for the journalist to be beaten up. In the taped conversation between the two OEs, Johnson agreed to find the address for his friend even though he knew exactly what Guppy was planning. Explaining his plan to Johnson, Guppy says: 'But I am telling you something, Boris, this guy has got my blood up all right, and there is nothing which I won't do to get my revenge. It's as simple as that.'

> Johnson: If this guy is seriously hurt, I am going to be fucking furious.
> Guppy: I guarantee you he will not be seriously hurt.

Johnson: How badly hurt will he be?

Guppy: He will not have a broken limb or a broken arm and he will not, er, he will not be put into intensive care or anything like that. He will probably get a couple of black eyes and a, and a cracked rib or something like that.

Johnson: A cracked rib.

Guppy: Nothing which you didn't suffer in rugby okay but he will get scared and that is what I want him to do, I want him to get scared, I want him to have no idea who is behind it okay, and I want him to realise that he's fucked someone off and whoever he's fucked off is not the sort of person he wants to mess around with. Because I guarantee you, Boris, I guarantee you these people are, you know, if someone hurts their boss or threatens their boss I promise you it's just total sort of, it's like they're like dogs, they are like Alsatians or rottweilers, they love their masters, they are affectionate towards them, they are evil bastards to everyone else.

Johnson: Yeah, yeah, good. Okay Darry now, yeah, I mean I but.

Guppy: You must have faith in me, Boris.[9]

Three years later Guppy was jailed for an insurance fraud committed several years earlier, which came close to being a perfect crime. He and an associate had paid someone to tie them up and fake a robbery in New York, so that he could claim £1.8 million in insurance. It was his revenge on Lloyd's, the insurance firm which had ruined his father during a notorious financial scandal in the late 1980s.

Public schools breed networks, not communities. The Guppy/ Johnson tape, secretly recorded by Guppy's suspicious business partner, is a very extreme case of the old boys' network but it illustrates the strength of the bonds between two Eton schoolmates. This perfectly understandable desire not to 'let the side down' can lead good people into bad situations, as C.S. Lewis understood: 'To nine out of ten of you the choice which could lead to scoundrelism will come, when it does come, in no very dramatic colours. Obviously bad men, obviously threatening or bribing, will almost certainly not appear. Over a drink, or a cup of coffee, disguised as triviality and sandwiched between two jokes… Just at the moment when you are most anxious not to appear crude, or naïf or a prig – the hint will come. It will be the hint of something which the public, the ignorant, romantic public, would never understand.'[10]

In the City and among our professions, where jobs are dominated by privately educated bankers, hedge-fund managers, lawyers and accountants, such associations create perceptions of injustice. What is said and done in the cosy dining rooms of gentlemen's clubs is based on a shared set of unwritten rules and values.

The London gentlemen's club scene grew out of a need for aristocrats and the wealthy middle classes to come together in smoke-filled, female-free dining rooms in pursuit of exclusively male pleasures. They quickly descended into dens of iniquity where drinking, gambling and prostitution were all part of the club's lively entertainment.

One of the most fashionable was Brooks's in St James's Street in the West End. Its gambling excesses are legendary, culminating in a story of how in 1785 Lord Cholmondeley placed a bet with Lord Derby that he would win 500 guineas 'whenever his lordship [fornicates with] a woman in a balloon one thousand yards from the Earth'.

Today these clubs, whose entry is still strictly controlled by the black ball, continue to honour some of their very un-PC traditions. To a greater or lesser degree they are extensions of the public school, an attempt to recapture a lost fraternity. Indeed, one of the most famous was named the Public Schools Club. But perhaps the most curious of them all, raising questions about the clubs' crossover into public life, is the little-known Beefsteak Club, located in Irving Street near Leicester Square.

In an earlier incarnation, its motto was 'Beef and liberty!' and members swore an oath of secrecy to the effect that 'what happens in the Beefsteak stays in the Beefsteak.' A similar aura of secrecy surrounds the club today. According to *Who's Who*, among its members are the disgraced former MP Brooks Newmark (also a member of White's; Bedford School) and the Tory minister Rory Stewart (Eton). Boris Johnson's father, Stanley Johnson (Sherborne), was a member and blocked Michael Gove from joining after Gove stabbed his son in the back during the Tory leadership race. An online version of *Who's Who* dated 1 December 2017 tells us that William Shawcross, the chair of the Charity Commission since 2012, was once a member. One of Shawcross's jobs was to make sure the public schools complied with their charitable status.[11]

These bastions of masculine entertainment can pose a danger to open democracy. It is the gentlemen's clubs of London where politicians, bankers and hedge-fund managers meet to do deals and form secret alliances. Because membership lists are not disclosed to the public it is impossible to tell when a minister proposes a policy that favours the interests of members of his club.

The vast majority of these old school tie connections remain hidden from public scrutiny. But in a public forum such as a court of law the dangers of relying on such a narrow group of professionals to run the City is laid bare.

In 2016 Luke Bridgeman, a Bullingdon Club contemporary of David Cameron and George Osborne, was accused of taking confidential client details when he left his job to join a rival firm. Bridgeman's former company, Marathon Asset Management, a leading London and New York investment manager entrusted with clients' pensions and savings, decided to sue Bridgeman for £15 million. The case went to the High Court where it was heard by the experienced Mr Justice Leggatt. After a three-week trial, Leggatt ruled that far from the documents being 'priceless', any benefit accrued to Marathon would have been 'extremely modest'.

So he ordered Bridgeman to pay just £1 in nominal damages. The case was a bitter blow to Marathon, which spent around £10 million in legal costs. What Marathon may not have been aware of was that George Leggatt, like Bridgeman, was also educated at Eton, although their school lives are separated by a decade.

The judicial rules of conflict of interest say nothing expressly about a judge sitting in judgment where both the judge and one of the parties went to the same school. But Leggatt, whose father also attended Eton, is not just any Old Etonian. In the same year he was presiding over the trial he was also nominated by the Lord Chief Justice to Eton College's governing body, where he was under a duty to promote and protect the interests of the school. Leggatt, in common with the other fellows of the governing body, made this declaration to the school: 'I George Leggatt do solemnly profess and declare that I will be faithful to the College of Eton, and do nothing detrimental to it, but will, to the utmost of my power, maintain and support the interests of the same.'[12] Leggatt is also bound by a judicial oath to uphold justice. So what was the judge supposed to do in this instance – uphold justice, or do his utmost to support the interests of Eton?

The Marathon litigation neatly illustrates the tiny pool from which the City and the professions are drawn. In 2017 there were 24,281 state and private schools in the UK. If the distribution of the judiciary and City fund managers was fairly drawn from all our schools, these potential conflicts of interest would be far removed.[13] But today people who went to private school dominate almost all walks of public life, including the media, the City, 'magic circle' law firms and the Bar. In the courts where disputes between the state and the citizen are settled it is exaggerated. Seven per cent of the population are privately educated and yet three-quarters of High Court judges come from private schools; half of them were at boarding schools, where fewer than 1 per cent of pupils go.

*

Descendants of Douglas McGarel Hogg, 1st Viscount Hailsham, have held down more top jobs in the law and the City than any other privately educated family. For more than 150 years they have sustained their influence and standing through the patronage of Eton and a number of girls' public schools.

Douglas McGarel Hogg was educated at Cheam School and Eton College before studying sugar plantations in the West Indies. After serving in the Boer War he was called to the Bar in 1902 and later, as Baron Hailsham, appointed Conservative lord chancellor and secretary of state for war.

His son is Quintin Hogg, an Eton King's Scholar and a scholar at Christ Church, Oxford, where he was president of the Oxford University Conservative Association and the Oxford Union. His ministerial career began in 1957 when he was made minister of education under Harold Macmillan and served two terms as lord chancellor under Heath and Thatcher. He had five children, all educated privately and with top jobs in the City, the law and Westminster.

The eldest, Douglas Hogg (Eton), became a barrister and Tory government minister. But his unwelcome claim to fame was to be named in the 2009 parliamentary expenses scandal when he asked taxpayers to foot the bill for cleaning the moat which encircles his fifty-acre country estate of Kettlethorpe Hall. His wife Sarah, the journalist and economist who became the first woman to head a FTSE 100 company, went on to take charge of John Major's Policy Unit. She went to St Mary's School Ascot and is a former member of the governing board of Eton, where she sent her son. Douglas Hogg's younger sister Dame Mary Hogg (St Paul's Girls' School) was the High Court judge who was criticised in the case of the murder of six-year-old Ellie Butler, whom she had ordered to be returned to her father.[14]

Douglas and Sarah's daughter, Charlotte Hogg, was also caught up in controversy recently. Charlotte, educated at the same prestigious school as her mother, had enjoyed a stellar career in the City before being made deputy governor of the Bank of England in 2017, the most senior position ever achieved by a woman in the bank's history. Indeed, she was tipped to become the first female governor when Governor Mark Carney was due to step down in 2019. But in March 2017 it emerged that she had failed to declare a potential conflict of interest concerning a member of her family: her brother, Quintin Hogg (Eton), also a rising star in the City, had been appointed director of Barclays Investment Bank Strategy Group.[15]

A key part of Charlotte Hogg's job was overseeing the regulation of the banks as well as advising on setting interest rates. But she hadn't disclosed her potential conflict concerning her high-flying brother to her employers at the Bank of England and when she came before a parliamentary hearing she compounded the error by saying she had.

The Treasury select committee, which had interviewed her after her appointment as deputy governor, was less than impressed and delivered a damning verdict. The committee's report found she had failed 'over a period of nearly four years to comply with the Code of Conduct, despite numerous procedural reminders and opportunities to do so'. Its report concluded that she had shown a 'failure to appreciate the seriousness of that history of non-compliance during her tenure as the Bank's Chief Operating Officer. For at least some of that period, as far as the Committee is aware, her brother was in a senior role at Barclays, dealing with important regulatory matters.'

It was difficult for Charlotte Hogg to defend her oversight. Even the society magazine *Tatler* had written about the fact the two Hoggs were working in the same industry when the magazine was touting Quintin Hogg's daughter as a prospective suitor for Prince

George.[16] Half an hour after the committee published its report, Charlotte Hogg wrote to the governor of the Bank of England, resigning her position.

It is hard not to feel sorry for Hogg because in one sense she was a victim of her own family's suffocating privilege. She would have been used to operating in a world where relatives and school friends already occupied senior positions of influence. If she had been forced to make a written declaration of a potential conflict every time her path crossed with a family member, she wouldn't have got much work done. For members of a dynasty like the Hoggs it must be difficult to know when a lunch or meeting with a brother, uncle, aunt or even distant cousin has actually crossed a line and represents a serious risk of conflict. It is only when an objective voice raises a question over these close connections that the obvious appearance of unfairness becomes clear. For this reason the City and its regulators generally turn a blind eye, given that the elite are drawn from such a narrow pool of schools and families.

Going to the right school is the start of the business of getting on in the City. In this respect the City hasn't really moved on since the days of the first London banking crisis of 1825 when a public school education was a non-negotiable prerequisite for a well-paid job in Threadneedle Street. Today, private education plays just as big a part in the recruitment of bankers and private-equity executives. In 2014 a report for the Sutton Trust by the Boston Consulting Group found that over 50 per cent of leaders of major banks and nearly 70 per cent of heads of private-equity firms were privately educated, while for new banking and private-equity recruits the figures were 34 per cent and 69 per cent respectively. Privately educated bankers tend to hire privately educated bankers, a situation even more likely in private equity.[17]

A Social Mobility Commission report into access in investment banking reveals why these applicants are likely to be successful. It found that hiring managers have a tendency to 'recruit for familiarity and similarity', and focus on perceived 'fit'. The commission concluded that this mounts a particular challenge for candidates from disadvantaged backgrounds, as it suggests the concept of 'fit' is often determined by 'whether aspirant bankers share a social educational background with current hiring managers'. Entrance is now so skewed that pupils from ten named public schools are one hundred times more likely to apply for the most prestigious business graduate schemes than their peers educated at the bottom 10 per cent of schools, regardless of which universities they went on to.[18]

★

In a healthy democracy it is incumbent upon our fourth estate to shine a light into murky dealings and diagnose the conditions that restrict open and fair competition in careers like banking. The media has shown little hesitation in blaming elites in general terms for everything from Brexit to the Grenfell Tower tragedy. Incestuous groups of fat-cat politicians or champagne-guzzling hedge-fund managers are held up as the cause of our national scandals. But there is much less appetite to investigate the overall complexion of these 'elites' or understand why a narrow privately educated class has been allowed to take charge of the country.

The key reason for this is that the media is muted by conflicted privilege just as much as the rest of society. Research carried out by the Sutton Trust found that half of one hundred leading journalists are privately educated. It also showed that the dominance of public schools at the highest levels of newspapers had actually increased since the 1980s.

The Trust considered editors at twenty-two of the country's leading national newspapers, periodicals and press agencies. In 1986, 41 per cent of those in these posts had been educated at independent schools, 50 per cent at grammar schools and 9 per cent at comprehensives. By 2015, 58 per cent were educated at independent schools, 21 per cent at grammar schools and 21 per cent at comprehensives.[19]

The industry has been unable to solve long-standing problems of diversity and pay gaps – especially since journalists have been reluctant to report on the shortcomings of a system to which they may owe their jobs. The elements of this conflict were partly exposed in July 2017 when the BBC was forced to publish a list of staff who earned more than £150,000. At first the media's fire was directed at the huge fees paid to BBC Radio 2 presenter Chris Evans and *Match of the Day* pundit Gary Lineker. Then attention was turned on the pay gap between the highest paid men compared to the women and the gap between white and non-white managers. The BBC's China editor Carrie Gracie resigned after she discovered she was being paid at least £40,000 less than the male international editors based abroad.

Only after the outrage had died down did it begin to dawn on one or two journalists that there was an even more serious problem that underpinned all the others. The big salaries were being paid to mostly privately educated men and women by men and women who all went to the same schools. BBC daytime TV presenter Steph McGovern said she had once been told by a manager she was 'too common' to be a presenter: 'It's not as simple as a gender issue, it's partly down to class. There are a lot of women who do a similar job to me who are paid a hell of a lot more… who are a lot posher than me.'[20]

One former BBC reporter who had moved on to Sky did his own investigation into the pay packages and the men and women who earned them. Lewis Goodall, who had spent five years at the BBC, including reporting for its flagship current-affairs programme *Newsnight*, found that forty-three of the BBC's best-paid stars went to private schools. Among the exceptions were Gary

Lineker and Chris Evans, who have both sent their children to public schools.

Goodall wrote: 'If we actually talked or even cared about this peculiar taboo, we might begin to see one of the reasons the gender and race pay gaps exist in the first place. Just think about that. If you send your child to private school it increases their chances of being one of the biggest names in TV and media by a factor of six.'

He added: 'The gender pay gap may be too large but it's not nearly as big as the class pay gap for the people who never made it in the first place because of their background. The injustice is pretty overwhelming: after all, are we really saying that those who are lucky enough to be born into households which can afford to pay for private school fees are six times more talented? Six times better imbued with the skills required to be a successful BBC actor, sports presenter or journalist?'[21] When grammar school-educated John Humphrys finally lays down his microphone, the entire complement of broadcasters (as well as the editor) of Britain's premier current-affairs programme will be public school-educated.

Former *Today* programme editor Rod Liddle says:

When I joined the BBC in the late 1980s I was astonished at the preponderance of public school monkeys: more than two-thirds of the people who worked on the *Today* programme were privately educated and five of them were from Eton. Not all of them were fantastically stupid but they nearly all subscribed to the same political agenda – a sort of self-effacing, if not self-hating, limp-wristed Corbyn-lite, which they thought was not really political at all, but merely an expression of well-bred civility.

There were one or two state-educated grammar school kids who viewed this anodyne morass with a certain contempt. And there was me from my comp. At the end of my first week I mentioned the high-born nature of the programme staff to a colleague, Justin Webb. 'Ah, but think how proud your mum and dad would be to know that you're mixing with people like us,' Justin replied with a smile, scything through my class chippiness with great elan. A good joke from a very good journalist. But my point still held.[22]

★

Today's public schools are perfectly set up to get the best possible academic and social results for their pupils. They use tried-and-tested systems to multiply the privilege and wealth that pupils bring with them to school. Given how far down the track these kids are before they start their lives, it's hardly surprising that they go on to land prosperous and successful careers. We have already seen how networking and unconscious bias can accelerate this success once students leave school and university.

But the most direct performance measurement for the modern public school is the number of its pupils who win places at top universities. This is because it is one of the most important factor for parents deciding where to send their children. And for some it means just one thing: can you get my child into Oxford or Cambridge?

In 2017 a dozen public schools in London and the home counties sent 500 students to Oxford and Cambridge, which that year had a combined intake of roughly 5,700 from state and public schools.[23] At Westminster School 44 per cent of its school leavers in 2016 secured Oxbridge offers.[24] One pupil at Haberdashers' Aske's in north London has claimed that so many of its pupils were winning places at Oxford and Cambridge (fifty-five per year in the 1980s) that the colleges tried to impose quotas.[25]

In 2016 the London school Merchant Taylors' announced its highest Oxbridge success rate for sixteen years. The school proclaimed:

An exceptional cohort of twenty-one boys received offers from Oxford (ten) and Cambridge (eleven) this year. This is the largest number since 2000, approximating to 15 per cent of the Upper Sixth Form and almost 50 per cent of all applicants. Our pupils have been offered places to read a range of subjects, including Engineering, English, History, Law, and Natural Sciences. Pupils can be extremely proud of their efforts, with the competition for places becoming more intense every year. They all grasped the enormity of the challenge and made great use of extension seminars and mock interviews, as well as engaging in sustained reading in their chosen discipline.[26]

At most state schools entry rates are meaningless because their pupils have never won a place at Oxbridge.

This disadvantage is compounded by the fact that many of the older public schools share long and esoteric associations with England's ancient universities. The public schools were founded as feeders to Oxbridge colleges. King's College, Cambridge was established in 1441 by Henry VI as a sister college to Eton, while Winchester College, our oldest public school, was expressly established as a feeder for New College, Oxford. Westminster School has similar ties to Christ Church, Oxford, and Trinity College, Cambridge.[27] These ties have been strengthened and formalised over the years through the government and stewardship of the schools. Eton's statutes still ensure that two of its fellows are senior members of Oxbridge colleges. Collaboration between the institutions is supported by the maintenance of links between the schools and their alumni who hold influential positions across the Oxbridge estate, including the admissions departments.

This incestuous relationship is one reason why the overall Oxbridge undergraduate intake from private schools is stubbornly stuck at 45 per cent. Of greater concern is evidence which suggests the state/private school attainment gap might be getting worse. Data released by the Higher Education Statistics Agency found that 55.7 per cent of Oxford's 2015–16 intake were from state schools, compared to 57.7 per cent in 2010. Latest figures show that the absolute numbers of state school students peaked at Oxford in 2002 and in 2008 at Cambridge. The number of state school undergraduates to Oxford has been steadily falling since. And while raw figures indicate a downward trend in privately educated pupils, this is not the case when the growing numbers of privately educated overseas students are taken into account. Overseas undergraduates to Oxbridge have more than doubled in the last fifteen years. The public school figure is further skewed by those who moved from private to state schools for their A-levels.[28] There is also a serious disparity in Oxbridge acceptance rates with state school applicants who win offers 25 per cent less likely to take up their place at Oxford or Cambridge than those offered to pupils at independent schools.[29]

A former headmaster of Westminster School was once candid enough to spell out exactly how the relationship between the private sector and Oxbridge worked in favour of public school admissions. John Rae told how Oxbridge dons and other influential figures from the colleges were regularly wined and dined at lavish events hosted at Westminster School. He happily explained how 'over dinner' deals were done to get their less able students places at the colleges.[30]

It is not possible to say how much of this kind of horse trading for Oxbridge admissions goes on today. The selection process is of course more transparent and rigorous but a word in the ear in support of a 'promising' public school applicant cannot be without influence. Nick Hillman, director of the Higher Education Policy Institute, says that when he went to university his school, Repton, always had a reserved place at Peterhouse College, Cambridge, for a History scholar: 'When I didn't get into Peterhouse my school tutor rang up the college to inquire why. This still goes on today.

The private school tutors, who often make it their business to know the admissions tutor, don't hesitate to pick up the phone. I'm not sure the same can be said for a busy comprehensive teacher who has many other roles in the school. This is an advantage that plays in favour of public schools. It's perfectly legal and above board but it is unfair.'[31]

The Oxbridge factor matters because an Oxbridge education still determines who runs Britain. This was demonstrable of David Cameron's second cabinet, where 60 per cent had Oxbridge degrees.

The Sutton Trust argues: 'Large educational gaps remain and entrenched privilege continues in higher education. Students from lower socioeconomic backgrounds are still far less likely to attend university and students from the poorest households are fifty-five times less likely than independent school students to attend Oxford or Cambridge.'[32]

Barnaby Lenon, the chair of the Independent Schools Council, accepts his schools do have an advantage over state schools but he says it's got nothing to do with the historical links between the public schools and the Oxbridge colleges. 'They do have a slightly unfair advantage. And I explained this once to Michael Gove, but he didn't seem particularly interested. The reason they have an unfair advantage is not because of contacts, it's not because of networks, it's because of experience. If you are a school that every year has, let's say, three students applying to read History at Oxford, and you compare that to a school that has one student every ten years applying to read History at Oxford, you've got a completely different level of experience.'[33]

In 2017 the Labour MP David Lammy decided to investigate the social backgrounds of Oxbridge students. What he discovered was that four-fifths of students accepted at Oxbridge between 2010 and 2015 had parents with top managerial or professional jobs. He also established that this trend in elitism was getting worse.

The direct link between an Oxbridge degree and political power was fully exposed in Andy Beckett's excellent analysis of how an Oxford University degree in Philosophy, Politics and Economics is the secret to getting a top job in the business of running Britain. Beckett began by setting the scene:

Monday, 13 April 2015 was a typical day in modern British politics. An Oxford University graduate in philosophy, politics and economics (PPE), Ed Miliband, launched the Labour party's general election manifesto. It was examined by the BBC's political editor, Oxford PPE graduate Nick Robinson, by the BBC's economics editor, Oxford PPE graduate Robert Peston, and by the director of the Institute for Fiscal Studies, Oxford PPE graduate Paul Johnson. It was criticised by the prime minister, Oxford PPE graduate David Cameron. It was defended by the Labour shadow chancellor, Oxford PPE graduate Ed Balls.

Elsewhere in the country, with the election three weeks away, the Liberal Democrat chief secretary to the Treasury, Oxford PPE graduate Danny Alexander, was preparing to visit Kingston and Surbiton, a vulnerable London seat held by a fellow Lib Dem minister, Oxford PPE graduate Ed Davey. In Kent, one of Ukip's two MPs, Oxford PPE graduate Mark Reckless, was campaigning in his constituency, Rochester and Strood. Comments on the day's developments were being posted online by Michael Crick, Oxford PPE graduate and political correspondent of Channel 4 News.

On the BBC Radio 4 website, the Financial Times statistics expert and Oxford PPE graduate Tim Harford presented his first election podcast. On BBC1, Oxford PPE graduate and Newsnight presenter Evan Davies conducted the first of a series of interviews with party leaders. In the print media, there was an election special in the Economist magazine, edited by Oxford PPE graduate Zanny Minton-Beddoes; a clutch of election articles in the political magazine Prospect, edited by Oxford PPE graduate Bronwen Maddox; an election column in the Guardian by Oxford PPE graduate Simon Jenkins; and more election coverage in the Times and the Sun, whose proprietor, Rupert Murdoch, studied PPE at Oxford.

Beckett concluded: 'More than any other course at any other university, more than any revered or resented private school, and in a manner probably unmatched in any other democracy, Oxford PPE pervades British political life.'[34]

Lee Elliot Major of the Sutton Trust says: 'All this would be fine if England's two ancient universities attracted bright teenagers from a diverse swathe of social and economic backgrounds. But we know despite valiant efforts by the universities, entry into their hallowed colleges continues to be dominated by those from the most privileged families. It means that those in charge of us are not reflective of the people they are intended to serve, or drawn from the widest pool of available talents.'[35]

There are other damaging aspects to an overabundance of graduates from privately educated backgrounds. By cramming such students into ancient colleges and indulging them in tradition, custom and costume, the transition from public school to university is made almost seamless.

Journalist and broadcaster Laura Barton, who wrote and presented a three-part series for BBC Radio 4 called The Confidence Trick, says: 'The design of a public school such as Eton has much in common with, say, the colleges of Oxbridge, as well as the Inns of Court (where barristers and judges are trained) and the Houses of Parliament. If you grow up among these kinds of buildings, you are not only less likely to be daunted by their grandeur but, on the contrary, you will feel at home, as if you belong there and they speak your language'.[36]

Such cloying familiarity helps to create the conditions for social segregation. Public school graduates gravitate to one another, joining clubs, societies and elites that reinforce the myth that their privileged world is commonplace. But Oxford's Bullingdon Club and Cambridge's private school-dominated Apostles and the many other invitation-only associations shut out the rest of society.

For Cambridge alumnus *Times* columnist Matthew Parris the experience made him feel like he was back in South Africa: 'At Clare College (and Clare was one of the least snooty colleges) a broad equivalence in intelligence and learning was more or less assumed, but there was a clear social divide between state-school and public-school boys. It was as sharp as it was intangible. Although privately educated in Swaziland, I was quietly assigned to the grammar school gang, and felt comfortable there. More than forty years later I still do.'[37]

Oxford and Cambridge are not alone in their popularity with the public schools. There is evidence that attempts to reduce the number of privately educated graduates is boosting public school pupil entry levels at other universities, which are developing their own elitist enclaves. Nearly 40 per cent of Durham's entrants were privately educated, along with 39 per cent of those starting at Bristol, and 34 per cent of starters at Imperial College London.[38]

Less academic public school children tend to club together at fashionable universities like Newcastle whose alumni include the current Duke of Westminster and his sister, and St Andrews, where Prince William first met Kate Middleton. In this respect the business and family connections acquired at school give them a critical advantage over their state-educated counterparts, and these graduates get better jobs and higher pay than their state-educated equivalents who leave the same university with the same degree. The Sutton Trust calls this 'opportunity hoarding'.[39]

A 2014 study by the Social Market Foundation found that UK children who are privately educated are likely to earn almost £200,000 more between the ages of twenty-six and forty-two than those attending state schools. This is particularly so at the 'magic circle' law firms, which in 2017 were still recruiting 57 per cent of their trainees from private schools. The correlation between bigger salaries and private education is perfectly illustrated by a 2018 study which showed that eight out of ten starting salaries of £100,000 are awarded to privately educated candidates.[40]

This financial advantage is described by Francis Green, professor of Work and Education Economics at the UCL Institute of Education, as an important part of the 'public school premium'.[41]

But Professor Green goes further, saying that even the choice of marriage partner is unconsciously guided by educational background. Professor Green and Dr Golo Henseke, from the Centre for Learning and Life Chances in Knowledge Economies and Societies (LLAKES), analysed survey data on 75,000 adults in the UK gathered from 1991 to 2013. They found that privately educated women are four times more likely than their state-educated counterparts to marry a man who was privately educated. The researchers suggested that one reason why 'like married like' was that men and women from private schools were more likely to have friends in common, work in similar careers and hold shared values. Professor Green found that the privately educated husbands of privately educated women earned an average of £35,900 a year, compared with the £25,900 earned by state-educated husbands of state-educated women.[42]

These public school families can secure and protect their wealth by ensuring their own children are privately educated. Public school education is the parent of nepotism which helps a narrow pool of people consolidate their hold on power and influence. In this way the cycle of privilege is completed and the factories of advantage continue churning out better-equipped children.

David Willetts concedes that public schools are agents of inequality because pupils are 'buying a host of special advantages including very good advice about how to get into the best universities… And that is in some sense unfair, but trying to assault it head on would be less effective than trying to offset these problems elsewhere.' He says that the 'ultimate justification' for intervention is that 'the kids who come from tougher backgrounds outperform them [public school students] at university.'[43]

The Office for Fair Access is trying to give universities the confidence to look beyond prior attainment and at the underlying potential of the students. Oxford and Cambridge have invested heavily in outreach projects to boost the numbers of disadvantaged and ethnic minority students. And a number of Russell Group universities, notably King's College and Queen Mary's College, University of London, are admitting people from a wide range of backgrounds but still turning out graduates with good degrees: 'So you can offset it,' says Willetts, 'by a combination of legitimising universities exercising some discretion in their admission procedures and even putting pressure on them to do it.' But the truth is that the Oxbridge colleges are sitting on £11 billion's worth of endowments and in receipt of £800 million of government funding each year. That's an awful lot of public money being used to maintain the huge advantage privately educated students have over those from disadvantaged backgrounds in securing a place at Cambridge or Oxford.[44]

★

Why does it matter that people who pay for their education end up with more power, better jobs, more money and greater success in sport and acting than those who don't? Where is the harm in letting rich people purchase better lives? After all, this is how capitalism has always worked.

On the most basic level such a system gravely offends the principle of equality of opportunity, the foundation of any democracy. It is also a form of corruption because it permits people to bypass the rules of professional advancement by paying membership fees to a self-selecting group of lottery winners. Unchecked, such a system works against meritocracy and establishes a socially divided society where a minority increasingly controls a majority of the national wealth, earned by the hard work of the majority. The test of a working democracy is how much trust the people place in it. When citizens no longer believe the system is serving everyone fairly and, no matter how hard they work or study, they will never escape the life into which they were born, then the glue that holds society together starts to come unstuck.

There is now research to show this is exactly what is happening in Britain. In 2017 just two-fifths of UK citizens surveyed by the Sutton Trust believe that 'people have equal opportunities to get on' in society. This is a significant drop on the 53 per cent of the public who agreed with those sentiments just a decade before.[45]

The established political parties no longer understand their membership, never mind the wider electorate. So a despairing electorate looks to demagogues who promise simple solutions to complex problems. Far-right groups and far-left populism have already started to change the character of our politics.

When Orwell was warning about the dangers of a divided education system, 35 per cent of the income went to the richest 10 per cent of the people. After the Second World War Britain gradually became a more equal society so that by 1979 just 21 per cent of the income went to 10 per cent of the population. But since then the trend has reversed so that today the distribution of wealth is much more similar to the period when Orwell was alive.[46] Today Britain is experiencing the longest wage stagnation since the end of the war, threatening the economic model of neoliberalism. The UK sits on its own as a rich economy in which profits have risen but wages continue to fall in real terms.[47] Since the crash Britain's wealth, supercharged by rocketing house prices, has risen by more than £4 trillion, almost half of which has accrued to the richest 10 per cent of households. Fifteen per cent of adults in Britain have either no share of the nation's record £11.1 trillion of wealth, or have negative wealth.[48] Fourteen million people, one in five of the population, live in poverty; 400,000 more children and 300,000 more pensioners have been added to this number since 2013.[49] 2021 is predicted to be the worst year for living standards for the poorest half of households since comparable records began in the mid–1960s.[50]

Britain's widening wealth gap has had a profound impact on social mobility, which has actually stalled since the 1980s. Instead of talking about upward mobility, we are confronting the dangers of downward mobility. This means it is now harder to climb up the ladder to a better job and easier to fall down the ladder to a worse job.[51] Indeed, Millennials (born from the 1980s) are likely to be the first generation in modern times to earn less than their parents. The biggest obstacle to social mobility is 'large educational gaps and entrenched privilege in higher education'.[52]

In London the helpless predicament of the non–property-owning classes is at its most bleak. Huge swathes of the capital are still owned by generational 'toffs' – a handful of grand families controlling many of its freeholds. Very little is known about most of them, and that is how they like it. A further tract of real estate has been bought up by foreign families using investment vehicles to take major stakes in the heart of the capital. Many of these families have made their fortunes in the chaotic liberalisations of the economies of the former Soviet Union and China and have chosen to base their lives in Britain. A key strategy in retaining and spreading their Western wealth is buying public school educations for their children. In turn, the public schools are committed to guarding the privacy of these mega-rich families who use them to assimilate into the British elite.

There is another cost to the country. The education and eleva-tion of a narrow group of people who come from boarding schools based in the south of England and focused on London, Oxford and Cambridge only exacerbates Britain's economic north–south divide. It perpetuates a mindset that puts the south and London at the centre of national affairs and treats the rest of the country as an economically irrelevant backwater.

So how will it all end?

Robert Halfon MP, the Conservative chair of the influential parliamentary education select committee, warns that social injustice is 'endemic' in the education system. He says we are failing our children's futures with far too few disadvantaged students going to the best universities.[53]

For Justin Madders MP, chair of the parliamentary committee on social mobility, it is the most pressing issue facing Britain. 'In some respects it's getting worse,' he warns. 'The number of professional jobs is going to contract over the next couple of decades and those people who have connections and advantages are going to be at the front of the queue... We look at how young people got into these professions in the first place. Work experience and internships are a big part of that, but actually there are shocking stats about how many work placements in some professions are settled on the basis of some prior connection to that particular institution. You're a City lawyer, your son is interested in architecture, one of your major clients is in architecture, so it's very easy to say, well, here's an idea for you.'[54]

He says that 50 per cent of people in law, banking and finance are filled by graduates who have already worked for that employer in some capacity. 'That says to me there is a network that still operates that puts people at the front of the queue. People obviously don't see anything wrong in getting work experience with clients or contacts, but what it does mean is that those people who are already known to these sorts of people and professions get these opportunities.' Everybody else has to take their chance on sending a blind CV in the post and hope it lands on the right desk.

But Madders predicts: 'I think it will be even more of a challenge because those elite professional jobs will be in shorter supply. Which means that to break through the class barrier you have to be even more outstanding.'

Since the close of the nineteenth century the world has been gradually evolving into a much fairer place. Basic human rights, like the right to food, shelter and education, have spread across the globe. At the end of the Cold War we could all expect to look forward to more years of even greater shared equality. But according to the Israeli historian Yuval Noah Harari, author of the bestselling book *Sapiens*, equality is about to take a very serious turn for the worse.

He argues that 'humans basically have just two types of skills – physical and cognitive – and if computers outperform us in both, they might outperform us in the new jobs just as in the old ones. Consequently, billions of humans might become unemployable, and we will see the emergence of a huge new class: the useless class.'[55]

Mankind has always depended on a hierarchical society led by an elite. In the future the elite will not just be those who hold most of the wealth, they will also be ones who have protected access to a skilled job. And privileged education will be at an even greater premium.

Unless we urgently tackle the drivers of inequality and break up networks of advantage there can be no equality of opportunity. Disenfranchisement has already set in, which, in turn, is beginning to breed resentment and grievance. This has already led to the protest movements that have seen the rise of Jeremy Corbyn and Momentum, and brought us Brexit and Donald Trump. But these are merely the symptoms of a much deeper malaise.

Conclusion

THE DISSOLUTION OF THE PUBLIC SCHOOLS

It was Plato who established the idea of selectively educating an elite group of citizens to rule over society. But the Greek philosopher also understood how power corrupts and so proposed first teaching the apprentice leaders temperance and justice. He knew that 'without controlling their education, the city cannot control the future rulers'.[1] Plato's Socrates argued that to ensure the guardians were true and faithful to their vows, they should be stripped of all wealth and property.

Today our guardian rulers frequently invoke the ideas of Plato and Socrates to try to show they are just and wise leaders who govern in the best interests of the people. David Cameron's signature refrain was his call for a 'big society' to demonstrate that we are 'all in it together'. He told us: 'Above all we must build a bigger, stronger society because in the end the things that make up that kind of society – strong families, strong communities, strong relationships – these are the things that make life worth living and it's about time we had a government and a prime minister that understands that.'[2] His 'big society' idea backfired spectacularly when he called a referendum over Europe, leaving the nation divisively split down the middle.

His successor, Theresa May, stood on the steps of Downing Street and also promised: 'The government I lead will be driven not by the interests of the privileged few, but by yours.'[3] And so the 'big society' became the 'shared society'.

Then, in August 2017, Jeremy Corbyn took to the pyramid stage at Glastonbury to urge us to build a society 'for the many not the few', which would 'mean sharing the wealth out in every part of our country, and looking to global policies that actually share the wealth, not glory in the levels of justice and inequality, where the rich seem to get inexorably richer and the vast majority continually lose out.'[4]

For hundreds of years the wealthy and influential have organised the public schools to sustain, protect and perpetuate their wealth, power and advantage. They have also made sure that these schools are not places of learning for ordinary families. The average salary in the UK is £26,500. Eton's school fees are £37,730. This is the widest ever difference between average earnings and fees charged by the top public schools.

There appears to be a growing political consensus that we don't live in one big, happy society, but in many fractured and segregated communities. The interactions between these communities are becoming more and more infrequent. Families who live behind the gated walls of luxury mansion estates in gentrified parts of our cities would rather drive to the other end of the country to find suitable friends for their children than let them socialise with the kids next door. Our once strong and bonded industrial communities have become diffuse, structureless places run by the exigencies of service industries. We are a deeply divided country and the divisions are deepening.

The writer and former Tory MP Matthew Parris has written that Britain has more in common with the class-riven societies of Africa than we realise. Describing his upbringing, he said: 'In white colonial Africa one was conscious of being among a few hundred thousand people, many of whom one knew, who ran everything. And then there were millions of another race in the encircling dark, whom one would never know. Britain, I expected, would be so different. We would all be similar, fifty million of us, slipping in and out of each other's social and career spheres.'

But instead when he arrived in Britain he found: 'From the minute I disembarked at Southampton, class screamed at me… From Cambridge [University] onwards I seemed to move among a surprisingly small number of people and kept bumping into them in positions of authority… and, outside, the encircling darkness; the natives, the nation "out there" as Westminster pundits like to say. People one would never meet. They might as well be holograms.'[5]

Today, communities of privileged elites coalesce around the social structures of the public schools. There are families, who live among us in well-resourced community pods and silos, who have simply opted out of mainstream society.

In 2015 David Cameron acknowledged the UK's serious social divisions by promising to tackle the privileges of 'Tim Nice-But-Dim'. He told the Tory Party conference: 'Listen to this: Britain has the lowest social mobility in the developed world. Here, the salary you earn is more linked to what your father got paid than in any other major country. I'm sorry, for us Conservatives, the party of aspiration, we cannot accept that.'[6]

Alan Milburn, the then social mobility commissioner, warned in 2017 that there was a greater need than ever for improved social mobility. 'As the general election seems to demonstrate,' said Milburn, 'the public mood is sour and whole tracts of Britain feel left behind.'[7]

In essence, we need to learn to mingle again.

The Harvard professor of Political Philosophy, Michael J. Sandel, noticed in 2012, long before anyone had called the rise of populism, Brexit or Trump, that wealthy people and those on modest means are coming to lead increasingly separate lives. He raised his concerns at the Labour Party Conference, telling the audience: 'We live and work and shop and play in different places, our children go to different schools. This is not good for democracy, nor is it a satisfactory way to live even for those of us who may end up on the top. Democracy doesn't require perfect equality but it does require that citizens share a common life. It is important that people from different walks of life bump up against each other.' For Sandel, schools are healthy 'class-mixing' places which allow people to witness the lives of fellow members of the community.

The tragedy of the Grenfell Tower fire has made us think more carefully about the neglect of our communities. Our troubled backwaters are no longer out of sight and out of mind. If we are concerned about segregated, poor communities then we should also have fears about the other side of the coin, the privatised, wealthy communities whose citizens live in gated estates and send their children to their own schools.[8] The Grenfell residents have repeatedly raised concerns about the social impact of too many private schools doing business in the verdant glades of west London. Of particular concern has been the high density of segregated prep schools which have set up in the gentrified streets a stone's throw from the tower.

Private schooling in the area has become so crowded that, in 2014, the wealthy parents of two prep schools, Notting Hill Prep and Alpha Plus, went to war over who should be allowed to spend millions of pounds leasing a building from Kensington and Chelsea Borough Council. Notting Hill Prep parents, who were paying up to £15,000 a year in fees, signed a petition to try to stop the council granting to Alpha a twenty-year rental of £2 million a year on a property on the same road as their children's school. One mother threw the full weight of her connections behind her protest over the council decision: 'My husband Tim Bevan produced the movie *Notting Hill*, so as a family we feel connected to the narrative of this area in more ways than one... Whatever your feelings about the film, the Royal Borough of Kensington and Chelsea will have certainly benefited economically from the project.'

Earl Spencer also wrote an eloquent letter, even though his nephews, Princes William and Harry, had attended another of Alpha Plus's schools in Wetherby, Yorkshire. He complained: 'The thought of another set of parents deluging the area at the same time is mind-boggling... The council chose to ignore what was best for the local area and chose instead merely to fall in with the highest bidder.'[9] But of course it was the voiceless, non-fee-paying residents who suffered the most.

Grenfell residents were so angry about the increasing use of 4x4 vehicles around the schools that they decided to speak out in 2016. In a letter to the council, they accused the two private schools of 'clogging up the surrounding area every morning and evening when picking up or dropping off their children at school in large four-wheel drive cars'.

They were also worried about the safety of the rich children who used the schools, warning: 'The parents of school users also frequently park their cars on yellow lines (with seeming impunity)... The Notting Hill Prep School also use yellow lines to park their coaches that frequently take pupils to and from external activities and already cause serious danger for other road users and pedestrians alike... we believe that this places the children at serious risk and any further increase in traffic will only increase the danger to these infants.'

In 2016, when their pleas were ignored, their anger and frustration spilled onto the streets after it emerged that Notting Hill Prep School had offered to pay Kensington and Chelsea Borough Council £365,000 to expand the school by buying up an old library on the same street. Local residents staged several protests outside the building, home to the North Kensington Library, which opened in 1891 and has been a much-loved and much-used resource for local people. And when they still weren't listened to, they stormed the council building to let councillors know how strongly they felt about the issue. The residents accused the council of 'asset stripping' in favour of a private prep school that served the interests of the wealthy minority. Edward Daffarn, of local community organisation the Grenfell Action Group, said:

> The library was built out of public funding so that local people could educate themselves. It was then given to the council to manage, but instead of managing it they've decided to strip it and give it to their friends at the prep school. They've told us for a long, long time that they couldn't afford to do it up and that's why they're moving the library, but they've offered the prep school a year's free rent to do it up. The building is so special to us and we just don't think it is appropriate to let it to a private school. The library is so loved by the public. That building sums up what North Kensington is – it's having that that makes this community great.[10]

The Grenfell Tower fire of June 2017, in which seventy-one people died, had a devastating impact on the community and its children. Four pupils from the nearby Kensington Aldridge Academy (KAA) died in the tragedy and the school was closed for several months afterwards.[11]

The KAA is run by a charity, the Aldridge Education Trust. But it has a very different ethos to the many private schools which operate in the area. Aldridge Education was established by Sir Rod Aldridge, the former head of Capita, whose central vision is to use non-selective schools to improve 'underprivileged communities'. Over a period of ten years, Aldridge has developed a group of sponsored community academy schools and colleges that 'create social change and community regeneration opportunities through enterprise and entrepreneurship to help young people to reach their potential and improve their communities'.

After the fire, one of the KAA teachers set up a JustGiving page. The teacher, Haley Yearwood, director of learning for Year 8, explained: 'As I watched the news at five o'clock in the morning, I just wanted to make sure residents affected were well cared for after the tragedy. Our school is in the heart of a fantastic community.'[12] The school's page has raised more than £660,000 for local residents. In January 2018 Ofsted judged KAA to be 'outstanding' in all categories.

*

When parents elect to send their children to a private school they are depriving the community of families who would otherwise take a close interest in the success and failure of the local school. Local schools need pushy parents to drive up the standards of the school for everyone. Every time someone resists sending their child to a private school, community cohesion is strengthened. Children from advantaged backgrounds also improve the education experience of less-advantaged children. Research shows that articulate, confident, able classmates are the greatest source of help for other pupils. Similarly, middle-class parents who can use their time, influence and experience boost the performance of their local school.[13]

Today, British state schools are being outperformed by the rest of the world and so we need these children and their family resources more than ever. We are the fifth-biggest economy but twenty-fifth on the world education tables. At the same time state schools are facing a bigger funding crisis than the NHS.[14] It doesn't take a Maths IGCSE to work out that this chronic underinvestment in education means the economy will suffer in the long run.

Our community schools need the support and resources of all the community. The historian David Kynaston, a private school pupil himself (Wellington), summed up the case for community schooling in a seminal article for the *New Statesman* in 2014. 'One has only to witness pushy private school parents on a touchline,' said Kynaston, 'to realise that the state sector will never achieve its full capability without them; and it can only be damaging that so many of our leading figures are not personally invested in this most crucial part of our society.'[15] By remaining outside the community, public schools are anti-community.

It seems paradoxical that state schools located in the richest parts of the south-east benefit less from the community's wealth, which is instead showered on private schools. I live in one of four former farm workers' cottages in a small rural community in Surrey, a county awash with private schools. Every morning the adults all get in our cars and drive in different directions all over the county and beyond to take our children to school. My three closest neighbours have children who are sent to schools of distances ranging from 5 to 150 miles away. The more expensive the education, the longer the drive. And because some of them are boarding, there are many mornings when the parents don't need to get up at all. As a result of us all sending our kids to different schools, we don't see very much of each other. Our children don't interact and so the adults don't have a reason to mix. Last year, an ambulance was called to one of the houses. It turned out that the old lady who had lived there for fifty years had died. But it had taken two days for anyone to notice.

★

In 2017 one Old Etonian published a book intended to explain to the public why our societies weren't working like they used to in the good old days. In *The Road to Somewhere: The Populist Revolt and the Future of Politics*, David Goodhart acknowledges that there are two distinct groups dominant in Britain. The *Somewheres* who are tied to a specific place or community, socially conservative, often less educated. Those who could come from *Anywhere* are mobile, often urban, socially liberal and university educated. Confronting his privilege and trying to make sense of it in the context of the wider world, Goodhart's diagnosis is that a 'good society' is a 'circle of mutual interests' where the best and brightest still rise to the top but the contribution of all is valued.[16] He goes on to argue that those who are serious about social mobility and meritocracy must not shy away from the 'hard solutions' including 'closing down private schools'.[17]

Government spending on education today is 50 per cent higher than it was in 1997. But according to the Social Mobility Commission there is no prospect of the gap between poorer and wealthier children being eliminated at either GCSE or A-level.[18] Education is the key to closing the gap between the 'haves' and the 'have-nots'. By building more inclusive communities from the schools up, people will stop distrusting those who govern us. A fairer education system can bring communities back from the abyss, by giving us each an equal stake in society.

The time is right for reform. Left-wing politicians have long spoken about structural and entrenched inequality in education, but now voices on the right are joining them. In 2013 Brixton-born and grammar school-educated John Major spoke out about something everyone knew but few politicians considered worth talking about. 'I remember enough of my past to be outraged on behalf of the people abandoned when social mobility is lost... Our education system should help children out of the circumstances in which they were born, not lock them into the circumstances in which they were born. We need them to fly as high as their luck, their ability and their sheer hard graft can actually take them. And it isn't going to happen magically.'[19]

Even Boris Johnson, when he was London mayor, concluded in 2013 that one way of reversing the decline in social mobility was to open up public schools by forcing them to take a quarter of bursary-funded pupils from poor backgrounds. Equally, Dominic Raab is no lily-livered liberal, but he sees a place for reform. The Conservative MP for Esher and Walton went to Dr Challoner's Grammar School and studied law at Oxford and international law at Cambridge. He started his career as a commercial lawyer at Linklaters in the City, and later spent six years at the Foreign and Commonwealth Office, including heading its war crimes team in The Hague. In a 2013 paper, Raab's first proposal for making Britain a more balanced society was to 'require public schools, as a condition of charitable status, to either subscribe to the Sutton Trust's Open Access Scheme or take 25 per cent of their pupils on a selective – and means-tested – basis, to give more low- and middle-income children access to the best education on merit'.[20]

Michael Gove, when he was education secretary, summed up the problem:

> We have one of the most stratified and segregated education systems in the developed world, perpetuating inequality and holding our nation back… but while the education these schools provide is rationed overwhelmingly to the rich, our nation remains poorer. From the England cricket team to the comment pages of *The Guardian*, the BAFTAs to the BBC, the privately educated – and wealthy – dominate. Access to the best universities and the most powerful seats around boardroom tables, influence in our media and office in our politics are allocated disproportionately to the privately educated children of already wealthy parents.[21]

But it was Theresa May, ironically brought to power in 2016 after a failed Tory coup orchestrated by Gove, who opened up the path for true reform. Standing before the electorate outside Downing Street, she pledged to fight 'against the burning injustice that, if you're born poor, you will die on average nine years earlier than others. If you're black, you're treated more harshly by the criminal justice system than if you're white. If you're a white, working-class boy, you're less likely than anybody else in Britain to go to university. If you're at a state school, you're less likely to reach the top professions than if you're educated privately.'[22]

In October that year she was as good as her word and published a green paper, 'Schools that work for everyone', which pledged to tackle the inequalities of private education head on. The consultation paper proposed that independent schools which have the 'capacity and capability' should either offer a certain proportion of places as fully funded bursaries, sponsor an academy or set up a new free school in the state sector and take responsibility for ensuring its success. Suddenly, the public schools were fair game. Had she not called a snap election, the private schools would be locking heads with government today over their right to keep their privileged charitable status.

In many respects these voices from the right are only echoing what Margaret Thatcher was saying shortly after she first took office and complained about the privileged educations of Shirley Williams and Tony Benn. Benn's daughter Melissa, a long-time education reform campaigner, argues the time is right for reform and that we have reached a critical moment in the debate about the future of education. She says that one reason for this is that a 'significant part of the political right have... come round to comprehensive schools'. She says that this is partly evidenced by 'Goveism' and the Conservative opposition to a revival of grammar schools, the second part of May's doomed education reforms.

Benn says: 'I think we could be at an important point in history and what we might see at the end result of this period is an integrated national system. That's what I'd like to see. However, I am not naive and I do not deny there are enormous obstacles to that, not least the inequality that we have in society; this means that if we had an integrated state system, we would continue to have all kinds of problems about postcodes, inequalities and a really difficult debate about what makes a good education... Certainly I'd rather see that than a continuation of wealthy children being educated separately – what I call the alchemy of privilege, with better-off children being given more resources, benefiting from their privileges, living, working and socialising separately from the 93 per cent.'

Fiona Millar, a founder of the Local Schools Network, argues that public schools are holding back radical change to education: 'For the most part, private schools are only interested in looking after themselves. Let's be honest: many of the parents who pay huge fees to send their children to these schools don't want them mixing with the great unwashed. They are paying for an elite education. I live in an area [north London] which is serviced by a great many private schools so I know what they do and what they don't do for the community. Our state primary school swimming pool was out of action for a while and so the children couldn't have swimming lessons [learning to swim is part of the national curriculum]. So the school approached the two nearest independent schools to see if we could use their swimming pools while the public pool was being fixed. Both schools declined to help.'

She acknowledges the huge scale of the challenge: 'You are up against a powerful vested interest and at the very top echelons of society – the judiciary, politics, the media, most of the professions. The privately educated are disproportionately represented. I would like to see a fully comprehensive system which would tackle the private/state school divide. In the first place, the private schools would lose their charitable status and those that remained would be forced to do much more to help the educational needs of the community.'

Public schools, independent schools, private schools, call them what you will, are facing their own crossroads. Many of the less well-known schools have fallen on hard times. Those that have been unable to take advantage of the tax breaks because they can't meet the charity criteria are run on increasingly tight margins. The emergence of Cameron's Eton government raised the profile of public schools, drawing the media's fire and making a private education unfashionable. As Tony Little puts it: 'Eton is now a four-letter word.'[23] Television shows like *Made in Chelsea* have only antagonised ordinary folk, who have an unflattering image of the public school student. And in the workplace, especially in the public sector, an education at Eton or Harrow can be as much a source of social embarrassment as a crowning entry on a CV.

A combination of political animosity, public disquiet and being out of fashion means public schools are vulnerable to change. But the agents of privilege will not go without a fight. The public schools are well organised and well financed. Among their ranks are government ministers, influential civil servants and money men from the City. The schools and their representative bodies also have the confidence and experience of more than 150 years of defeating the most determined reformers.

The Independent Schools Council acknowledges that change may be coming down the track, but if it comes it will be change that enhances and preserves the cherished independent status of the schools — after all, the best defence is always attack. Barnaby Lenon, chairman of the ISC, argues that the right to a private education is inalienable and is enshrined in the United Nations Universal Declaration of Human Rights. 'I don't think anyone seriously believes you can abolish paying for education. That argument was lost as soon as Labour brought in tuition fees for university education. There have always been socialists who want to abolish private schools.' Neither does Lenon think Theresa May or her advisers 'understand how social mobility works… Scrapping public schools will do very little to bridge the achievement gap. A pupil's achievement is 20 per cent to do with the school and 80 per cent due to parenting, upbringing and genetic heritage.'

He argues that the 'top 500 state schools have a much greater influence on social segregation. It's a postcode lottery... if education reformers were really serious about social mobility they would do more to help raise the standards of half the school population who don't get good grades in English and Maths.' Lenon, who was David Cameron's Geography teacher at Eton, is scornful of the Tory proposal, included in the dormant 2017 manifesto, to force the one hundred top private schools to partner with state schools. He reserves special criticism for May's former adviser, Nick Timothy, whom he has identified as the architect of the reform.

'Nick Timothy doesn't know what he is talking about if he thinks he can improve social mobility by forcing independent schools to form partnerships with state schools. If you want a fairer and more equal society then tackle the kids who are not getting good GCSEs. Improve their chances in life by bringing them up rather than knocking down the top performers. Tories are supposed to stand for small businesses, which is what a lot of our schools are, and of course parental choice.'

Speaking at a Westminster Education Forum shortly after publication of the green paper, Lenon said: 'The Green Paper is actually quite hostile to us. I dare say it is partly a reaction against the Cameron government. It is partly because they are, quite understandably, trying to attract the C1 and C2 voters that are not always going to send their children to our schools.' It is a rich irony that, had it not been for the stellar achievements of Lenon's own pupils, particularly Cameron, the public schools might have escaped such political scrutiny.

In a bid to outflank the government, the ISC has tried to muddy the waters by offering to educate 10,000 state pupils paid for by the government. Lenon said his schools wanted to support the government's overall aim of increasing the number of 'improved places' at state schools.[24] But the ISC proposal would be a return to the assisted-places scheme, abolished under Tony Blair, where the state ended up part-funding private schools, saving some from going out of business. Even Lenon acknowledges that such an idea in the current political climate is politically toxic.

★

A parent's choice of school for their children is a topic of conversation that is best avoided at a dinner party. Many who went to public school find it hard to rationalise private education. They may recognise it bestows an unfair advantage but to suggest the system is broken is a repudiation of the person they have become. It also means invalidating the role of well-meaning parents, who may have spent hundreds of thousands of pounds trying to give them a better life. And of course it means a rejection of the school that many pupils still regard as their 'family' where they forged their closest friendships.

Everyone wants a good education for all children but nobody wants their kids to do worse than their neighbours'. Under our present system, for one child to succeed, others must fail.

Privately educated media commentator Mehdi Hasan candidly addressed the public school taboo in 2012 when he confided that he and his wife disagreed about where to school their children. He wrote then: 'It's one of the biggest taboos in British politics; the educational elephant in the room. Too many politicians and pundits would much rather argue about the challenge of grade inflation, the future of "gold-plated" A-levels or the role of the teaching unions than address the reality that, in the words of Deputy Prime Minister Nick Clegg, the "great rift in our education system" is between our best schools, most of which are private, and the schools ordinary families rely on. Shamefully, the rest of us also turn a blind eye to this grotesque educational apartheid in our midst.'

He went on:

My own parents paid for me to be educated at private school. I understand why they did so and there is no point in me pretending that I would be where I am today without the (unfair) advantage that their investment provided me with. Yet there is no escaping the big picture: a two-tier education system produces a two-tier society, divided between the rich and the rest. It is morally and socially untenable. Our schools should be at the forefront of promoting civic solidarity and guaranteeing social mobility; private schools, however, do the opposite. They produce not a meritocracy but a plutocracy, in which a tiny minority is able to entrench its power and privilege. Thus the inconvenient truth is this: if we genuinely want to create a level playing field for our children, and ensure equality of opportunity and social justice, there can be no place for private schools. It is time to abolish our educational caste system.[25]

In December 2017 David Cameron's cousin, Harry Mount, the Westminster School-educated editor of *The Oldie*, acknowledged the injustice of his class's advantage over the rest of society: 'Us white public schoolboys, very unfairly, still have that much more access to great offices of state and all the rest of it. I don't think they are being set aside for us just because we have expensive educations, posh voices and a certain confidence. But it's crazy to say that life is equal. I don't think life can ever be equal.'[26]

While some of those who went to public school are prepared to confront the iniquity of the education system, many from the left are not. When Owen Jones and Zadie Smith were invited to discuss social mobility on BBC Radio 4's *Start the Week* in 2014 they were conspicuously silent on the issue of private education. Instead it was left to the privately educated David Kynaston to make the case for reform. As we have learned, recent Labour politicians have also been equally mute on this subject: if the case for abolishing public schools were solely a hard-left enterprise as Barnaby Lenon suggests, wouldn't you expect to hear more about it from Jeremy Corbyn?

The public school problem is not confined to these shores. Private education has become an engine of inequality all over the world. From the new Arab states of the Middle East to the former colonies of the West in East Asia and the developing countries of Africa, the ruling classes and despots rely on private schools to sustain their grip on power. But in America, the debate has also shifted towards reform, particularly after the triumph of Trump and his 'billionaire cabinet' of privately educated advisers.

In November 2016 Warren Buffett said one of the greatest challenges facing America was the rich opting out of the public education system. 'I imagine that if I used the local golf courses, I'd care a lot about how they were managed and maintained – it's the same with schools. There's a two-tiered system right now.'[27] Similarly Bill Gates, who went to the private Lakeside School in Seattle, has tried to raise standards in the state education system by pouring millions of dollars into charter schools that cater for disadvantaged pupils.[28]

If we are all agreed – that there is a private education problem – then we need to decide what kind of changes will bring about the social mobility and restored faith in meritocratic democracy that public schools are working against. The popular approach to the problem since the end of the Second World War has been to encourage the leaders of private schools to do more to bridge the gap between state and private education. This has ranged from threats of expropriation by the state to bribery under various school places subsidy schemes. Winston Churchill, Clement Attlee, Harold Wilson and Tony Blair all, to some degree, made efforts to get public schools to return to the communities where they were born. But progress has been glacial. Such slow progress led in 2016 to Theresa May's government publishing plans to force one hundred leading public schools to sponsor state schools or lose their charitable status. But in 2017, only twelve public schools were involved in full sponsorships with state academy schools or free schools.[29] Many of these arrangements are sited in carefully chosen catchment areas and on terms favourable to the public school.

At Dulwich College in south London a new reality is dawning: if the schools don't change and embrace their foundation principles, change will be forced upon them. Joe Spence is rare among public school heads in that he is committed to returning Dulwich to the philanthropic mission of its original founder. As recently as the 1950s, during what has become known as the 'Dulwich Experiment', 90 per cent of school pupils were on free places funded by local authorities under the 11-plus scheme. Spence now talks of the 'new Dulwich Experiment' which will see 50 per cent of all pupils in Year 7 and above on some kind of 'fee remission', compared to 30 per cent today. 'In a lifetime I want our bursary fund to grow from £12 million to £100 million so it is large enough to make us needs blind… We know that no political party likely to govern in the 2020s is going to support us unless we can properly articulate this vision.'

Spence, who is state educated, says that only if 'you have a balanced school that represents all elements of society, in terms of ethnicity, creed and class, will it properly prepare people for the twenty-first century.' He has crossed swords with Michael Gove over his claim that private schools need to save all of Fagin's boys, not just Oliver Twist: 'We are not going to raise whole communities of people to a high standard of holistic education in one generation. What we can do is raise a sufficient number of individuals and that can have an impact on whole communities.' Nevertheless, he concedes that if he was handed the task of creating an education system he wouldn't start with public schools.

Yet he insists they can be agents of social mobility: 'That is my social mission – and why I came to Dulwich to help restore our foundational values. I'm in education because I want social mobility. I think the state sector has stopped it happening. Much that they are directed to do has nothing to do with properly creating young people ready to face the challenges of work and a good life in the twenty-first century. It is criminal watching schools being forced to get five A*s to C for candidates who, as soon as they are out of school, five A*s to C is going to mean nothing. There are a number of state schools who we work with who want more than that. And that is an integral part of what I am about.'

But even the more progressive schools like Dulwich are regarded as obstacles to social mobility because they can only ever hope to help a very small number of genuinely disadvantaged pupils and then only the bright ones or the poor kids with strong family support. And Spence knows he can't achieve his far-sighted ambition of a needs-blind admissions policy without a return to some form of assisted-places scheme which will require a massive financial input from the state.

Headmasters like Joe Spence are good people who believe in strong liberal values. But they find themselves in charge of insti-tutions founded on philanthropic ideals that can't be matched by their schools today. Most are happy to bury their heads in the sand and blindly carry on with the business of educating the elites. But others, like Spence, are brave enough to acknowledge the divergence from the original foundation mission and even commit to making efforts to return the school to the service of the community.

Anthony Seldon, who has done perhaps more than any other public school figure to address the problem, says his colleagues have failed to rise to the challenge of reaching out into the communi-ties: 'There needs to be real and substantial mixing and learning and sharing on a deep level, and not just with staff but the students also. And there are models that work very well at that. There are so many things both sides can still learn from each other. And it's been a lifelong passion and maybe I haven't made any impact at all but it certainly isn't for want of trying.'

It has been a similar story in the provision of bursaries for poorer children. The ability of the public schools to fund poor pupils has reached a natural limit. Many medium-sized and small public schools have seen a drop in donations, particularly at girls' schools whose alumnae aren't willing or able to make gifts. This means the schools can't afford to pay the full bursaries that justify charitable status. Even schools with large endowments rely on donations to keep their bursary schemes ticking over. The bigger public schools' solution to the problem is a commitment towards a needs-blind selection where all pupils are given places purely on their ability, turning public schools into glorified grammar schools. But we have discovered that this is pie in the sky for even the richest schools. To turn Eton into a needs-blind institution would require a bursary fund worth more than £1 billion. Today, fewer than 6,000 children of the 600,000 who are schooled privately benefit from a totally free education.

Seldon argues that, after years of trying to make public schools more charitable, or play a greater part in the community, more radical action is needed to improve the lot of disadvantaged pupils. His idea is for the creation of one hundred state schools with selective admissions and teaching support from a nearby private school. He says they will differ from grammar schools because their only class intake will be the brightest of the poor, effectively barring children of ambitious middle-class parents. Seldon says: 'The school population will thus be 150 in the sixth form, meaning that every year 15,000 bright pupils from disadvantaged backgrounds will be looking to join university, which is 15,000 more gaining a top education than might have had the chance today.'[30]

But there are big drawbacks to the Seldon plan. The private sector would be left untouched and public schools would continue to frustrate social mobility by pumping out 100,000 sixth-formers every year. Seldon's reliance on the private schools to support his new enterprise by helping with the teaching is prone to the same failures that have made the schools such reluctant partners in the past. The private sector has a vested interest in the failure of schools that threaten their own client base.

Andrew Adonis and Robert Halfon MP favour a tax or levy to be imposed on private schools that would generate funds for places for genuinely disadvantaged students. But these reforms also envisage the survival of our two-tier education system. The elite schools would educate more very bright, poor kids alongside the children of the very rich, while the state schools, now educating fewer poor bright pupils, would be left alone to do the best they could educating everyone else.

This is not radical change.

Radical change is needed because we haven't seen any real changes in 500 years. The public schools have been exploited and then hijacked by the rich in their desire for a greater share of the nation's wealth. Today we have a well-oiled system of private education that efficiently divides society into winners and losers. For the losers the loss is terminal. In the north of England there has been a rise in the number of people who are dying from so-called diseases of despair such as alcoholism.[31] There are small sections of our ethnic communities who no longer trust their own government. A community is only as strong as the trust and respect its members have for one another. That trust is fatally undermined if too many community members are allowed to opt out and follow different rules.

People need to feel confident that they can express their grievances against the system. But when anyone ceases to recognise the system that controls their lives they will look for ways to protest, undermine or abstain from the political life of the country. Segregated and divided societies are tinder boxes that can explode at the touch of a spark, as they did in the London riots of 2011.

This violent social upheaval was presaged in the late 1980s by the American right-wing sociologist Charles Murray, famous for his controversial book *The Bell Curve*, who identified Britain's own underclass. He found parallels with America's excluded urban communities, pinpointing a surge in the number of families without resident fathers who relied on social benefits. Murray predicted that in British inner cities this would lead to communities adopting counter-culture value systems outside mainstream society. A direct consequence of this trend would be low school attendance leading to high youth unemployment, leaving some young people vulnerable to gangs that might seek to drag them into crime as a means of getting by.

It is not only libertarian political scientists who recognise these dangers. In the midst of the 2011 riots a *Telegraph* leader grimly warned: 'Today, the benefits system sustains the underclass and poor state schooling is unable to compensate for the harm caused by broken homes and absent fathers. Inadequate policing cannot suppress the symptoms of crime and disorder. These communities are trapped in a vicious circle, where violence, crime, intimidation and hopelessness are quotidian. It is a world from which most of us are insulated until it spills into the wider community, as it did so nightmarishly this week.'[32]

As far back as 1968 the Newsom Commission, which was tasked with investigating public schools, tried to forestall the breakdown in society by questioning the system that creates Britain's 'leaders':

Justice and efficiency both demand that nobody of character and ability should be denied the chance of achieving professional competence which is the prerequisite of leadership. Our country would prosper more if greater efforts were made to attain this ideal.

Indeed, the biggest single disadvantage of having two sectors of education – one fee-paying and privileged in the matter of class sizes, the other subject to teacher rationing – is that those who can afford to opt out of the maintained system care less about its development. People who are themselves professionally concerned with education – whether as politicians, administrators, or even as members of the Public Schools Commission – do not always make use of the maintained sector for their own children. If all influential parents had children in maintained schools, they would have brought pressure to bear on Parliament and Whitehall to make them better than they are.[33]

Diane Reay says that the public school 'hangs like a shadow' over the state education system which prevents the education of the working classes. In her book *Miseducation* she argues: 'The faltering commitment to comprehensive schooling is fundamentally undermined by structures, such as private schools, that perpetuate advantaged and segregated schooling.'[34]

Perhaps the public school system seems like a legacy issue, a little remnant of the society that came before, with the monarch at the helm and the classes neatly ordered behind – harmless as an ermine collar on a Westminster gown. In the days of Empire, Britain was governed by a much smaller, more easily defined, ruling class serviced by far fewer public schools than today. But since the end of the Second World War the classes of government and influence have mushroomed into a diffusive mass spread across all of society and sustained by a new service industry of private education. Today 7 per cent of the population attends an independent school and over five million of the population have benefited from a private education.

If we carry on with this piecemeal approach to public school reform, it will take 120 years before disadvantaged teenagers are as likely as their better-off counterparts to get equivalent qualifications.[35] The Social Mobility Commission, which assessed government policies on social mobility from 1997 to 2017, warns that without radical and urgent reform, the social and economic divisions in British society will widen even further, threatening not only community cohesion but our economic prosperity. While we sit on our hands, communities are becoming more disjointed, detached and untrusting.[36]

In December 2017 Milburn and his deputy, Gillian Shephard, a former Tory education minister, resigned over fears that the government's failure to address deepening divisions in Britain's communities was fuelling political alienation and creating a breeding ground for populism. In his letter to the prime minister, Milburn cited the urgent need to close the attainment gap between poor students and their more affluent classmates, which has risen to 27 per cent by the age of sixteen.[37] A day later, Robert Halfon and the Joseph Rowntree Foundation called on the government to tackle social injustice by 'radically redefining' its relationship with private schools: 'The current social contract between government and private schools clearly isn't working.'[38]

★

There are those, like Warren Buffett, Alan Bennett, Diane Reay and David Kynaston, who want public schools abolished. It is the most radical of reforms which raises both seen and unforeseen troubles. Abolition would at a stroke create a truly national education system that would lead to a seismic change in the education landscape.

Alan Bennett, who advocates abolition of the private school sixth form, put the case succinctly when he presented his 'sermon' at King's College Chapel, Cambridge, on 1 June 2014: 'My objection to private education is simply put. It is not fair. And to say that nothing is fair is not an answer. Governments, even this one, exist to make the nation's circumstances more fair, but no government, whatever its complexion, has dared to tackle private education.'

One reason why no government has dared to act is because radical reform would mean curtailing the right of a parent to pay for their child's education. But what about the rights of the overwhelming majority of children who can't afford to attend public schools? As David Kynaston has suggested: 'As a society, do we prioritise the right for individuals to educate their child as they wish (a phantom right for most people, given that fees are not an option), or the right of every child, including the poorest, to an even start? It is not the child's money that is spent on fees; no child has earned the right to a better education, just as no child has failed to earn that right. It is a question of liberty – the maximum possible liberty consistent with a like liberty for others. Do some parents have the right to pay for an education that indirectly harms the life chances of other children by blocking their path?'[39]

The counter-argument runs that all parents must be allowed to buy the best education for their children in the same way they buy all their other services in a capitalist economy. But education is not a commodity to be traded on the high street like a new model car. Nor is it the same as buying a service like a private healthcare plan. The education we choose for our children defines the very terms of the kind of society in which we wish to live. When we select a school we are also choosing our community.

For educators and politicians like David Willetts, Joe Spence, Anthony Seldon and former education secretary Lord Baker, the law stands in the way of the abolition of public schools. But the legal case against abolition is far from open and shut. The Human Rights Act merely declares that no person shall be denied the right to education; it gives individuals a right to access education facilities that already exist. The law does not require the state to provide or fund private schools and our sovereign parliament has enacted legislation abolishing many different kinds of schools, including grammar schools in most counties. The human right of a parent to send their child to a state-funded selective school has already been curtailed. Why shouldn't the state change the character of non-state schools? Should the human-rights bar prove insurmountable perhaps we should consider turning all our schools into fee-paying private institutions, issuing the poorest pupils with school vouchers which they could spend at Eton, Harrow and Winchester or any school they chose. By sending everyone to public schools run by companies like Capita and G4, no one would unfairly benefit from a privileged education and the taxpayer would save tens of billions of pounds a year in funding primary and secondary schools. Privatising all schools would, at a stroke, neutralise the elitist appeal of the public school. After all, the reason why the rich and powerful patronise them with their business is partly because 93 per cent of the population can't afford to.

But many believe abolition or even universal privatisation would solve one problem by creating another. Wealthy parents faced with no choice might send their children abroad to private schools established in British dependencies or to Switzerland, America and Australia. The globalisation of private education over recent years would make this possible and may even suit some families who have business and property interests spread all over the world. A similar scare-mongering argument was mounted against a cap on bankers' bonuses in the aftermath of the 2008 financial crisis and Brexit because of a fear of an exodus in capital creators. How often have we heard celebrities threaten to emigrate because of high taxation? The bankers haven't left the City and, despite their whingeing, celebrities like Griff Rhys Jones and Rod Stewart, who returned to the UK in 2014 so his children could be educated here, have happily adjusted to the new tax regime. The same thing would happen if we moved to a truly integrated education system. There would be much carping and stamping of feet but there would not be a mass evacuation of rich kids to foreign schools. A more appropriate analogy might be the M6 private toll road, an expensive alternative to the M6 that drivers only use because it is there. If it was closed but more lanes were added to the M6 so that everyone's driving experience was improved, we would soon forget about the toll road.

The eradication of the power and influence of the public schools cannot happen overnight. Melissa Benn believes the process could take between ten and fifteen years: 'I think it's important not to use aggressive language around this issue. One of the things I've learned over the course of my personal and political life is that people don't listen to you if you attack but they do listen if you suggest and you have good ideas and you make the alternatives sound more interesting than the status quo. So there could be a very interesting discussion to be had about what you would do with the great public schools in an integrated education system.'

She argues the dismantling or the nationalisation, of the public school system would open opportunities and new horizons for state education in the UK. 'I always thought Eton would make a fine sixth-form college. I think sixth-form colleges would be one very good use for them, or maybe inner-city schools for children who want to develop their interest in history or sport – some kind of specialist centre, but for the use of all.'

The abolition of the private schools would strengthen our comprehensive system and help raise the standards of all schools. There would be no need for academies, grammar schools or free schools. Everybody would share a community-based education system that catered for all children regardless of their intelligence and social background.

To achieve all this, it is important to carry the argument to the public schools. Michael Wilshaw made just such an appeal in 2013 when he reminded private school teachers why they became teachers:

> I think you all became teachers because you love learning and want to see the next generation learn to love learning. If you became a teacher because you understand that great learning and great educational outcomes aren't restricted to those whose parents have deep pockets, far more unites us than divides us. If you don't believe that, then what I'm about to say will fall on deaf ears. If you believe, as so many of your original founders believed, that how you deal with wider society, and how you relate to those children less fortunate than your students defines you as schools, then I have a proposition for you.[40]

Wilshaw went on to tell the schools that whether they liked it or not they were part of the community and that they were working in institutions that were founded to improve the education of the poor. The obliteration of the public schools and the return of their ancient estates to the communities from whom they were stolen must be a long-term goal. But it needn't involve a violent overthrow of the elite system and its citadels.

I advocate a slow and peaceful euthanasia. By introducing a series of policies and initiatives designed to weaken the appeal of the public school, the private education sector could be put to sleep.

This will not be easy. We as a nation commit a greater share of our spending (15 per cent of the combined private/state annual budget of roughly £75 billion[41]) to educating pupils at private schools than any other rich country on earth.[42] So the first step must be to withdraw state funding for private schools. Each year more than £200 million of taxpayers' money is spent on independent school places, making our private schools the most subsidised schools in the Western world (although there is a case for keeping the specialist schools which educate children with behavioural problems).

The second step must be to strip the schools of their charitable status. For too long, politicians have failed to challenge the bizarre assertion that the education of the privileged few is a charitable pursuit. This would liberate around £2.5 billion each year, enough for 100 new state schools. In Scotland it has already begun. In December 2017 the SNP government announced it was to abolish tax relief on business rates for private schools, raising £5 million for the state. It was hardly reported across the border but this was the first policy reform of private education since Tony Blair's government ended the assisted-places scheme in 1997.

And what should we do with the ancient endowments which have made some of the public schools the richest institutions in the country, owning billions of pounds' worth of land and property? These endowments were entrusted to the schools to educate the poor and the needy. They should perform that function once again by a compulsory transfer programme so that the endowment funds are directly administered by the state for the benefit of those for whom they were originally intended. Many smaller schools will then be faced with the choice of withering on the vine or accepting the offer of maintained status in an integrated education system. In 1978 more than fifty direct-grant private schools opted to become comprehensives when the government pulled the plug on part of their funding.[43]

At the same time there must be a concerted effort to make a private education a disadvantage rather than an essential stepping stone to success. There have already been moves to combat the impact of the old school tie in the workplace. Theresa May's government has brought in plans to block a favourite route used by private school pupils to secure good jobs. The internship has

become a fast track to a job in sought-after trades and professions like the media and the law. They directly discriminate against
poorer applicants who don't have the contacts to get them or can't
afford to spend months working for free until a paid vacancy pops
up. Under May's proposals all internships would be paid and part
of a formal application process.

Matt Hancock, the former Cabinet Office minister, went
further and drew up proposals in 2016 to force job applicants to
disclose whether they were educated by the state or the independent sector.[44] Predictably, this didn't go down well in the
public schools, which saw it for what it was – an attempt to flag
up unfair advantage. First to complain was the provost of Eton,
Lord William Waldegrave, a former Tory minister, who threatened
to resign from the party because he said it discriminated against
people who went to fee-paying schools. My own view is that this
approach might backfire by helping employers who are interested
in favouring private school over state school applicants. The old
school tie is a formidable secret society that will not be defeated
by a question on a job application form.

A far better way to impose a disincentive on private education is to curb their greatest appeal – fix a limit on the number
of pupils they send to leading universities. As we have discovered,
public schools trade on their records of securing high entry levels
to top institutions like Oxbridge and the Russell Group. In 2016, a
private school student had a 1 in 20 chance of entering Oxbridge
compared to a student from a poor background, who had odds
closer to one in 2,000. To put this in perspective, the bookies' odds
on Bono becoming the Pope are one in 1,000.[45] Some state schools
have never had a pupil win a place at Oxbridge, which suggests a
factor other than raw talent is at work. Public schools can train their
pupils to appear clever to secure a place at a good university, while
smarter but disadvantaged undergraduates fall into the education
trap of securing a degree at a bog-standard university that does

little to improve their job prospects yet at the same time saddles them with unmanageable debt. They leave university further down the wealth and career ladder than when they entered.

The top universities do use their outreach funds and bursaries to recruit more state-educated undergraduates. But like the public schools, progress has been stagnant. It is now time that admissions departments of the leading universities operate a system that positively discriminates in favour of state school applicants. The best way to level the playing field would be to make sure A-levels attained at a poorly performing school were awarded higher university admission points. Labour MP David Lammy says top universities expect a student living on the twentieth floor of Grenfell Tower to 'jump through the exact same hoops as a student at Eton or Harrow'.[46] He wants Oxbridge and the Russell Group universities to reserve places for the best-performing free-meals pupil at every school in the country. This would soon drive sharp-elbowed parents towards local schools and in turn raise standards across the school. Pupils would get the message that a poor teacher or a challenging studying environment need not end their chance of going to a good university. Because nothing succeeds like success, high-achieving students would act as trailblazers that other pupils would emulate.

Should all this fail then more radical measures must be considered, including the introduction of quotas so that the number of top jobs in certain fields would be restricted to the proportion of all privately educated pupils in the country. If 7 per cent of pupils are at fee-paying schools in the year of application, only 7 per cent of High Court judges or army majors could be appointed from the private sector.

In time, public schools would become pariah institutions and parents would see only a snobbish advantage in paying for an education. That may still leave the big schools in business, albeit on a reduced scale, but at least society would accept them for what they are – anachronistic institutions of inequality which no longer serve the nation's best interests. Other countries have created better societies by remodelling their education systems so that parents no longer pay for their children's schooling. It has been achieved in Finland and Sweden. Germany has no need for a shadow private school sector to boost its enviable productivity levels.

And of course talking about the problems with the current system invites the same tired criticisms, intended to stifle debate: those who benefit from the current system are bound to say that it works well enough at it is; that those who have the temerity to make criticisms are suffering from 'chippy' jealousy; that these schools represent the last bastion of excellence; that someone has to be the elite; that this is how it has always been.

They say it is anachronistic to try to apply the values of medieval Britain to a modern, liberal democracy. But surely the values championed by philanthropists like William Wykeham and Thomas Sutton, who established the first public schools, are no different to the values we aspire to today: fair access to a fair education system.

And we must not forget these schools belong to all of us. They were established to improve the education in our communities, to help the weak and poor escape the disadvantages of their birth. These schools, which were as much a part of the community as the village church is today, were once the cornerstones of town and country life. They are part of our shared heritage but were misappropriated by the nobility and moneyed classes for the education and advancement of their own.

The public school movement refuses to be held back by their past. But remember: the founders of the colleges of Eton and Winchester could not have been clearer in their expressed wishes that the poor should benefit from their gifts. This was what they intended to be their legacy. That was how they wanted God to know them and how they wanted their communities to remember them.

ACKNOWLEDGEMENTS

A long time ago I came across a book about the rules and tactics of rugby first published in 1918. It was the only prize my grandfather ever won at school. Inscribed on the leather-bound cover are the words 'Sedbergh, *suaviter in modo, fortiter in re*' (gentle in manner, powerful in deed), which, at the time, meant nothing to me.

It was only when I was researching *Posh Boys* and I encountered the incredible tale of Brendan Bracken (Chapter 8) that it dawned on me my grandfather had also been educated at one of England's oldest public schools. One hundred years after he had received his scholarly prize (awarded for a rather average mark in a French exam), I wonder what he would have made of my book. He was born into a different age when millions of men and women gave up their lives to keep Britain and its Empire free. Sedbergh and the other ancient public schools, which supplied the army and government with leaders, were emblematic of British rule. Yet my grandfather's education did not equip him very well for the modern world. He died in middle age, a violent and embittered alcoholic who never came to terms with his place in a fading empire. He was neither gentle in manner nor powerful in deed.

★

In 2017 an old friend wrote to tell me he had returned with his family to our former secondary modern school in Kent. Outside the sports hall, sitting in the bushes, he had encountered an old drunk sipping from a can of Tennent's Super. The man looked ten or even twenty years older than my friend. His name was Nick and he informed my friend that they were in the same year at school. I remember Nick. He had struggled academically so the teachers put him to work on the school farm. Like many of the boys and girls from the out-of-town estates, he left school weeks before suffering the humiliation of sitting any exams. It was the local plastic injection-moulding factory or nothing. Written off at such a young age he never really stood a chance.

I had a hunch that the life chances of the children who come from Nick's part of town haven't improved in the last forty years. So I checked the school's 2017 Ofsted report. The school is now a comprehensive and overall it is doing well, but this is what the inspectors had to say about the new 'Nick' generation: 'There is a large group of pupils who do not have special educational needs or disabilities and are a long way behind their classmates. Often they find the work too hard and are at risk of falling further behind. A few pupils are persistently absent despite the school's best efforts to help them to attend regularly.' The inspectors explained: 'Sometimes pupils are absent because they miss the one and only bus from their area that drops off at the school.' Nick used to miss the bus on purpose because he couldn't see the point of getting up early to spend the day shovelling shit.

★

I dedicate this book to my parents who taught me that for someone to succeed, someone else must fail. I wish to pay special thanks to my partner Linda King and our two sons, Stanley and Walter, without whose love and support nothing would have got done. Thanks, Stan, for the hours of patient and underpaid transcription.

I owe a particular debt of gratitude to my editor, Alex Christofi, for the invaluable work he has done on the script and for his encouragement and guidance throughout. I suspect lots of authors are told, like I was, to 'follow your nose' but it takes nerves of steel for an editor to stick to this advice. It may seem strange that in the two years researching and writing this book, Alex and I never enquired of each other's education. *Posh Boys* is not intended as criticism or judgement of any individual on the basis of his or her education, only a critique of a system that so obviously produces unfair outcomes. It shouldn't matter where someone went to school. What matters is where we choose to educate our children.

I'm also grateful to Jonathan Bentley-Smith of Oneworld for helping to give the book early shape, and all the brilliant team at Oneworld.

Thank you to all those who have given so generously of their time, expertise, inspiration and support:

Lord Kenneth Baker, former Secretary of State for Education

Lord David Willetts, Chair of the Resolution Foundation and former Minister of State for Universities and Science

Sir Anthony Seldon, former head of Wellington College

Dillibe Onyeama, second black schoolboy to attend Eton and author of *Nigger at Eton*

Melissa Benn, author and education campaigner

Barnaby Lenon, former headmaster of Harrow School and chair of the Independent Schools Council

Tony Little, former headmaster of Eton and chief education officer of GEMS Education

Fiona Millar, journalist and education campaigner

Nick Hillman, director of the Higher Education Policy Institute

Simon Dudley, founder and chair of Holyport College, sponsored by Eton College

Professor Diane Reay, Emeritus Professor of Education, Cambridge University

Conor Ryan, director of research and communications, Sutton Trust, and former education adviser to Tony Blair and David Blunkett

Lord Kenneth Baker, former Secretary of State for Education

The comedians David Baddiel and Jim Davidson

Trenton Oldfield, class activist who disrupted the 2012 Oxford Cambridge Boat Race

David Kynaston, historian and author

Andrew Turner, deputy Head of Charterhouse School

Robert Halfon MP, chair of the House of Commons select committee on education

Justin Madders MP, chair of the House of Commons select committee on social mobility

Dr Joseph Spence, Master of Dulwich College

Dr Cameron Pyke, deputy Master (External Relations), Dulwich College

Andrew Smith, former headmaster of Rodborough School

Ian Mason, head of media and communications, Independent Schools Council

John McLellan, parent who sued a public school over the education of his children

Nick Duffell, psychotherapist and author of *The Making of Them* and *Wounded Leaders*

David Greenwood, solicitor representing victims of child abuse

Steve Turner, trade union official

Journalists Jonathan Ames, Robert Mendick, Dominic Turnbull, Oliver Duff and Katherine Butler

Former schoolboys Paul Ferris, Amandla Thomas-Johnson, Dr Mike Hamblin, David Cheskin, Dan Hayes, Robert Bilsland,

Robert Barr, Babar Ahmed, Isaac Verkaik, Rocky Leanders, Tom Tanner, Ben Jackson, Ekwall Singh Tiwana, Peter Veitch, Claire and James Garthwaite, Bobby Egbuna, Piers and Sally Le Marquand, Bill and Mary Anne Verkaik, Michael Evans and David Nugent

And hundreds of other unnamed teachers, schoolboys and schoolgirls, both private and state, who wittingly and unwittingly contributed to this book.

NOTES

Prologue

1 George Orwell, *The Lion and the Unicorn* (London: Secker & Warburg, 1941), available at https://www.orwellfoundation. com/the-orwell-foundation/orwell/essays-and-other-works/ the-lion-and-the-unicorn-socialism-and-the-english-genius/

2 Gary McCulloch, *Philosophers and Kings: Education for Leadership in Modern England* (Cambridge: Cambridge University Press, 1991), pp. 27–30.

3 http://www.independent.co.uk/news/uk/this-britain/newly-published- ss-handbook-gives-blueprint-for-nazi-britain-5371959.html

4 The Sutton Trust reports, 2015/17.

5 http://www.suttontrust.com/wp-content/uploads/2010/05/1MPs_ educational_backgrounds_2010_A.pdf

6 Rosemary Bennett and Nicola Woolcock, *The Times*, 20 November 2017.

7 Office for National Statistics report, *Persistent Poverty in the UK and EU*, 2014.

8 According to a 2011 study by the Sutton Trust.

Part One: Selling Education by the Pound

1 http://www.educationengland.org.uk/documents/fleming/fleming.html. Quoted from John Strype, *Memorials of Thomas Cranmer*, Book 1, Chapter 22, in Board of Education, *The Public Schools* (Fleming Report) (HMSO, 1944), p. 10.

1 Poor Schools

1   William A. Smith, *Ancient Education* (New York: Philosophical Library, 1955), p. 184.

2   *Oxford Classical Dictionary*, ed. Simon Hornblower and Antony Spawforth, Third Edition (Oxford: Oxford University Press, 1996).

3   Frederik Poulsen, *Glimpses of Roman Culture* (Leiden: E.J. Brill, 1950), p. 228.

4   http://www.educationengland.org.uk/history/chapter01.html

5   A.F. Leach, *The Schools of Medieval England* (London: Methuen & Co., 1915), p. 2.

6   Ibid., p. 7.

7   Nicholas Orme, *Medieval Schools: From Roman Britain to Renaissance England* (New Haven, CT: Yale University Press, 2006), p. 131.

8   Leach, p. 119.

9   Virginia Davis, *William Wykeham: A Life* (London: Hambledon Continuum, 2007), p. 31.

10.   Michael Wood, *The Story of England*.

11   David Turner, *The Old Boys: The Decline and Rise of the Public School* (New Haven, CT: Yale University Press, 2015), p. 6.

12   Henry B. Wheatley, *London Past and Present: Its History, Associations, and Traditions* (London: J. Murray, 1891), p. 403.

13   Geoffrey Brown, *A Brief History of Merchant Taylors' School*. https://www.mtsn.org.uk/fileadmin/content/MTSN/_Admissions/History/450History_Concordia.pdf

14   https://www.cityoflondonschool.org.uk/about/history

15   Winchester College Statutes, Turner, p. 7.

16   Leach, p. 231.

17   http://archiveblog.westminster.org.uk/?p=142

18   http://www.westminster.org.uk/westminster/admissions/scholarships/

19   Dr Stephen Porter, archivist of Charterhouse, *Charterhouse: A 400th anniversary portrait*, p. 18.

20   http://www.charterhouse.org.uk/suttonshospital

21   Richard L. DeMolen, *Richard Mulcaster and the Profession of Teaching in Sixteenth-Century England* (Philadelphia, PA: University of Pennsylvania Press, 1974), p. 15.

22   http://www.bl.uk/learning/langlit/sounds/case-studies/received-pronunciation/

23 Turner, p. 20.

24 Christopher Tyerman, *A History of Harrow School* (Oxford: Oxford University Press, 2000), p. 183.

25 Ian Williams, *The Alms Trade: Charities, Past, Present and Future* (London: Unwin Hyman, 1989), p. 61.

26 Tyerman, p. 180.

27 Attorney-General v. Earl of Lonsdale (1827).

2 Nurseries of Aristocracy

1 Nick Fraser, *The Importance of Being Eton* (London: Short, 2006).

2 John Nelson Miner, *The Grammar Schools of Medieval England: A. F. Leach in Historiographical Perspective* (Montreal: McGill-Queen's University Press, 1990), p. 25.

3 Ralph Nevill, *Floreat Etona: Anecdotes and Memories of Eton College* (London: Macmillan, 1911), p. 5.

4 Foster Watson, *English Grammar Schools to 1660* (Cambridge: Cambridge University Press, 1908), p. 12.

5 Miner, p. 22.

6 Kenneth Lindsay, *English Education* (London: William Collins, 1941), p. 14.

7 Basil Williams, *The Life of William Pitt, Earl of Chatham, Vol. 1* (London: Cass, 1966), p. 34.

8 Turner, p. 57.

9 Tyerman, p. 180.

10 Select Committee on the State of Education, 1834, p. 225; https://babel.hathitrust.org/cgi/pt?id=umn.31951d00029127a;view=1up;seq=233

11 Colin Shrosbree, *Public Schools and Private Education: The Clarendon Commission, 1861-64, and the Public Schools Acts* (Manchester: Manchester University Press, 1988), p. 57.

12 https://www.shrewsbury.org.uk/features/school-history (although con-eveniently the school has left out the second part of this quote!)

13 Shrosbree, p. 57.

14 Ibid., p. 59.

15 Turner, p. 87.

16 Tyerman, pp. 227, 229, 250.

3 Empire of the Sons

1 *Imperialism and Popular Culture*, ed. John M. Mackenzie (Manchester: Manchester University Press, 1992), p. 118.

2 Clarendon Report, p. 11.

3 'Winston S. Churchill: The Battle of Omdurman, 1898', at https://sourcebooks.fordham.edu/halsall/mod/1898churchill-omdurman.asp

4 Jasper Ridley, *Lord Palmerston* (New York: Dutton, 1972), p. 10.

5 *The Invention of Tradition*, eds. Eric Hobsbawm and Terence Ranger (Cambridge: Cambridge University Press, 1984).

6 Brian Dobbs, *Edwardians at Play: Sport, 1890–1914* (London: Pelham, 1973), p. 89.

7 C. Brad Faught, *Gordon: Victorian Hero* (Washington, DC: Potomac, c.2008), pp. 6–8.

8 Author interview with Sir Brian Barttelot 2017.

9 Tim Jeal, *Stanley: The Impossible Life of Africa's Greatest Explorer* (New Haven, CT: Yale University Press, 2007), pp. 357–8.

10 Walter George Barttelot, *The Life of Edmund Musgrave Barttelot, Captain and Brevet Major Royal Fusiliers, Commander of the Rear Column of the Emin Pasha Relief Expedition* (London: Richard Bentley and Son, 1890).

11 Bernard Glassman, *Benjamin Disraeli: The Fabricated Jew in Myth and Memory* (Lanham, MD: University Press of America, 2002), p. 8.

12 https://www.mtsn.org.uk/about-us/old-boys/

13 http://www.historyhome.co.uk/people/hastings.htm

14 Basil Williams, *Cecil Rhodes* (London, 1921), p. 8.

15 Robert Anderson, *British Universities Past and Present* (London: Continuum, 2006), pp. 92–3.

16 Turner, p. 190.

17 Peter Parker, *The Old Lie: The Great War and the Public School Ethos* (London: Constable, 1987), p. 55.

18 Jeffrey Richards, *Happiest Days: The Public Schools in English Fiction* (Manchester: Manchester University Press, 1988), p. 145.

4 A Victorian Reckoning

1 Jenny Holt, *Public School Literature, Civic Education and the Politics of Male Adolescence* (Farnham: Ashgate, 2008).

2 Shrosbree, p. 48.

3 *The Times*, 16 February 1861, p. 9.

4 Shrosbree, p. 97.

5 https://archive.org/stream/lifelettersgeorge01maxw#page/14/mode/2up

6 Sir George Lewis, *Hansard*, CLXII, 23 April 1861, col. 984.

7 http://www.educationengland.org.uk/history/chapter03.html

8 Clarendon Commission Report, Vol. 1, p. 6.

9 Embodied in the Endowed Schools Act of 1869.

5 Eton Rifles

1 A.H.H. Mclean, *Public Schools and the Great War 1914–1919* (London: Edward Stanford, 1923).

2 Parker, p. 63.

3 Ibid., p. 54.

4 Ibid., p. 55.

5 Anthony Clayton, *The British Officer: Leading the Army from 1660 to the Present* (Harlow: Pearson Education, 2006), p. 125.

6 Alec Waugh, *Public School Life: Boys, Parents, Masters* (London: Collins, 1922), p. 259.

7 This figure is based on 1914 battalion requirements of 3,000 officers leading 100,000 men. We can be confident that these ratios can be applied to public schools because obtaining a commission in 1914 was strictly a matter of class.

8 https://www.army.mod.uk/documents/general/history_of_rmas.pdf

9 Roland Wales, *From Journey's End to the Dam Busters: The Life of R. C. Sherriff, Playwright of the Trenches* (Barnsley: Pen & Sword Military, 2016).

10 http://www.exploringsurreyspast.org.uk/themes/subjects/military/surreys-first-world-war/sherriff/; http://discovery.nationalarchives.gov.uk/details/r/D5133419; Anthony Seldon and David Walsh, *Public Schools and the Great War* (Barnsley: Pen & Sword Military, 2013); Michael Lucas, *The Journey's End Battalion: The 9th East Surrey in the Great War* (Barnsley: Pen & Sword Military, 2012).

11 Parker, p. 68.

12 http://www.etoncollege.com/ArmedServices.aspx

13 http://www.nationalarchives.gov.uk/pathways/firstworldwar/service_records/courts_martial.htm

14 Elizabeth Speller, *Daily Express*, 24 February 2010.

15 http://www.spectator.co.uk/2014/04/book-review-private-lord-crawfords-great-war-diaries-edited-by-christopher-arnander-public-schools-and-the-great-war-by-anthony-selden-and-david-walsh/

16 Tim Card, *Eton Renewed* (London: John Murray, 1994), p. 301.

17 The net result of the initiative appears to be more funding being ploughed into public schools cadet corps which continue to supply officers to our armed forces.

18 https://www.thegazette.co.uk/London/issue/32868/page/6728/data.pdf

19 Seldon and Walsh, p. 1.

20 http://noglory.org/index.php/articles/112-lions-and-donkeys-dan-snow-s-10-myths-about-world-war-one-answered-by-no-glory. The total number of privately educated officers who served is harder to ascertain, unless someone between 1914 and 1920 kept careful records. One would, however, expect these numbers to be at least three times the size of the school in 1914. Even if there were differences between schools in the numbers volunteering in 1914–15, conscription from 1916 should have meant that all medically fit alumni between the ages of 18 and 40 would be called up. Seldon and Walsh, p. 254.

21 Ibid., p. 172.

22 Ibid., p. 6.

6 Survival of the Fittest

1 http://www.telegraph.co.uk/education/educationopinion/11005281/The-Great-War-and-education.html

2 Section 26 provided for the Abolition of Fees in Public Elementary Schools: 'No fees shall be charged or other charges of any kind made in any public elementary school, except as provided by the Education (Provision of Meals) Act, 1906, and the Local Education Authorities (Medical Treatment) Act, 1909.'

3 George Bernard Shaw, Introduction, *Man and Superman* (1911).

4 *Bernard Shaw's Book Reviews: 1884–1950*, ed. Brian Tyson (University Park, PA: Pennsylvania State University Press, c.1996), p. 480.

5 H.V. Marrot, *The Life and Letters of John Galsworthy* (London: William Heinemann, 1935), pp. 703–5; Tyerman, p. 304.

6 Alec Waugh, pp. 8, 271.

7   Gary McCulloch, *Cyril Norwood and the Ideal of Secondary Education* (New York: Palgrave Macmillan, 2007), pp. 131–2.

8   Turner, p. 166.

9   Ibid.

10 Ibid., p. 167.

11 Frank Fletcher, *After Many Days: A School Master's Memories* (London, 1937), p. 274.

12 Board of Education Circular 1381. David Donnison, *The Public Schools Commission* (1970).

13 H.C. Dent, *Secondary Education for All: Origins and Development in England* (London: Routledge & K. Paul, 1949), p. 106.

14 Turner, p. 168.

15 Mika LaVaque-Manty, *The Playing Fields of Eton: Equality and Excellence in Modern Meritocracy* (Ann Arbor, MI: University of Michigan Press, 2009), p. 101.

16 Turner, p. 180.

17 https://www.theguardian.com/lifeandstyle/2011/nov/26/peter-waugh-alec-wagh-evelyn-waugh

18 Evelyn Waugh, *Decline and Fall* (1928).

19 Turner, p. 178.

7 Churchill, the Public School Reformer

1   Patrick Bishop, *Daily Telegraph*, 29 May 2005.

2   David Boyd, *Elites and Their Education: Patterns of Recruitment and Mobility* (Thesis (D.Phil.), University of Oxford, 1972), pp. 41, 82.

3   Ibid.

4   Orwell, *The Lion and the Unicorn*.

5   Turner, p. 189.

6   *Winston S. Churchill: His Complete Speeches, 1897–1964*, Vol. VI, ed. Robert Rhodes James (New York: Chelsea House, 1974), p. 6315.

7   Nick Hillman, 'The parallels between admissions to independent boarding schools and admissions to selective universities', *Higher Education Review*, Vol. 46, No. 2, 2014, p. 7.

8   Turner, p. 188.

9   Nick Hillman, 'The Public Schools Commission: "Impractical, Expensive and Harmful to Children"?', *Contemporary British History*, Vol. 24, Issue 4, 2010.

10 http://www.bbc.co.uk/schoolreport/25751787

11 Sir Bernard Lovell, *Echoes of War: The Story of H2S Radar* (Bristol: Adam Hilger, 1991).

12 Ibid., p. 3.

13 Fleming Commission, pp. 3, 4.

14 Clive Griggs, *The TUC and Education Reform, 1926–1970* (London; Portland, OR: Woburn Press, 2002), p.144.

15 *The Trusty Servant*, No. 121, 2016, p. 13; https://www.joomag.com/magazine/trusty-servant/0441241001463133573?short

16 C.H. Batteson, 'The 1944 Education Act reconsidered', *Educational Review* 51.1 (1999), pp. 5–15.

17 Turner, p. 190.

8 Post-War Privilege

1 https://www.winstonchurchill.org/publications/finest-hour/finest-hour-113/brendan-bracken-the-fantasist-whose-dreams-came-true; http://www.irishtimes.com/life-and-style/people/the-irish-spoofer-who-was-churchill-s-right-hand-man-1.2698575

2 http://labourlist.org/2010/11/ellen-wilkinson-forging-a-new-path/

3 http://www.newstatesman.com/node/195453

4 Turner, p. 183.

5 Martin Francis, *Ideas and Policies Under Labour, 1945–1951: Building a New Britain* (Manchester: Manchester University Press 1997), p. 163.

6 *Haileybury News*, 9 October 2017.

7 Francis, p. 161.

8 Interview with Dr Joseph Spence, Master of Dulwich College, 12 January 2018.

9 Nick Hillman, 'Public Schools and the Fleming Report of 1944: shunting the first-class carriage on to an immense siding?', *History of Education*, Vol. 41, issue 2, 2012.

10 McCulloch, *Philosophers and Kings*, p. 27.

11 Sir John Newsom, *The Public Schools Commission: First Report* (1968).

12 David Donnison, *The Public Schools Commission* (1970).

13 Interview with the author, January 2017.

14 http://www.telegraph.co.uk/news/uknews/1322534/Forget-the-school-its-the-teaching-that-counts.html

15 Author's interview with Melissa Benn, July 2017.
16 http://hansard.millbanksystems.com/commons/1965/dec/22/
public-schools-commission
17 Hillman, 'The Public Schools Commission'.
18 Ibid.
19 Newsom, The Public Schools Commission: First Report, Vol. 1.,
para. 320.
20 Ibid., paras. 238–9
21 Hillman, 'The Public Schools Commission'.
22 Ibid.
23 Mark Peel, *The New Meritocracy: A History of UK Independent Schools 1979–2015* (London: Elliott and Thompson Ltd, 2015), p. 28.
24 Ibid.
25 Ed Vaizey was best man at Michael Gove's wedding in 2001.
26 https://www.standard.co.uk/lifestyle/esmagazine/ed-vaizey-the-
dedicated-minister-of-fashion-8514939.html
27 Hillman, 'The Public Schools Commission'.
28 Ibid.
29 Social Market Foundation report; http://www.smf.co.uk/wp-content/
uploads/2014/01/Publication-Schools-United-Ending-the-divide-
between-independent-and-state-Anthony-Seldon.pdf
30 http://www.suttontrust.com/newsarchive/
assisted-place-holders-enduring-social-networks-better-jobs/
31 https://www.theguardian.com/politics/2012/dec/28/
margaret-thatcher-role-plan-to-dismantle-welfare-state-revealed

9 Education Education Education

1 Jon Sopel, *Tony Blair: The Moderniser* (London: Bantam, 1995), p. 10.
2 Tony Blair, *A Journey* (London: Arrow Books, 2011), p. 561.
3 Sopel, pp. 17–18.
4 Ibid., p. 20.
5 Andrew Gimson, *The Spectator*, 5 May 2001.
6 Ibid.
7 Blair, p. 43.
8 Peel, p. 18.
9 http://www.bbc.co.uk/programmes/b090213q
10 Blair, p. 87.

11 In Labour's 2017 manifesto the imposition of VAT on school fees was the only policy tackling private education.

12 Author interview with Conor Ryan (July 2017), former education adviser to Tony Blair and David Blunkett.

13 Paul Bolton, 'Oxbridge "elitism"', House of Commons Library, 19 June 2017.

14 Twenty years later the Conservatives made the threat more explicit in their May 2017 manifesto when they ordered 100 top public schools to sponsor an academy or set up a free school. Those that didn't would no longer enjoy charity status.

15 Joe Murphy and Rosie Waterhouse, *Mail on Sunday*, 23 November 1997.

16 *The Independent*, 2 October 1997.

17 Interview with the author, September 2017.

18 https://assets.publishing.service.gov.uk/
media/575bd0a740f0b66bda00000e/The_Independent_Schools_
Council_v_The_Charity_Commission_for_England___Wales_and_The_
National_Council_for_Voluntary_Organisation__2__HM_Antorney_
General_v_The_Charity_Com_and_The_ISC.pdf

19 http://www.scotsman.com/news/education/
parents-angry-as-gordonstoun-sells-school-1-509725

20 *Daily Mail*, 17 July 2003.

21 Peel, pp. 50, 52.

22 http://www.telegraph.co.uk/news/uknews/1511429/50-public-schools-
fined-for-fixing-their-fees.html

23 *The Times*, 22 September 2003.

24 http://www.thenational.ae/business/aviation/
gems-education-reports-increase-in-six-month-revenue

25 *Today* programme, 14 July 2009.

26 http://www.dailymail.co.uk/news/article-1199761/Who-better-lead-
attack-private-education-class-war-activist-yes-went-public-school-herself.
html

27 https://www.theguardian.com/society/2012/jul/10/
suzi-leather-chair-charity-commission

28 *The Chronicle*, Issue 4093, 2009.

29 Julie Henry, *Sunday Telegraph*, 4 October 2009.

30 https://assets.publishing.service.gov.uk/
media/575bd0a740f0b66bda00000e/

The_Independent_Schools_Council_v_The_Charity_Commission_
for_England___Wales_and_The_National_Council_for_Voluntary_
Organisation__2__HM_Antorney_General_v_The_Charity_Com_and_
The_ISC.pdf

31 Christopher Hope, *Daily Telegraph*, 5 December 2012.

32 Helen Wright, 'Class war: the independent school heads reply', *Sunday Telegaph*, 25 November 2012.

33 https://www.suttontrust.com/researcharchive/
the-sutton-trust-cabinet-analysis/

34 http://www.dailymail.co.uk/news/article-4305312/We-NOT-bullied-
private-schools-tell-May.html;
http://www.telegraph.co.uk/education/2016/10/03/
dont-point-a-gun-to-our-heads-teachers-tell-theresa-may/

35 https://inews.co.uk/opinion/
isnt-labour-pledging-reform-private-schools/

36 https://www.conservatives.com/manifesto

Part Two: Bad Education

1 *The Oxford Myth*, ed. Rachel Johnson (London: Weidenfeld & Nicolson Ltd., 1988), pp. 70–1.

10 Did You Go to School?

1 Greg Hurst, *The Times*, 1 September 2016.

2 http://www.pravoslavie.ru/english/96686.htm

3 http://everyday-saints.com/13.htm

4 *The Times*, 1 September 2016.

5 http://www.telegraph.co.uk/news/politics/david-cameron/8757576/
David-Cameron-tells-Russian-hosts-KGB-tried-to-recruit-me-but-I-
failed-the-test.html

6 @MichaelLCrick, Twitter, 7 September 2107.

7 https://www.theguardian.com/news/2016/apr/04/
panama-papers-david-cameron-father-tax-bahamas

8 *The Times* obituary, 9 December 1930.

9 Francis Elliott and James Hanning, *Cameron: Practically a Conservative* (London: Fourth Estate, 2012), p. 369.

10 Michael Ashcroft and Isobel Oakeshott, *Call Me Dave: The Unauthorised Biography* (London: Biteback Publishing, 2015), p. 17.

11 Ashcroft and Oakeshott, p. 17.

12 http://www.financemagnates.com/executives/moves/exclusive-broctagon-solutions-onboards-peter-romilly-as-chief-operating-officer/

13 https://relationshipscience.com/edward-g-mallinckrodt-p3617968

14 https://www.1843magazine.com/features/eton-and-the-making-of-a-modern-elite

15 Ashcroft and Oakeshott, p. 32.

16 http://www.express.co.uk/expressyourself/235077/A-very-exclusive-club-called-pop

17 Ashcroft and Oakeshott, p. 37; http://www.telegraph.co.uk/news/uknews/1542289/Cameron-the-bad-boy-of-Eton-who-wouldnt-split-on-druggy-friend.htm

18 http://d56ddea33f0f1bf171c7-0d3b9304851da04b7a689f475e7e240f.r47.cf2.rackcdn.com/850215%20Eton%20College%20Chronicle%20iv%20THCR%201-3-15%20f85.pdf

19 *Evening Standard*, 7 April 2008

20 http://www.dailymail.co.uk/news/article-2572544/Files-Britain-NOT-support-military-action-against-Russia.html

21 www.etoncollege.com/TheOEA.aspx

22 https://development.mtsn.org.uk/city-network---september-2016

23 https://www.theguardian.com/politics/2011/sep/02/bullingdon-club-david-cameron-riots

24 Ashcroft and Oakeshott, p. 73.

25 *Mail on Sunday*, 18 March 2007; Ashcroft and Oakeshott, p. 79.

26 http://www.telegraph.co.uk/men/thinking-man/10377728/Clubland-were-all-members-now.html

27 Ashcroft and Oakeshott, p. 80.

28 https://www.theguardian.com/politics/2011/sep/02/bullingdon-club-david-cameron-riots; Ashcroft and Oakeshott, p. 111.

29 Ashcroft and Oakeshott, p. 198.

30 http://www.dailymail.co.uk/news/article-3461103/The-torture-watching-husband-choose-beliefs-old-friend-PM-Daily-Mail-columnist-SARAH-VINE-s-intensely-personal-account-momentous-decision.html

31 Michael Green was educated at Haberdashers' Aske's Boys' School, in
    Elstree, Hertfordshire on a scholarship and left, aged seventeen, with four
    O-levels. Contemporaries included David Elstein, the former head of
    Channel 5, and Nicholas Serota, director of the Tate galleries. But there
    were a number of former Haberdashers who were moving in Cameron's
    circle including David Lidington. Following the 2010 general election,
    Cameron appointed Lidington minister for Europe. In August 2016, fol-
    lowing Cameron's resignation, Lidington was awarded a CBE in the Prime
    Minister's Resignation Honours for his services to the government in
    that role. Haberdashers' also provided Cameron with his closest friend and
    oldest political ally, David Feldman. They first met at Brasenose College,
    Oxford. Feldman later ran the operations and fundraising for Cameron's
    2005 Tory leadership bid and was later made chief executive of the party.
    He was credited with accusing Conservative Associations of being 'all mad,
    swivel-eyed loons'.

32 Ashcroft and Oakeshott, p. 118.

33 Ibid., pp. 127, 128.

34 Ibid., pp. 149–50.

35 Elliott and Hanning, p. 208.

36 Ibid., p. 292.

37 Ibid., p. 375.

38 Other notable additions were Nick Boles, son of Sir Jack Boles, the former
    head of the National Trust and the great-nephew of Conservative MP
    Dennis Boles. Boles was a scholar at Winchester before studying PPE at
    Magdalen College, Oxford. In 2008 Boris Johnson made him his chief
    of staff when he became London mayor. Others now part of Cameron's
    tightknit group were George Bridges (Eton) and Kate Fall (King's,
    Canterbury), a friend of Cameron's since Oxford who later became his
    deputy chief of staff. Fall was the daughter of a former ambassador to
    Moscow and an old girlfriend of George Osborne. She was ennobled
    after the 2015 general election. It took a year until she made her maiden
    speech. She is now a partner at PR company Brunswick, which is
    run by close Cameron friend Sir Alan Parker. Another was Kate Rock
    (Sherborne School for Girls) who was appointed deputy chair of the Tory
    Party. She is married to Caspar Rock, an OE who is chief investment
    officer at Cazenove Capital Management, the wealth management arm
    of Schroders in the UK, Channel Islands and Asia. One of Cameron's key

confidantes moving up the rails was James O'Shaughnessy (Wellington). He was already a well-connected lobbyist and was brought into the fold by Gove whom he knew him from their time together at the think tank Policy Exchange in the early noughties. O'Shaughnessy later followed Gove, the then newly appointed shadow education secretary, to work for the Conservative Party in opposition. He helped write the 2010 general election manifesto and then co-drafted the deal between the coalition parties in 2010, before doing a stint as Cameron's director of policy. But his expertise was always in education. In 2012 he left the government set up the Floreat Education Academies Trust (Feat) and its parent charity, Floreat Education, a charity and free schools operator. He was later accused of profiting from his conflicts of interests.

39 David Anderson QC, at Eton before Cameron, was appointed in 2011 by the home secretary. He reported directly to the prime minister and parliament. Anderson's predecessor Sir Alex Carlile actually went to same school (Epsom College) as Sir John Scarlett, the head of MI6, one of the agencies Carlile had oversight of. When both men retired they set up an intelligence consultancy.

40 https://www.ft.com/content/ e78f9402-ab61-11e3-aad9-00144feab7de?mhq5j=e3

41 The Sutton Trust.

42 Cameron hired his non-contemporary George Young (chief whip), also Oliver Letwin, Henry Bellingham (under secretary of state at the Foreign and Commonwealth Office until 5 September 2012), Jo Johnson, Boris Johnson, Rupert Harrison, Jesse Norman and Zac Goldsmith, whose billionaire father James did so much to sow the seeds for Brexit. All were Old Etonians.

43 https://www.ft.com/ content/3c5ebc20-1300-11e7-80f4-13e067d5072c?mhq5j=e3

44 http://www.telegraph.co.uk/news/2016/06/02/ patrick-rock-ex-david-cameron-aide-to-be-sentenced-for-making-in/

45 Cameron's loyal political ally and Notting Hill neighbour George Osborne was made a Companion of Honour. OEs Oliver Letwin and Hugo Swire were both given knighthoods. There was, of course, a peerage for Ed Llewellyn, his tennis partner and OE contemporary. Cameron also recommended him to become the UK's next ambassador to France. Gabby Bertin, Cameron's press secretary, and later responsible

for forging Downing Street's relations with business, pressure groups and charities, was given a peerage, which made her the youngest member of the House of Lords. His head of operations Liz Sugg was also made a peer. Camilla Cavendish (Putney High School, another member of the Girls' Day School Trust), head of the Policy Unit, joined her in the Lords. Even Samantha Cameron got in on the act by ensuring her stylist, Isabel Spearman, who went to boarding school with Clare Balding and Miranda Hart at Downe House in Berkshire, was given an OBE.

46 Among them was Richard Benyon who had been a childhood friend of Cameron. Benyon is one of the richest MPs. The great-great-grandson of three-times Tory prime minister Lord Salisbury, he can trace his ancestry back to William Cecil, the chief political adviser to Elizabeth I. He attended Bradfield College, a low-key member of the influential Rugby Group, which also includes Harrow, Wellington and Charterhouse. Benyon's father was also an MP and the family still carries influence among the hunting and shooting set of the Conservative Party. Cameron later made Benyon a minister in the Department for the Environment, Food and Rural Affairs. Greg Barker (Lancing) and three more OEs joined the Cameron camp, Hugo Swire, Oliver Letwin ('I would rather beg in the street than send my children to a state school') and significantly Nicholas Soames, grandson of Winston Churchill. Swire was married to the daughter of former Tory bigwig John Nott (Bradfield). But of course Soames's influence went to very the heart of the Tory Party. Added to his group was another influential Tory, Andrew Robathan (Merchant Taylors'). Two key individuals resigned from the Tory press office to help Cameron with his leadership campaign. George Eustice (a former member of UKIP who later became Tory MP for Camborne and Redruth) went to ancient Truro Cathedral School, which during the Second World War accommodated boys evacuated from St Paul's, London. The other was Gabby Bertin, who attended Croydon High School, a fee-paying member of the Girls' Day School Trust. Alumnae include Susanna Reid, Anneka Rice and Sandra Howard, former model and wife of Cameron's mentor Michael Howard.

47 http://www.standard.co.uk/news/howard-attacked-for-choosing-eton-7201922.html

48 http://www.dailymail.co.uk/news/article-3724567/
    Dave-s-two-fingers-voters-brazen-contempt-public-opinion-Cameron-
    showers-honours-chums-cronies-second-raters.html
49 http://www.dailymail.co.uk/news/article-3723197/
    David-Cameron-s-resignation-honours-list-reveals-type-
    British-CORRUPTION-friend-ex-policy-guru-Steve-
    Hilton-says.html
50 https://www.ft.com/content/4c3b9c90-0422-11e7-ace0-
    1ce02ef0def9?mhq5j=e3; http://www.mirror.co.uk/news/politics/
    greedy-george-osborne-facing-furious-10049285
51 https://www.byline.com/column/67/article/2049

11 Boys' Own Brexit

1 Stuart Jeffries, *The Guardian*, 26 May 2014.
2 http://www.dulwich.org.uk/college/about/history
3 http://www.telegraph.co.uk/news/politics/ukip/11291050/
   Nigel-Farage-and-Enoch-Powell-the-full-story-of-Ukips-links-with-the-
   Rivers-of-Blood-politician.html
4 https://www.channel4.com/news/
   nigel-farage-ukip-letter-school-concerns-racism-fascism
5 Michael Crick, *Channel 4 News*, 19 September 2013.
6 http://www.independent.co.uk/news/uk/politics/
   nigel-farage-open-letter-schoolfriend-brexit-poster-nazi-song-dulwich-
   college-gas-them-all-a7185336.html
7 http://www.independent.co.uk/news/uk/politics/
   nigel-farage-fascist-nazi-song-gas-them-all-ukip-brexit-schoolfriend-
   dulwich-college-a7185236.html
8 Interview with the author at Dulwich College, 12 January 2018.
9 www.facebook.com/myiannopuolos, accessed 24 January 2018.
10 https://www.linkedin.com/in/sam-farage-85b406b2; http://
   www.telegraph.co.uk/news/politics/nigel-farage/11467039/
   Nigel-Farage-My-public-school-had-a-real-social-mix-but-now-only-
   the-mega-rich-can-afford-the-fees.html
11 Simon Kupar, *Financial Times*, 7 July 2016.
12 http://www.telegraph.co.uk/news/2017/01/05/project-
   fear-brexit-predictions-flawed-partisan-new-study-says/;

http://www.telegraph.co.uk/news/2016/06/25/
how-project-fear-failed-to-keep-britain-in-the-eu--and-the-signs/

13 Odey declined to be interviewed.

14 *Sunday Times*, 23 April 2017, p. 4; http://www.independent.co.uk/news/
uk/politics/brexit-leave-eu-campaign-arron-banks-jeremy-hosking-five-
uk-richest-businessmen-peter-hargreaves-a7699046.html

15 https://inews.co.uk/news/technology/cambridge-analytica-facebook-
data-protection/

16 http://www.bbc.co.uk/news/technology-43581892

17 https://inews.co.uk/news/technology/cambridge-analytica-facebook-
data-protection/

18 https://www.reuters.com/article/us-facebook-cambridge-analytica-leave-eu/
what-are-the-links-between-cambridge-analytica-and-a-brexit-campaign-
group-idUSKBN1GX2IO

19 https://www.theguardian.com/uk-news/2018/mar/24/aggregateiq-data-
firm-link-raises-leave-group-questions https://www.businesstimes.com.sg/
government-economy/brexit-campaigners-breached-uk-vote-rules-
lawyers-say

20 https://dominiccummings.com/2016/10/29/on-the-referendum-20-the-
campaign-physics-and-data-science-vote-leaves-voter-intention-
collection-system-vics-now-available-for-all/

21 *A Very British Coup*, BBC2, 22 Sepptember 2016.

22 http://www.standard.co.uk/business/business-focus-the-billionaire-
hedge-fund-winners-who-braved-the-brexit-rollercoaster-a3284101.html

23 http://fortune.com/2014/12/03/
heineken-charlene-de-carvalho-self-made-heiress/

24 http://www.cityam.com/262239/
david-camerons-ex-adviser-daniel-korski-launches-major

25 Tim Shipman, *All Out War: Brexit and the Sinking of Britain's Political Class*
(London: William Collins, 2017), p. 610.

12 For the Few, Not the Many

1 http://www.telegraph.co.uk/news/politics/Jeremy_Corbyn/11818744/
Jeremy-Corbyn-the-boy-to-the-manor-born.html

2 http://www.castlehouseschool.co.uk/about-the-school/fees/

3 Rosa Prince, *Comrade Corbyn: A Very Unlikely Coup* (London: Biteback
Publishing, 2017), p. 29. Castle House is a leading institution among the

private school movement. Its former headmaster, Richard Walden, is former chairman of the Independent Schools Association.

4 In the 1960s it was still being run as a voluntary aided school which received state and private fee funding. All entrants had to pass the 11-plus. Like many grammar schools, it was influenced by the ethos of the public schools with which it was also competing for high-paying boarders. Jeremy's brother Andrew had been a boarder at the school, although the family allowed the other three to stay at home.

5 Prince, pp. 24–5

6 Ibid., p. 28.

7 Ibid., p. 29.

8 Ibid., p. 34.

9 https://www.stjos.co.uk/stjos-prod/assets/File/Fees%20and%20 conditions%202017-18.pdf

10 https://www.stjos.co.uk/senior/prospectus/senior-prospectus-pdf/

11 @johnmcdonnellMP, Twitter, 7 June 2017.

12 https://www.theguardian.com/politics/2015/aug/15/ jeremy-corbyn-world-supporters-mentors-influences

13 http://www.peoplesmomentum.com/about

14 Michael Wilkinson, *Daily Telegraph*, 8 March 2016.

15 https://www.linkedin.com/in/laura-murray-4a940b73/

16 https://life.spectator.co.uk/2016/09/letting-the-hard-left-off-the-leash/

17 *The Times*, 2 November 2016.

18 http://labourpartymarxists.org.uk/jon-lansmans-coup-in-momentum/

19 *The Times*, 2 November 2016.

20 http://www.independent.co.uk/news/uk/how-could-labour-fail-this-one-1326206.html

21 http://news.bbc.co.uk/1/hi/uk_politics/3229453.stm

22 Abbott's decision revealed that when it was something that had a direct impact on her own family's life she was happy to contravene sacred Labour doctrine. Yet in 2017, at the height of the Harvey Weinstein-inspired sex scandal that was sweeping male-dominated institutions, she complained that when she was a single mother MP she and other MPs were victims of sexism from MPs 'educated at all-boy private schools'. She omitted to mention she had sent her son to one.

23 Both Chakrabarti and her former husband Martyn Hopper went to comprehensives. Hopper is a partner at City law firm Linklaters, earning more

than £1 million a year. Chakrabarti is the former head of human rights group Liberty. Yet the inevitable political backlash which followed lacked the bitterness that had been directed at Abbott or even Harman.

24 https://vimeo.com/170152625

25 Corbyn's front bench also features prominent members who were privately educated, including Barry Gardiner, a key Corbyn supporter and his shadow international trade secretary. Valerie Vaz, shadow leader of the House of Commons, paid for her daughter to attend the exclusive Latymer Upper School in west London. It was the same school that her uncle and Labour MP Keith Vaz attended. Debbie Abrahams, shadow secretary for work and pensions, sent her two daughters to the fee-paying Bury Grammar School.

26 https://www.steve-howell.com/grammar-schools-how-pupil-power-overthrew-delusion-division/

27 Stephen Crone, Democratic Audit, 11 March 2011.

28 Interview with the author, September 2017.

13 The Class Ladder

1 http://www.etoncollege.com/CurrentFees.aspx

2 https://www.goodschoolsguide.co.uk/choosing-a-school/independent-schools/fees-financial-assistance-scholarships-and-bursaries

3 http://www.netsalarycalculator.co.uk/70000-after-tax/

4 http://www.1879zuluwar.com/t3657-major-william-joseph-myers

5 The consultant market for public school pupil placement is dominated by privately educated advisers who use their own networks and contacts to succeed in this highly competitive and lucrative industry. One of the most blue-blooded operators in this field is the Eton-educated Charles Bonas, the managing director of education consultants Bonas MacFarlane. Bonas is half-brother of Cressida Bonas, a former girlfriend of Prince Harry. Bonas MacFarlane promises to take children from 'cradle to career' by offering a bespoke advisory service which has an 'unparalleled set of relationships with leading schools'. Bonas claims 'the admissions departments of these schools respect our appraisals of students and work closely with us to facilitate entrance even after registration lists have closed'. The company says it has placed 'hundreds of children into all of the top schools (e.g. Eton, Harrow, Winchester, Westminster, Wycombe Abbey, Cheltenham Ladies College)'.

6 Interview with the author, August 2017.

7 http://www.etoncollege.com/userfiles/files/Destination%20of%20 Etonians%202015.pdf

8 http://www.smf.co.uk/wp-content/uploads/2014/07/Open-Access-an-independent-evaluation-Embargoed-00.01-030714.pdf

9 http://www.smf.co.uk/wp-content/uploads/2014/01/ Publication-Schools-United-Ending-the-divide-between-independent-and-state-Anthony-Seldon.pdf

10 http://www.etoncollege.com/TheOEA.aspx

11 https://www.pscl.org.uk

12 https://www.channel4.com/news/factcheck/ do-the-freemasons-claims-stack-up

13 http://www.etoncollege.com/userfiles/files/ Chronicle%20%234090.pdf

14 www.harrowschool.org.uk/recent-guest-speakers

15 https://www.isc.co.uk/media/4069/isc-census-2017-final.pdf

16 Interview with the author, 31 August 2017.

17 https://www.spectator.co.uk/2017/04/ how-private-schools-are-risking-their-charitable-status/

18 http://www.tatler.com/article/ school-fees-private-education-high-cost-eton-harrow

19 http://www.mirror.co.uk/3am/celebrity-news/ gary-linekers-son-fails-to-get-grades-243105

20 http://www.telegraph.co.uk/news/2016/10/21/ exclusive-top-public-school-head-resigns-after-year-of-controver/

21 *The Times*, 14 June 2017.

22 http://www.telegraph.co.uk/news/worldnews/europe/ germany/11745098/German-expat-banker-tells-countrymen-dont-send-your-kids-to-disappointing-British-private-schools.html

23 https://www.isc.co.uk/media/4069/isc-census-2017-final.pdf; https:// www.isc.co.uk/research/

24 http://www.independent.co.uk/news/education/education-news/ rich-foreign-families-brexit-public-school-rush-to-send-children-harrow-eton-st-pauls-uk-falling-a7609181.html

25 http://www.dailymail.co.uk/news/article-3796892/Son-China-s-richest-man-buys-eight-iPhone-7s-DOG.html#ixzz4dweOrLMg

26 Interview with the author, 31 August 2017.

27 Francis Green, Jake Anders, Morag Henderson and Golo Henseke,
    LLAKES, 'Who Chooses Private Schooling in Britain and Why?',
    Research Paper 62.
28 http://www.telegraph.co.uk/news/2016/12/09/
    top-public-school-willing-accept-donations-secure-places-overseas/
29 *Daily Telegraph*, 5 October 2017.
30 http://www.manchestereveningnews.co.uk/news/
    greater-manchester-news/david-lawson-fraud-allied-london-13605598
31 http://www.independent.co.uk/news/education/
    top-private-schools-unwittingly-accepting-laundered-money-wealthy-
    foreign-criminals-moldovan-police-a7640811.html
32. http://www.dailymail.co.uk/news/article-5481713/Calls-grow-UK-
    freeze-assets-London-based-Russian-oligarchs.html
33 http://www.dulwich.org.uk/college/about/dulwich-international
34 https://www.economist.com/news/britain/21577077-some-englands-
    best-known-private-schools-are-rushing-set-up-satellites-abroad
35 Interview with the author at Dulwich College, 12 January 2018.
36 https://www.economist.com/news/britain/21577077-some-englands-
    best-known-private-schools-are-rushing-set-up-satellites-abroad
37 @Andrew_Adonis, Twitter, 11 December 2017.
38 https://www.isc.co.uk/media/4069/isc-census-2017-final.pdf
39 www.gemseducation.com
40 *The Times*, 2 May 2017.
41 John Jerrim and Lindsey Macmillan, 'Income Inequality, Intergenerational
    Mobility and the Great Gatsby Curve: Is Education the Key?', *Social Forces*,
    Vol. 94, issue 2, 1 December 2015.

14 Dormitories of Abuse

1 Interview with the author, 19 July 2017.
2 http://www.dailymail.co.uk/news/article-2552175/Top-prep-school-PE-
   teacher-82-killed-hit-train-two-days-sentenced-abusing-
   young-boy.html
3 https://www.jordanssolicitors.co.uk/2013/12/
   caldicott-boys-school-former-headteacher-guilty-of-child-abuse/
4 https://www.theguardian.com/commentisfree/2017/feb/05/john-smyth-
   public-school-christianity-brutality-thrashings-evangelical-decency
5 Turner, p. 5.

6 http://www.telegraph.co.uk/news/2017/02/05/
john-smyth-school-predator-beat-five-years/

7 https://www.channel4.com/news/
police-investigate-alleged-brutal-lashings-by-christian-leader

8 https://www.theguardian.com/society/2017/feb/03/british-bar-
rister-john-smyth-child-abuse-allegations-church-england-charged-
zimbabwe-killing; http://www.telegraph.co.uk/news/2017/02/02/
archbishop-canterburys-delightful-friend-accused-killing-teenager/

9 Interview with the author via Twitter, February 2017.

10 http://www.bbc.co.uk/news/av/uk-39560235/
further-abuse-allegations-uncovered-against-leading-qc

11 http://www.titustrust.org/about.php

12 http://www.telegraph.co.uk/news/2017/02/10/
now-archibishop-sees-toll-child-abuse-claims-true-not/

13 https://www.theguardian.com/commentisfree/2017/feb/05/john-
smyth-public-school-christianity brutality thrashings evangelical-
decency

14 https://www.churchofengland.org/media/3999908/report-of-the-peter-
ball-review-210617.pdf

15. https://www.gov.uk/government/news/charity-commission-appoints-
interim-manager-to-ampleforth-abbey-and-the-st-laurence-
education-trust

16 http://www.itv.com/news/2018-02-18/shocking-scale-of-sexual-abuse-
at-uk-boarding-schools-revealed-by-itv-documentary/

15 Bad Charity

1 Lionel Cust, *A History of Eton College* (London: Duckworth, 1899).

2 Ibid.

3 http://apps.charitycommission.gov.uk/Accounts/Ends86/0001139086_
AC_20160831_E_C.PDF

4 Jeremy Paxman, *Friends in High Places: Who Runs Britain?* (London:
Penguin, 1991), p. 171.

5 http://apps.charitycommission.gov.uk/Accounts/Ends97/0001151597_
AC_20151231_E_C.PDF

6 Answer to Freedom of Information Act request to Ministry of Defence,
January 2017.

7 Laura Suter, 'Your Money', *Daily Telegraph*, 6 May 2017, p. 3.

8   *The Good Schools Guide: Boarding Schools*, 2018.

9   Email answer from ISC, 10 January 2018.

10 Tony Little, *An Intelligent Person's Guide to Education* (London: Bloomsbury Continuum, 2016), p. 197.

11 Interview with the author, August 2017.

12 *The Times*, 4 March 2017.

13 Green, Anders, Henderson and Henseke.

14 *Eton Onwards*, Summer 2017.

15 https://wincollsoc.org/new-design/pages/support-us/golf-bursary-fund

16 http://www.tatler.com/news/articles/august-2016/school-fees-private-education-high-cost-eton-harrow

17 https://www.theguardian.com/education/2015/aug/13/eton-college-borrows-45m-fund-scholarships-improve-sports-facilities

18 Interview with the author, 31 August 2017.

19 Interviews with the author, April to June 2017.

20 http://www.winchestercollege.org/bursaries

21 http://www.winchestercollege.org/UserFiles/Winchester%20College%20Financial%20Statements%2031%20August%202016%20-%20Signed.pdf

22 http://www.telegraph.co.uk/finance/property/news/7996693/The-Battle-for-Trevalga-residents-win-partial-victory-in-fight-to-stop-public-school-selling-hamlet.html

23 http://apps.charitycommission.gov.uk/Accounts/Ends39/0000310639_AC_20160831_E_C.PDF

24 Interview with the author, January 2018.

25 http://themediasociety.com/krishnan-guru-murthy-employing-black-privately-educated-women-isnt-diversity.php

26 http://www.telegraph.co.uk/education/secondaryeducation/3536588/Eton-aims-to-remove-financial-barriers-for-pupils.html; http://www.telegraph.co.uk/news/uknews/1563899/Eton-Private-schools-will-be-for-the-super-rich.html

27 *Eton Onwards*, Summer 2017.

28 https://harvardmagazine.com/2017/09/harvard-endowment-37-1-billion-on-8-1-per cent-return

29 Figures given by head of admissions in 2009 http://www.etoncollege.com/userfiles/files/Chronicle%20%234090.pdf

30 http://www.telegraph.co.uk/education/educationnews/8598930/Gove-highlights-Eton-in-public-school-criticism.html

31 FOI Department for Education 13 February 2018. https://www.gov.uk/government/uploads/system/uploads/attachment_data/file/636291/RR682_-ISSP_evaluation.pdf

32 https://www.tes.com/news/school-news/breaking-news/dulwich-college-pulls-out-academy-sponsorship

33 https://www.theguardian.com/teacher-network/teacher-blog/2013/oct/02/ofsted-michael-wilshaw-independent-schools

34 https://www.theguardian.com/education/2016/mar/09/ofsted-chief-criticises-independent-schools-lack-of-help-for-state-schools

35 @Andrew_Adonis, Twitter, 9 December 2017.

36 Interview with the author, 12 January 2018.

37 Holyport College founder and chair Simon Dudely's correspondence with the author, 9 December 2017.

38 Interview with the author.

39 https://www.theguardian.com/commentisfree/2016/mar/18/sponsoring-an-academy-private-schools-ofsted-michael-wilshaw

40 https://www.gov.uk/government/speeches/statement-from-the-new-prime-minister-theresa-may

41 https://www.conservatives.com/manifesto

42 https://data.oecd.org/eduresource/private-spending-on-education.htm

43 https://www.nfer.ac.uk/election-2017/school-funding-summary-of-evidence/labour-pledges-2017

44 http://www.cvsuk.com/news-resources/news/private-schools-get-%C2%A3522million-tax-breaks

45. I asked an accountant expert in charity education to look at the ISC figures and other publicly available financial reports from leading public schools.

46 http://www.schoolfeesadvice.org/school-fees-planning/why-do-you-need-to-plan-school-fees/

47 http://www.thisismoney.co.uk/money/bills/article-2558653/The-5-sneaky-perfectly-legal-ways-Britains-richest-parents-cut-tax-bill-private-school-fees.html

48 https://www.theguardian.com/teacher-network/teacher-blog/2013/oct/02/ofsted-michael-wilshaw-independent-schools

49 http://www.telegraph.co.uk/news/politics/nigel-farage/11467039/
Nigel-Farage-My-public-school-had-a-real-social-mix-but-now-only-
the-mega-rich-can-afford-the-fees.html

16 All That Glitters

1 @NadineDorriesMP, Twitter, 30 March, 2017.

2 http://www.independent.co.uk/news/uk/politics/
james-o-brien-nadine-dorries-tory-mp-posh-boy-daughter-goes-to-same-
public-school-lbc-presenter-a7658236.html

3 http://www.bbc.co.uk/news/av/uk-politics-35134966/
rees-mogg-on-question-time-heathrow-question-prompts-eton-quip

4 https://www.theguardian.com/music/2015/may/10/
paul-weller-miss-the-chaos-and-madness

5 http://www.independent.co.uk/arts-entertainment/music/features/
changing-man-an-audience-with-paul-weller-1950369.html

6 https://www.theguardian.com/education/2018/feb/06/
ofsted-chief-inspector-amanda-spielman-hijab

7 http://www.dailymail.co.uk/tvshowbiz/article-2188010/Im-tempted-
quit-posh-bashing-UK-says-star-Sherlock-Benedict-Cumberbatch.html

8 http://www.mirror.co.uk/tv/tv-news/
lewis-star-laurence-fox-says-7404545

9 *Daily Telegraph*, 4 December 2011; http://www.telegraph.co.uk/culture/
tvandradio/8933362/Laurence-Fox-how-fatherhood-made-me-a-better-
actor.html

10 https://www.theguardian.com/lifeandstyle/2011/nov/26/
peter-waugh-alec-wagh-evelyn-waugh

11 Interview with the author, April 2017.

12 http://www.independent.co.uk/life-style/profile-the-duke-of-
westminster-private-property-keep-out-1147573.htm

13 Alex Renton, *Stiff Upper Lip* (London: Weidenfeld & Nicolson, 2017), p. 149.

14 Jonathan Aitken, *Pride and Perjury: An Autobiography*, p. 226.

15 Simon Henderson, Eton College headmaster, Evidence to House of Commons education committee, 28 November 2017.

16 https://www.mumsnet.com/Talk/education/
1748079-Is-private-education-really-worth-the-cost

17 Interview with the author, August 2017.

18 Interviews with the author, April to June 2017.

19 Interview with the author, March 2017.

20 Interview with the author, December 2017.

21 *Sunday Times*, 7 May 2017.

22 http://www.dailymail.co.uk/news/article-482985/TOM-UTLEY-Universities-minister-learn-private-schools.html

23 *Surrey Magazine*, Autumn 2017, p. 70.

24 Differences in exam performance between pupils attending selective and non-selective schools mirror the genetic differences between them.' Kings College, London, https://kclpure.kcl.ac.uk/portal/en/journals/npj-science-of-learning(792ccdd8-9959-4675-a5e9-55b0bd3a67bc).html, Science of Learning, 13 November 2017.

25 Pisa, 2015, www.oecd.org/pisa/

26 *Sunday Times*, 24 September 2017.

27 Interview with the author, November 2017.

28 The German constitution enshrines the right to a private or independent education. This right was drawn up as part of a set of laws enacted to prevent a return of the Nazification of the education system.

17 The Entitlement Complex

1 Nick Duffell, *Wounded Leaders. British Leaders and the Entitlement Illusion* (London: Lone Arrow Press, 2014).

2 Johnson (ed.), p. 73.

3 Paxman, pp. 170–71

4 Address to the 27 Club, 11 May 1987.

5 *The Observer*, 11 December 2011, p. 40.

6 http://www.bbc.co.uk/news/uk-politics-39318829

7 https://www.theguardian.com/commentisfree/2017/mar/21/george-osborne-story-britain-ruled-never-ending-dinner-party

8 Private information.

9 https://www.politicshome.com/news/uk/political-parties/conservative-party/george-osborne/news/82772/pressure-mounts-george

10 http://www.smf.co.uk/wp-content/uploads/2014/07/Open-Access-an-independent-evaluation-Embargoed-00.01-030714.pdf

11 http://bigthink.com/experts-corner/decisions-are-emotional-not-logical-the-neuroscience-behind-decision-making

12 https://www.theguardian.com/politics/2017/sep/30/
boris-johnson-caught-on-camera-reciting-kipling-in-myanmar-temple

13 http://www.dailymail.co.uk/news/article-3668972/
If-charlatan-sexual-adventurer-Prime-Minister-d-emigrated-says-former-
boss-MAX-HASTINGS.html

14 http://www.hmc.org.uk/blog/
pushy-parents-endanger-children-eton-head-warns/

15 Interview with the author.

16 http://www.telegraph.co.uk/women/life/
did-boy-fail-cambridge-interview-went-eton/

17 http://www.etoncollege.com/userfiles/files/Destination%20of%20
Etonians%202015.pdf

18 http://www.telegraph.co.uk/education/2017/08/15/
private-school-pupils-forced-take-degrees-options-seen-disgrace/

19 Jeanne Ballantine and Floyd M. Hammack, *The Sociology of Education: A
Systematic Analysis* (Abingdon: Routledge, 2016), p. 72.

20 Jerome Karabel, *The Chosen: The Hidden History of Admission and Exclusion
at Harvard, Yale, and Princeton* (Boston, MA: Houghton Mifflin Company,
2006), p. 121.

21 https://www.nyma.org/tuition-and-fees/

22 Gwenda Blair, *The Trumps: Three Generations That Built an Empire* (New
York: Simon & Schuster, 2015), p. 237.

23 Ibid., p. 238.

24 Kristina Webb, *Palm Beach Post*, 11 July 2017.

25 CNN, 14 November 2016.

26 Rupert Murdoch first sent his eldest daughter Prudence to a state sec-
ondary school in London in the 1960s where he was based at the time.
Reports suggest this was not a happy experience and so he turned to
America's private education system for his children's secondary schooling.
Prudence was despatched to the Dalton School in Manhattan, founded
in 1919 and part of the exclusive Ivy Preparatory School League, where
current annual fees are $46,050. His eldest son Lachlan was educated at the
Trinity School, one of the five oldest private schools in America, founded
in 1709. In 2004 the *Wall Street Journal*, now owned by the Murdochs,
ranked Trinity as third-best at getting its students accepted to the country's
most exclusive colleges. Other alumni include Eric Trump and Britain's
attorney general Jeremy Wright. Murdoch's second daughter Elisabeth

went to The Brearley School, an all-girls private school, while London-born James, CEO of 21st Century Fox and chairman of Sky plc, went to the very expensive Horace Mann School in New York, founded in 1887 and still run as a tax-exempt charity.

27 https://www.newstatesman.com/politics/2014/04/ukips-own-privately-educated-clique

28 Adam Howard, *Learning Privilege: Lessons of Power and Identity in Affluent Schooling* (New York; London: Routledge, c2008).

29 Interview with the author, October 2017.

18 A Class Apart

1 Hillman, *Higher Education Review*.

2 http://www.educationengland.org.uk/documents/psc1/newsom1968-1.html

3 William Pitt the Younger, whose last term of office ended in 1806, was home-schooled.

4 ICS Census 2017.

5 Shrosbree, p. 8.

6 Turner, p. 161.

7 https://www.debretts.com/debretts-500-2017/

8 Dr Aaron Reeves and Dr Sam Friedman, 'The Decline and Persistence of the Old Boy: Private Schools and Elite Recruitment 1897 to 2016', *American Sociological Review*, Vol. 82, Issue 6, 2017.

9 http://www.independent.co.uk/news/uk/politics/darius-boris-and-a-blast-from-the-past-1658043.html

10 C.S. Lewis, 'The Inner Ring', Memorial Lecture at King's College, University of London, 1944.

11 https://www.theguardian.com/commentisfree/2018/jan/27/to-drain-the-swamp-of-men-only-clubs-there-must-be-a-public-register

12 http://www.etoncollege.com/userfiles/files/Eton%20College%20Statutes%20(approved%20October%202016).pdf

13 https://www.gov.uk/government/uploads/system/uploads/attachment_data/file/623124/SFR28_2017_Main_Text.pdf

14 http://www.dailymail.co.uk/news/article-3653858/Judge-sent-Ellie-Butler-father-killed-REFUSES-apologise-saying-merely-s-not-personal.html

15 https://www.linkedin.com/in/quintin-hogg-3562b2/?ppe=1

16 http://www.tatler.com/news/articles/october-2013/
who-will-marry-prince-george/viewgallery/274

17 https://d3n8a8pro7vhmx.cloudfront.net/labourclp269/pages/941/
attachments/original/1484611647/APPG_Report_-_Access_to_Leading_
Professions_Inquiry.pdf?1484611647

18 http://www.telegraph.co.uk/education/2017/05/06/
pupils-ten-private-grammar-schools-dominate-applications-top/

19 https://www.suttontrust.com/wp-content/uploads/2016/02/Leading-
People_Feb16.pdf; https://www.suttontrust.com/wp-content/
uploads/2017/07/BCGSocial-Mobility-report-full-version_WEB_
FINAL-1.pdf

20 http://www.bbc.co.uk/news/entertainment-arts-43195847

21 http://news.sky.com/story/
the-bbc-pay-gap-is-bad-its-class-gap-is-worse-10957166

22 Rod Liddle, *Sunday Times*, 17 September 2017.

23 Rosemary Bennett and Nicola Woolcock, *The Times*, 20 November 2017.

24 www.tatler.com/school/westminister-school

25 http://dorian.skoosh.com/serve-and-obey-my-arse/

26 https://development.mtsn.org.uk/april-2016/oxbridge-success

27 http://www.westminster.org.uk/wp-content/uploads/2017/01/
Prospectus-2016-1.pdf

28 Bolton, 'Oxbridge "elitism"'.

29 Ibid.

30 John Rae, *Delusions of Grandeur: A Headmaster's Life 1966–1986* (London:
HarperCollins, 1993), p. 125.

31 Interview with the author, July 2017.

32 https://www.suttontrust.com/wp-content/uploads/2017/07/BCGSocial-
Mobility-report-full-version_WEB_FINAL-1.pdf

33 Interview with the author.

34 https://www.theguardian.com/education/2017/feb/23/
ppe-oxford-university-degree-that-rules-britain

35 http://www.suttontrust.com/newsarchive/race-top/

36 *The Confidence Trick*, BBC Radio 4, 8 November 2017, 13 November
2017, 15 November 2017.

37 Matthew Parris, *The Times*, 9 June 2012.

38 Higher Education Statistics Agency figures.

39 https://www.suttontrust.com/research-paper/
social-mobility-2017-research/

40 http://www.chambersstudent.co.uk/where-to-start/newsletter/
    school-background-of-trainee-solicitors
41 http://onlinelibrary.wiley.com/doi/10.1002/berj.3256/full
42 http://www.ucl.ac.uk/ioe/news-events/news-pub/april-2017/
    privately-educated-women-marriage
43 Interview with the author, January 2017.
44 Sathnam Sanghera, *The Times Magazine*, 14 April 2018.
45 https://www.suttontrust.com/research-paper/
    social-mobility-2017-research/
46 https://www.equalitytrust.org.uk/how-has-inequality-changed
47 http://www.bbc.co.uk/news/business-41160748
48 https://www.theguardian.com/inequality/2017/jun/17/
    wealth-gap-rises-as-uk-home-ownership-falls-resolution-foundation
49 UK Poverty 2017, Joseph Rowntree Foundation.
50 https://www.theguardian.com/business/2017/jan/31/
    theresa may inequality margaret thatcher resolution-foundation
51 https://www.suttontrust.com/wp-content/uploads/2017/07/BCGSocial-
    Mobility-report-full-version_WEB_FINAL-1.pdf
52 https://www.suttontrust.com/wp-content/uploads/2017/07/
    BCGSocial-Mobility-report-full-version_WEB_FINAL-1.pdf
53 Robert Halfon, *Channel 4 News*, 3 December 2017.
54 Interview with the author, August 2017.
55 https://www.theguardian.com/inequality/2017/may/24/
    are-we-about-to-witness-the-most-unequal-societies-in-
    history-yuval-noah-harari?CMP=share_btn_tw

Conclusion: The Dissolution of the Public Schools

1 Plato, *The Republic*.
2 https://www.gov.uk/government/speeches/speech-on-the-big-society
3 https://www.gov.uk/government/speeches/
   statement-from-the-new-prime-minister-theresa-may
4 http://www.nme.com/festivals/jeremy-corbyn-glastonbury-2017-speech-
   full-2093107#YpxzkTZV5LV6UhQ0.99
5 Matthew Parris, *The Times*, 9 June 2012.
6 James Kirkup, *Daily Telegraph*, 7 October 2015.
7 http://www.independent.co.uk/news/uk/home-news/britain-divided-
   society-social-mobility-commission-alan-milburn-a7811386.html
8 https://www.oecd.org/education/school/50293148.pdf

9 http://www.dailymail.co.uk/news/article-2572643/SEBASTIAN-SHAKESPEARE-Dis-brother-joins-war-Notting-Hill-yummy-mummys.html#ixzz4q9BgN9l1

10 http://www.getwestlondon.co.uk/news/west-london-news/council-denies-asset-stripping-community-11216646

11 https://www.theguardian.com/uk-news/2017/jul/21/temporary-school-built-pupils-academy-grenfell-tower

12 http://www.kensingtonaldridgeacademy.co.uk/grenfell-tower-justgiving-page/

13 https://www.theguardian.com/commentisfree/2016/oct/10/shami-chakrabarti-education-system-grammars-private-schools-local-comprehensive?CMP=share_btn_tw

14 http://www.telegraph.co.uk/education/2016/12/14/schools-face-bigger-funding-crisis-nhs-select-committee-chair/

15 https://www.newstatesman.com/2014/01/education-private-schools-berlin-wall

16 *The Road to Somewhere: The Populist Revolt and the Future of Politics*, p. 191.

17 *The Road to Somewhere*, p. 183.

18 https://www.gov.uk/government/news/an-analysis-of-2-decades-of-efforts-to-improve-social-mobility

19 http://www.smf.co.uk/wp-content/uploads/2014/06/Publication-The-Meritocrats-Manifesto-Dominic-Raab.pdf

20 http://www.smf.co.uk/wp-content/uploads/2014/06/Publication-The-Meritocrats-Manifesto-Dominic-Raab.pdf

21 https://www.newstatesman.com/2014/02/gove-michael-our-segregated-education-system

22 https://www.gov.uk/government/speeches/statement-from-the-new-prime-minister-theresa-may

23 Interview with the author.

24 https://www.isc.co.uk/media-enquiries/news-press-releases-statements/joint-funding-could-see-10-000-free-new-independent-school-places-every-year/; https://www.tes.com/news/school-news/breaking-news/private-schools-should-receive-state-cash-educate-poor-pupils-if

25 http://www.huffingtonpost.co.uk/mehdi-hasan/warren-buffett-is-right-ban-private-schools_b_1857287.html

26 *The Westminster Hour*, BBC Radio 4, 3 December 2017.

27 http://www.warrenbuffett.com/buffetts-thoughts-on-public-education/

28 https://seattleducation2010.wordpress.com/2015/09/07/15765/

29 http://www.hmc.org.uk/about-hmc/partnerships/

30 https://inews.co.uk/opinion/sir-anthony-seldon-plan-solve-educations-inequality-problems-just-100-new-schools/

31 *Journal of Epidemiology and Community Health* suggests that 2,698 people aged 25–44 died in the north in 2015 who would have survived had they lived in the south.

32 http://www.telegraph.co.uk/comment/telegraph-view/8698227/A-palpable-change-inthenational-mood.html

33 http://www.educationengland.org.uk/documents/psc1/newsom1968-1.html

34 Diane Reay, *Miseducation: Inequality, Education and the Working Classes* (Bristol: Policy Press, 2017), p. 44.

35 Social Mobility Commission, *Time for Change*.

36 Ibid.

37 *The Observer*, 3 December 2017.

38 Joseph Rowntree Foundation annual report 2017. Caroline Wheeler, *Sunday Times*, 3 December 2017.

39 https://www.newstatesman.com/2014/01/education-private-schools-berlin-wall

40 https://www.theguardian.com/teacher-network/teacher-blog/2013/oct/02/ofsted-michael-wilshaw-independent-schools

41 https://www.isc.co.uk/research/independent-schools-economic-impact-report/; https://www.oecd-ilibrary.org/education/private-spending-on-education/indicator/english_6e70bede-en; https://www.ifs.org.uk/tools_and_resources/fiscal_facts/public_spending_survey/education

42 Reay, p. 44; Danny Dorling, *Social Injustice: Why Social Inequality Persists* (Bristol: Policy Press, 2011), p. 68.

43 http://hansard.millbanksystems.com/written_answers/1978/mar/22/direct-grant-schools

44 https://www.theguardian.com/society/2016/nov/12/unpaid-interns-elitist-uk-social-mobility-alan-milburn

45 https://www.theguardian.com/education/2014/oct/14/poor-pupil-oxbridge-less-likely-pope-bono

46 @DavidLammy, Twitter, 26 January 2018.

INDEX

1

POSH
BOYS

ABOUT THE AUTHOR

Robert Verkaik is an author and journalist specialising in extremism and education. He writes for the *Guardian, Independent,* the *i, Observer, Sunday Telegraph* and *Sunday Times*. In 2013 he was runner-up in the specialist journalist category at the National Press Awards and he has previously been longlisted for the Orwell Prize and the Paul Foot Award. Before becoming a freelance journalist, he was the security editor for the *Mail on Sunday* and the home affairs editor and law editor for the *Independent*, where he worked for twelve years.

Since the 9/11 attacks, Verkaik has covered the 'War on Terror', visiting the US detention camp at Guantánamo Bay and interviewing victims of torture in Syria. He has also headed media campaigns against 'secret justice' and in support of greater press freedoms. More recently he has been writing about the causes of extremism and social immobility. In 2016 he tracked Mohammed Emwazi's path from London schoolboy to Islamic State executioner in *Jihadi John: The Making of a Terrorist*, which is also published by Oneworld.

As well as being a journalist, Verkaik is a qualified non-practising barrister, called to Bar in 2007. He lives in Surrey.

POSH BOYS

How the English Public Schools Ruin Britain

Robert Verkaik

ONEWORLD

A Oneworld Book

First published by Oneworld Publications Ltd, 2018

Copyright © Robert Verkaik 2018

ISBN 978-1-78607-383-9
ISBN 978-1-78607-384-6 (eBook)

Typeset by Divaddict Publishing Solutions Ltd.
Printed and bound in Great Britain by Clays Ltd, Elcograf S.p.A

Oneworld Publications Ltd
10 Bloomsbury Street
London WC1B 3SR
England

Stay up to date with the latest books,
special offers, and exclusive content from
Oneworld with our newsletter

Sign up on our website
oneworld-publications.com

MIX
Paper from
responsible sources
FSC® C018072